ANIMALS AND MAN:
A State of Blessedness

by
Joanne Stefanatos,
DOCTOR OF VETERINARY MEDICINE

LIGHT AND LIFE PUBLISHING COMPANY
P.O. Box 26421
Minneapolis, Minnesota 55426

Address all correspondence to:
Dr. Joanne Stefanatos
Animal Kingdom Veterinary Hospital
1325 Vegas Valley Drive
Las Vegas, Nevada 89109

Cover: Collage by the author.

Illustrations compiled by the author.

Library of Congress Cataloging in Publication Data
92-72802

Stefanatos, Joanne, DVM.
    Animals and Man: A State of Blessedness.
    1. Christianity — Eastern Orthodox Saints and Theology.
2. Animals. 3. Ecology.
    I. Title

Library of Congress Catalogue Number
ISBN 0-937032-90-5

To

Blessed Abbot Herman

(St. Herman of Alaska Monastery,
Platina, California)

...for his intense love and compassion for Man and Beasts

...for his undying love and courage to be a living witness for our Lord
and Savior

...for exemplifying the Passion of the Spirit and bringing so many
God seekers to Jesus Christ

AND

To All Fathers and Brothers of the St. Herman of Alaska Monastery
and Mothers and Sisters of St. Xenia Skete in Wildwood, California

...who endeavor to live saintly lives

The author dedicates this book to *"Simba,"*
a magnificent member of God's Animal Kingdom,
who reflects the majesty of her Creator, and to

Michael Christian Stefanatos, our beloved nephew,
who will be graced by living in the future age of blessedness.

Table of Contents

INTRODUCTION:

PART II: SAINTS AND ANIMALS

"O GOD, enlarge within us the sense of fellowship with all living things, our little brothers to whom Thou hast given this earth as their home in common with us.

"May we realize that they live not for us alone, but for themselves and for Thee, and that they love the sweetness of life even as we, and serve Thee better in their place than we in ours."

—St. Basil the Great, 370 A.D.

Introduction

Animals and Man:
A State
of Blessedness

O Lord, our Lord,
how wonderful is Thy Name in all the earth!
For Thy magnificence is lifted high above the heavens....
For I will behold the heavens, the works of Thy fingers,
the moon and the stars, which Thou hast founded.
What is man that Thou art mindful of him?
Thou hast made him a little lower than the angels,
with glory and honor hast Thou crowned him,
and Thou hast set him over the works of Thy hands....
O Lord, our Lord, how wonderful is Thy Name in all
the earth! (Ps. 8:1, 3-5, 8)

BLESSEDNESS was the original state of existence of Adam
and Eve in the Garden of Eden, and of all the animals before
the Fall. Blessedness in God is the ultimate aim of man's
existence on earth. God created man as the crown of earthly
creation, as the "image of God"—the King of Nature, responsible for proclaiming the will of God in the world by word and
deed. Man, by linking the material creation with the spiritual,
can bring down upon earth blessings from heaven and unite all
things of earth with God, and maintain all earthly creatures in
a state of love, harmony, and order.

11

Through the grace of God, the Saints of the Church restored in themselves the blessedness which had been man's from the beginning, and thus it was that they lived in loving communion with animals just as Adam and Eve once did. By leading a life of virtue, prayer, and Christian struggle, we too can live with animals in this state of grace and blessedness.

Man, animals, and plants are living expressions of the Grace of the Creator. Man can have a common language with the animals, consisting of the purest thoughts and blessings we bestow upon them. We can talk to animals "mind to mind," and through the silent, universal language of the heart. Love for animals is nourished from the depths of our heart, by the deepest longing of our soul to respond with God's unconditional love (agape) to our fellow earthly creatures.

PART I:

Man and Animals

CREATION: THE VISIBLE
AND THE INVISIBLE

THE STORY OF CREATION is a cosmic symphony beginning in Genesis and triumphantly ending in Revelation. Genesis is the account of God's Creation as seen through Divine Revelation by the God-seer Moses, and confirmed by the experiences of later Holy Fathers who were in direct succession from the Holy Apostles of Jesus Christ.

The Creator is of one Essence and three Persons. He is One Triune God: God the Father, Jesus Christ the Son, and the Holy Spirit. The Trinity is uncreated energy, uncreated light, bodiless and all Spirit. God's imperishable Spirit is in all things for the preservation of the universe: *The Spirit of the Lord fills the world.* (Wisdom of Solomon, 1:7) God is the source and the life of all things: *For in Him we live and move and have our being.* (Acts 17:28) *God created everything to exist, and the generative forces of the world are wholesome.* (Wisdom of Solomon, 1:14)

God first created the invisible world which we call heaven—the world of bodiless spirits. This is the world of archangels, angels, dominions, principalities, and powers—beings more perfect than and superior to man. Angels were given free will, and they were at liberty to sin or not to sin.

When the highest of the angels, Lucifer, chose to sin against God through pride, one third of all the angels fell with him, and together with him were cast out of heaven and sent to earth. These fallen angels are called demons, because they continuously persevere in evil and rage against the works of God. They are here on earth, constantly tempting man to sin. The angels that remained faithful to God established themselves in holiness. Their function is to glorify God with a burning zeal, and to minister to man for the salvation of our souls. They are God's ministering spirits—angels. (cf. Hebrews 7)

On the third day of Creation,

God said, Let the earth bring forth the herb of grass bearing seed according to its kind and according to its likeness, and the fruit-tree bearing fruit whose seed is in it, according to its kind on the earth, and it was so.... (Gen. 1:11)

On the fifth day of Creation,

God said, Let the waters bring forth reptiles having life, and winged creatures flying above the earth in the firmament

of heaven, and it was so. And God made great whales, and every living reptile, which the waters brought forth according to their kinds, and every creature that flies with wings according to its kind, and God saw that they were good.... And God said, Let the earth bring forth the living creature according to its kind, quadrupeds and reptiles and wild beasts of the earth according to their kind, and cattle according to their kind, and all the reptiles of the earth according to their kind, and God saw that they were good. (Gen. 1:20-22, 24-25)

God created millions of kinds of creatures—spiritual, physical, animate, inanimate, rational and irrational—and adorned them with a variety of essences, powers, organs, energies, and perfections. In our visible world, God created very tiny living organisms that are completely invisible to our eyes but readily seen through a microscope.

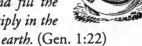

Before the end of the fifth day of Creation, God blessed His birds and sea creatures: *Be fruitful and multiply and fill the waters in the seas, and let fowl multiply in the earth.* (Gen. 1:22)

Each animal was made with its own nature, instincts, and characteristics. *All flesh is not the same flesh, but there is one kind of flesh of men, another flesh of beasts, another of fishes, and another of birds.* (I Cor. 15:39)

All of creation is called to glorify the Creator according to its ability.

Let everything that hath breath praise the Lord.
(Ps. 150:6)

How great are Thy works, O Lord! In wisdom hast Thou wrought them all: the earth is filled with Thy creation. So is this great and wide sea: there are things creeping innumerable, small animals and great. (Ps. 103:24-25)

O all ye fowls of the air, bless ye the Lord, Praise and exalt Him above all forever. (Song of the Three Holy Children, 58)

Jesus said, *Behold the birds of the air; they sow not, neither do they reap or gather into barns.* (Matt. 6:26)

God cares for every one of His creatures, from the smallest sparrow to the largest whale.

Consider the lilies of the field, how they grow and toil not.... Seek ye the King-dom of God, and all things will be added unto you. (Luke 12:24-31)

On the sixth day, God created man:

And God said, Let us make man according to our image and likeness, and let them have dominion over the fish of the sea, and over the flying creatures of heaven, and over the cattle and all the earth, and over all the reptiles that creep on the earth. And God made man, according to the image of God He made him, male and female He made them.... (Gen. 1:26-27)

Man is composed of body and soul. The earthly body is visible and destructible, the soul invisible and indestructible. Man was created to be the liaison between the angelic, spiritual realm and the earthly, material realm.

God created first the invisible world and then the visible one, "in order to reveal a greater wisdom and the manifold purposes of nature."[1] (St. Gregory the Theologian)

According to St. Caesarius, the brother of St. Gregory the Theologian, Adam was forty days in Paradise.

CREATION: THE WILL, WISDOM AND POWER OF GOD

GOD existed before the world began, both in His uncreated Essence and in His uncreated Energies, revealed to us as uncreated Light. God created the universe by His Word, by His Will, and by His Command, with a divine purpose and destiny. He created all things from nothing and brought them into being by His Word:

> *For He commanded and they were created.* (Ps. 148:5)

> *In the beginning was the Word, and the Word was with God, and the Word was God.... All things were made by Him; and without Him was not any thing made that was made. In Him was life....* (John 1:1,3-4)

God did not make heaven and earth out of things that already existed. (cf. 2 Macc. 7:28) He created the world from nothing; there were no pre-existing atoms, molecules, or elements, no energies of any kind.

> *For from Him and through Him and to Him are all things. To Him be glory forever.* (Romans 11:36)

> *The heavens are telling the glory of God; and the firmament proclaims His handiwork.* (Ps. 19:1)

Therefore, the creation of the universe occurred as the result of the Will, Wisdom, and Power of the Triune God, and was accomplished by His Word. The creation of the universe out of nothingness is an eternal mystery which can never be understood by man's finite mind.

> *By faith we understand that the world was created by the Word of God.* (Heb. 11:3)

The primordial wisdom of God was laid as a foundation to nature at the time of Creation.[2]

God endowed creation with a self-sustained natural law and order within time and space, giving man the wisdom to know the constituents of the world and the working of the elements.

> *God had granted me wisdom, it is He that leadeth unto wisdom and directed the wise,... for in His hand are both wisdom and knowledge.* (Wisdom of Solomon, 7:17-22 LXX)

God the Creator continuously provides for the preservation and well-being of His creatures.

> *The beast of the field shall honor Me,*
> *the dragons and the owls,*
> *because I give waters in the wilderness*
> *and rivers in the desert*
> *to give drink to My people, My chosen.*
> *This people have I formed for Myself,*
> *they shall show forth My praise.* (Isaiah 43:20-21)

God called creation into existence in order that other beings, glorifying Him, might share in His goodness and happiness.

The earth is the Lord's and the fullness thereof, the world and they that dwell therein. (Ps. 24:1)

For every beast of the forest is Mine, and the cattle upon a thousand hills. I know all the fowls of the mountains, and the wild beasts of the field are Mine. (Ps. 50:10-11)

But ask now the beasts,
and they shall teach thee,
and the fowls of the air,
and they shall tell thee.
Or speak to the earth,
and it shall teach thee,
and the fishes of the sea
shall declare unto thee.
Who knoweth not in all these
that the hand of the Lord hath wrought this?
In Whose hand is the soul of every livng thing
and the breath of all mankind. (Job. 12:7-10)

Praise ye the Lord!
Praise ye the Lord from the heavens,
praise Him in the heights!...
Praise the Lord from the earth....
Mountains and all hills,
fruitful trees and all cedars,
beasts and all cattle,
creeping things and all flying fowl.
Kings of the earth and all people,
princes and all judges of the earth...
let them praise the name of the Lord,
for His name alone is excellent.
His glory is above the earth and heaven....
Praise ye the Lord! (Ps. 148:1-14)

In the Image of God

GOD CREATED only man in "His image." What is the image of God? It is the direct reflection of all God's attributes. Man bears the image of God in the higher qualities of the soul, such as the soul's immortality, freedom of will, reason, the capacity for pure love, and spiritual power.[3]

While according to physical ability man is among the weakest of the creatures in the universe, only he has the gift of a spiritual nature. Man's soul is immortal not by its nature, but by the Grace of God. God is Spirit; therefore, the image of God can be seen only in the soul, not in the body. *Man was created of earthly body and spiritual soul as the crown of the universe.* (Ps. 8:5b) Man's physical body was created to serve his spiritual life. It is the temple of the Holy Spirit. Thus, the body participates in all the life-giving energies of Christ.

And in the Likeness of God

THE IMAGE OF GOD gives us the power to grow to become more like God. The "likeness" consists in the perfecting of man in virtue and sanctity, in acquiring the gifts of the Holy Spirit. The "likeness" is obtained by our continuous efforts towards deification, by our own will, and through our own endeavors to fulfill the potential with which God endowed us.

We obtain it by growing in devoutness and righteousness and striving to acquire Christ's perfect nature.

> *Man's first purpose is to glorify God in all that he does, to acknowledge Him as his Creator, to persevere towards Him with his soul, to rejoice in union with Him, to live in Him.* (Sirach 17:6-10)

God created Adam and Eve of one nature. "Adam" means "earth," and "Eve" means "life," for she is the mother of all living. To Eve, the Lord also gave the same wisdom, strength, and unlimited power, and all the holy qualities necessary to grow in grace. He created her, not from the dust of the ground, but from Adam's rib in the Garden of Delight, in the Paradise which He had planted in the midst of the earth.[4]

Adam and Eve were created by the Grace of God and placed in the Garden of Delight to live in harmony and happiness with the rest of creation. They could converse with the animals.

> *And God formed the man of the dust of the earth, and breathed upon his face the breath of life, and the man became a living soul.* (Gen. 2:7)

"Owing to the gift of the supernatural grace of God which was infused into Adam by the breath of life, Adam could see and understand the Lord walking in Paradise and comprehend His words and the conversations of the Holy Angels, and the language of all the beasts, birds, and reptiles, and all that is now hidden from us fallen and sinful creatures, but was so clear to Adam before the fall."[5]

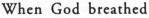

When God breathed upon Adam, Adam's soul was given life-giving power over his body, thus uniting God with man and the spiritual realm. Adam was created as the crown of God's creation—sinless, passionless, and holy. But his nature was created alterable, and only with God's help could he stay steadfast in the Lord.

And the Lord God took the man whom He had formed, and placed him in the Paradise of Delight, to cultivate and keep it. And the Lord God gave a charge to Adam, saying, Of every tree which is in the garden, thou mayest freely eat, but of the tree of the knowledge of good and evil—of it ye shall not eat, but in whatsoever day ye eat of it, ye shall surely die. (Gen. 2:15-16)

God gave Adam the commandment to not eat of the fruit of the tree of knowledge of good and evil so that he might know that he was alterable and change-able, and might freely choose to live in a divine state. God gave Adam and Eve everything inside and outside of Paradise through grace, requiring nothing in re-turn either for His creation of them or for the glory in which He clothed them.

In his book *Orthodox Dogmatic Theology* (p. 158), Fr. Michael Pomazansky writes:

> Man was created immortal in his soul, and he could have remained immortal also in body if he had not fallen away from God. The Wisdom of Solomon says: *God did not make death* (Wis. 1:13). Man's body, as was well expressed by Blessed Augustine, does not possess the "impossibility of dying," but it did possess "the possibility of not dying," which it has now lost. The writer of Genesis informs us that this "possibility of not dying" was maintained in Paradise by eating the fruit of the *Tree of Life,* of which our first ancestors were deprived after they were banished from Paradise.

Adam was given all the spiritual and physical gifts necessary for his perfection. It was up to Adam's free will to decide whether to continuously grow in grace. If the man and woman had properly cultivated all the excellences bestowed upon them by God in Paradise, then, by the grace of God, they would have become holy and righteous and attained the likeness of God.[6]

God created each of us to exercise our free will to choose the direction we take in life.

God destined us in love, to be His sons through Jesus Christ, according to the purpose of His will, to the praise of His glorious grace which He freely bestowed upon us in the Beloved Christ. (Eph. 1:5-6)

The purpose of creation is the salvation of man in Christ, for "in Him all things were created in heaven and on earth." (Col. 1:16)

Adam and Eve transgressed God's commandment because they allowed the evil words of the serpent to penetrate their heart and take charge of their whole being. When Adam and Eve fell from grace, the rest of creation which served them fell with them. Through Adam, death gained power over the creation. When Adam fell and was dead in the eyes of God, the Creator wept over him. The angels, all the powers, heaven and earth, bewailed his death and fall. The material creation lamented, seeing its king now become a servant of an opposing evil power. Therefore darkness became the garment of his soul, a bitter and evil darkness, because he was made a subject of the prince of darkness.[7] After Adam violated God's commandment and entered into a sinful state, continuous thoughts of fear and every sort of disturbance and depravity of passion infiltrated the whole world.

Because man's nature is changeable, he has the power to turn away from God. Man must decide whether he will fix his gaze on the spiritual world or on the material world. Adam wanted to obtain perfection and happiness independent from God, by himself, without advancing through the grace of God. His sin was arrogance, disobedience, selfishness, and lack of reliance on God. When Adam and Eve transgressed, they lost the "garment of glory" they wore in the Garden of Eden, and their bodies suffered pain, disease, and lifelong toil. They lost the pure possession of their nature as created according to the image and likeness of God; they lost their full heavenly inheritance.

Sin came into the world through Adam and Eve. Man's nature, being God's creation, is not inherently evil; however, God had graced man with freedom of will, allowing him to choose between good and evil. When Adam transgressed, he was given the opportunity to repent and receive forgiveness from God, because he and Eve had been deceived by Satan. But instead of repenting before God, Adam blamed Eve, the woman God had given him.

> *And Adam said, The woman whom Thou gavest to be with me—she gave me of the tree and I ate. And the Lord God said to the woman, Why hast thou done this? And the woman said, The serpent deceived me and I ate.* (Gen. 3:13-14)

Through death God stopped the spread of sin, thus revealing His love for man through this very chastisement.

> *They cry out by reason of the arm of the mighty. But none saith, "Where is God my maker, Who giveth songs in the night, Who teacheth us more than the beasts of the earth, and maketh us wiser than the fowls of heaven?" There they cry, but none giveth answer, because of the pride of evil men.* (Job 35:9-12)

God loved His creation so much that He sent His Only Son, Jesus Christ, to the world to die to save sinners. Christ reunited divinity with humanity, and raised from hell the souls of Adam and Eve and all the righteous and took them to heaven. Adam and Eve, the ancestors of the human race, caused all men to die, but all men are resurrected and have life in Jesus Christ.

> *For as by one man's disobedience, many were made sinners, so by one man's obedience, many will be made righteous.* (Rom. 5:19)

The salvation of man is God's supreme desire. The Father sacrificed His Son to save fallen man.

Jesus Christ raising Adam and Eve from hell.

DOMINION OVER THE EARTH

MAN, created in the image of God, was made the highest of all forms of life. As the crown of God's creation, Adam was given dominion over beasts and fowls. (cf. Eccles. 16:24) Adam had the responsibility of preserving and maintaining God's creatures, as they live in their perfection, beauty, and unique natures. God provided food for all the creatures—"every seed-bearing herb" (Gen 1:11)—from the abundance of the earth. To have dominion of the fowl of the air means to furnish whatever the nature of the fowl of the air may have need of, that they may live and be happy. Dominion over the cattle and over all the earth means to feed and pasture cattle for the sake of their happiness, in praise of the Lord, Who abundantly furnishes all breath and life and all things necessary.

Man is God's appointed leader of all the visible creation, and man is capable of gathering up to himself all the creatures that are subjected to him to live harmoniously. The Prophet David acknowledged the magnificent value of man:

> *What is man, that Thou art mindful of him?*
> *And the son of man, that Thou visitest him?*
> *For Thou hast made him a little lower than the angels,*
> *and hast crowned him with glory and honor.*
> *Thou madest him to have dominion over the works of Thy*
> *hands; Thou hast put all things under his feet: all sheep and*
> *oxen, yea, and the beasts of the field; the fowls of the air, and*
> *the fish of the sea, and whatsoever passeth through the paths of*

the seas. O Lord, our Lord, how excellent is Thy name in all the earth! (Ps. 8:4-9)

Man on this earth today must seek to shed the "old man," who as a ruler sacrifices and destroys his dominion, yielding to his selfish desires. We have misused our God-given authority, and we destroy ourselves by not sparing the interests of the rest of creation. We must take on the "new man"—full of wisdom and piety, governing ourselves and the world in devoutness and righteousness, being at peace with God, ourselves, and the rest of our dominion.

THE PEACEFUL KINGDOM

Behold, I have given you
every herb and every fruit of every tree to eat.
And all the animals of the earth and of the air
shall feed upon plants and trees
like you. "(Gen. 1:29)

THE EATING of herbs and fruits befitted man in his state of innocence and sinlessness; meat-eating befits the life of man in sin. Because death came into the world as a result of Adam and Eve's transgression, God gave man the animals to eat, as He had before given them the green herbs. Therefore, living in blessedness with animals and sparing their lives is an act of repentance to God. Refraining from eating meat does not necessarily make us more virtuous in God's eyes, however, for we are still fallen men, sinners. But out of love for His creation, we can refrain from eating meat as a sacrifice.

O Lord, how manifold are Thy work
In wisdom hast Thou made them all;
the earth is full of Thy creatures. (Ps. 104:24)

The animals did not share man's willfulness and apostasy. Animals did not rebel against God, because all creatures were not entrusted with freedom of choice. Animals lived faithfully according to God's ordinances.

32

Yea, the stork in the heaven knoweth
her appointed times; and the turtledove
and the crane and the swallow observe
the time of their coming; but my people
know not the judgment of the Lord.
How do ye say, "We are wise, and the
law of the Lord is with us"? ...lo, they
have rejected the word of the Lord,
and what wisdom is in them?" (Jer.
8:7-9)

Throughout history, nature has suffered because of the wickedness of mankind. Violence, greed, wastefulness, and destruction prevail. God is not known, truth and mercy disappear, and morality is jeopardized. The Lord's heritage has succumbed to man's fallen nature.

The earth shall be utterly laid waste and utterly despoiled...for
they have transgressed the laws, violated the statutes, broken the
everlasting covenant. (Is. 24:3,5)

How long shall the land mourn, and the herbs of every field
wither, for the wickedness of them that dwell therein? The beasts
are consumed and the birds. (Jer. 12:4)

If Adam and Eve had not sinned,

they could have maintained to all eternity the full powers
of their body, soul and spirit in a state of immortality and
everlasting youth, and they could have continued in this
immortal and blessed state of theirs forever.... [When they
transgressed], they lost the priceless gift of the grace of the
Holy Spirit, so that until the actual coming into the world
of the God-Man Jesus Christ, *The Spirit of God was not yet*
in the world *because Jesus was not yet glorified.* [John 7:39]
(St. Seraphim of Sarov)[8]

ADAM NAMES THE ANIMALS

AND GOD formed yet farther out of the earth, all the wild beasts of the field, and all the birds of the sky, and He brought them to Adam, to see what he would call them. And whatever Adam called any living creature, that was the name of it. And Adam gave names to all the cattle and to all the birds of the sky and to all the wild beasts of the field. (Gen. 2:19-20)

Everything was subject to [Adam] as the beloved of God, as the king and lord of creation; and everything looked up to him as the perfect crown of God's creatures. Adam was made so wise by this breath of life which was breathed into his face from the creative lips of God the Creator and Ruler of all, that there never has been a man on earth wiser or more intelligent than he, and it is hardly likely that there ever will be. When the Lord commanded him to give names to all the creatures, he gave every creature a name which completely expressed all the qualities, powers, and properties given it by God at its creation.[9]

The Fall: Adam and Eve Fear the Animals

AFTER THE FALL of Adam and Eve, the animals wanted to turn against them, since all the material creation had fallen together with them.

This is confirmed by St. Symeon the New Theologian:

"Then also all creatures, when they saw that Adam had been banished from Paradise, no longer wished to submit to him,

the criminal: the sun did not wish to shine for him, nor did
the moon and the other stars wish to show themselves to him;
the springs did not wish to gush forth water, and the rivers
to continue their course; the air thought no longer to blow
so as not to allow Adam, the sinner, to breathe; the beasts and
all the other animals of the earth, when they saw that he had
been stripped of his first glory, began to despise him, and all
immediately were ready to fall upon him. The heaven, in a
certain fashion, was about to strive to fall upon him, and the
earth did not wish to bear him any longer. But God, Who
created everything and made man—what did He do? Knowing before the creation of the world that Adam would transgress His commandment, and having foreordained for him
a new life and a re-creation, which things he was to receive
in rebirth in Holy Baptism by virtue of the economy of the
Incarnation of His only-begotten Son and our God, He
restrained all these creatures by His power, and in His
compassion and goodness did not allow them immediately
to strive against man, and commanded that the creation
should remain in submission to him, and having become
corrupt, should serve corrupt man for whom it had been
created, with the aim that when man again should be renewed
and become spiritual, incorrupt, and immortal, then also the
whole creation, which had been subjected by God to man to
serve him, might be delivered from this servitude, might be
renewed together with him, and become incorrupt and as it
were spiritual...."[10]

One apocryphal source attempts to recount the conversation that might have occurred when Adam begged God to
preserve him and Eve from being devoured by the beasts:

"But now, O Lord God, that I have transgressed Thy
commandment, all beasts will rise against me and will devour
me, and Eve Thy handmaid; and will cut off our life from
the face of the earth. I therefore beseech Thee, O God, that,

since Thou hast made us come out of the garden, and hast made us be in a strange land, Thou wilt not let the beasts hurt us." When the Lord heard these words from Adam, He had pity on him.... Then God commanded the beasts and the birds and all that moves upon the earth, to come to Adam and to be familiar with him, and not to trouble him and Eve; nor yet any of the good and righteous among their posterity.

And the beasts did obedience to Adam, according to the commandment of God; except the serpent, against which God was wroth. It did not come to Adam with the beasts.[11]

GOD CURSES THE SERPENT

THE SERPENT is the animal into which the Deceiver entered, and which in turn deceived Eve. The serpent was the most crafty and beautiful animal created, and he conversed with Adam and Eve in the garden.

Now the serpent was the most crafty of all the brutes on the earth, which the Lord God made, and the serpent said to the woman, Wherefore has God said, Eat not of every tree of the garden? And the woman said to the serpent, We may eat of the fruit of the trees of the garden, but of the fruit of the tree which is in the midst of the garden, God said, Ye shall not eat of it, neither shall ye touch it, lest ye die. And the serpent said to the woman, Ye shall not surely die. For God knew that in whatever day ye should eat of it your eyes would be opened, and ye would be as gods, knowing good and evil. And the woman saw that the tree was good for food, and that it was pleasant to the eyes to look upon and beautiful to contemplate, and having taken of its fruit she ate, and she gave to her husband also with her, and they ate. (Gen. 3:1-6)

And the Lord God said to the woman, Why hast thou done this? And the woman said, The serpent deceived me, and I ate. And the Lord God said to the serpent, Because thou hast done this

thou art cursed above all cattle and all the brutes of the earth.
On thy breast and belly thou shalt go, and thou shalt eat earth
all the days of thy life. (Gen. 3:13-14)

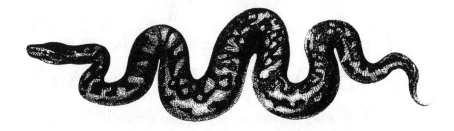

Adam and Eve, the serpent, and all the fallen creation were
sent out of the Garden of Delight. God stationed cherubim with
fiery swords to keep them out of the garden and to prevent them
from eating from the tree of life.

GOD'S COVENANT WITH NOAH AND THE ANIMALS: THE RAINBOW

AFTER many generations of men had sprung from Adam and Eve, God saw that apostasy had spread over the entire earth due to man's wickedness. Grieved that He had created everything on earth, God vowed to blot out man and the rest of creation by sending a great flood. However, one man, Noah, found grace with the Lord, together with his wife and three sons, and their wives. God also loved the animals, so to save their species He commanded each of their kinds to enter Noah's ark in pairs.

And it came to pass after forty days Noah opened the window of the ark which he had made. And he sent forth a raven; and it went forth and returned not until the water was dried from off the earth. And he sent a dove after it to see if the water had ceased from off the earth. And the

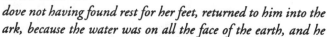

dove not having found rest for her feet, returned to him into the ark, because the water was on all the face of the earth, and he

stretched out his hand and took her, and brought her to himself
into the ark. And having waited yet seven other days, he again
sent forth the dove from the ark. And the dove returned to him
in the evening, and had a leaf of olive, a sprig in her mouth; and
Noah knew that the water had ceased from off the earth. And
having waited yet seven other days, he again sent forth the dove,
and she did not return to him again any more. (Gen. 8:6-12)

After the flood subsided, God spoke to Noah and established a covenant with him and his future generations and with
every living creature coming out of the ark:

And God spoke to Noah, and to his sons with him, saying, And
behold I establish My covenant with you, and with your seed
after you, and with every living creature with you, of birds and
of beasts, and with all the wild beasts of the earth, as many as
are with you, of all that come out of the ark. And I will establish
my covenant with you and all flesh shall not any more die by the
water of the flood, and there shall no more be a flood of water to
destroy all the earth. And the Lord God said to Noah, This is the
sign of the covenant which I set between me and you, and between
every living creature which is with you for perpetual generations.
I set My bow in the cloud, and it shall be for a sign of covenant
between Me and the earth. And it shall be when I gather clouds
upon the earth, that My bow shall be seen in the cloud. And I
will remember My covenant, which is between me and you, and
between every living soul in all flesh, and there shall no longer
be water for a deluge, so as to blot out all flesh. And My bow
shall be in the cloud, and I will look to remember the everlasting
covenant between Me and the earth, and between every living
soul in all flesh, which is upon the earth. And God said to Noah,
This is the sign of the covenant, which I have made between Me
and all flesh, which is upon the earth. (Gen. 9:8-17)

Every time we look at a rainbow, we should remember the
covenant between God, us, and the animals.

GOD'S ANIMAL KINGDOM

AS ALL living things are God's creation, they are related to each other and to God, Whose Spirit sustains their life. This energy—the divine, universal presence of God—permeates all things. Everything was created by God with its own nature, power, purpose, and essence; and each part of creation has its own intrinsic worth independent of human appraisal. Animals who are governed mostly by instinct are much more consistent in their natures than men. Each species of animal is joined to its own nature, blessed by God. All of life has a divine purpose and spiritual progression, for God created all things good. To all of creation, we owe an allegiance of service and admiration.

In the Garden of Eden, animals could communicate thoughts and feelings. All living things were in communion with each other, and all lived and moved in harmony and common accord.

How great is the wisdom which God has infused into the little creatures! The turtledove conceals her nest with onion sprouts to prevent wolves from attacking her young. Yet man doesn't know how to protect himself from the wiles of the devil.

Each animal has an innate wisdom to share with us, if we have the patience to cooperate with and understand them. Animals remain within the boundaries of their natures, not altering in any way what God has ordained; but we who have been honored with the power of intellect have completely abandoned His commandments.

God or-
dained a simple,
natural life for
humans and an-
imals. In the Garden of Eden, man and animals shared the same diet of fruits and herbs. They were not responsible for procuring their own food, but all were fed and cared for by the bounty of God.

God entrusted Adam and Eve with sovereignty over the animal kingdom so that animals could be governed with love and justice. That is why He established a kind of communication between man and animals. Thoughts and feelings between them were pure, with no mental barriers. These barriers came after the Fall, when men chose no longer to communicate with animals. That is why today animals are constantly trying to evaluate our motives, actions, and intentions. Animals know Who created them—it's man who wants to forget.

> But ask now the beasts, if they may speak to thee; and the birds of the air, if they may declare unto thee. Tell the earth, if it may speak to thee: and the fishes of the sea shall explain to thee. Who then has not known in all these things that the hand of the Lord has made them? Whereas the life of all living things is in His hand, and the breath of every man. (Job 11:7-10)

In dealing with animals, human beings today try to exert superior power over them instead of seeking a loving, silent communication, with the awareness that they are worthy of respect, life, and freedom. Animals respond better to non-verbal communication, and by patient listening we can understand what they are trying to tell us. Animals are close to the Creator, and are a reflection of His goodness.

THE HUMAN SOUL

OF ALL the things that God created, there is nothing closer to Him, nothing superior to the human soul. Even the moon, sun, stars, and animals are inferior to a single human soul.

What is the soul? The soul is a living incorporeal essence, invisible to the bodily eyes. The soul dwells in the body but is not of the body. The soul is the inward part of man. It is a spirit similar to the angels and demons, who are spirits.

The soul is immortal: it does not die, but returns to God. This aspect of the soul's nature is not inherent, but is a gift of

God's grace. The soul is the life of the body, and the spirit is the life of the soul; it is the higher part of the soul, capable of apprehending God.

"The whole world is not equal in worth to the soul, for the world passes away, while the soul is imperishable and remains imperishable." (St. John of Kronstadt) [12]

MEATBALL

STRESSBALL

Stress less this holiday... leave your party to Buca

Buca
di BEPPO
Italian Restaurant

This Holiday Season, think of Buca when planning office parties or family get-togethers. Whether you bring them to Buca, or bring Buca to them, we know how to feed a crowd.

Perfect for

HOLIDAY GATHERINGS | GIFT CARDS | PARTY PANS TO GO

AN AMERICAN FEAST WITH AN *Italian Twist!*

N AT 11AM
ANKSGIVING

...B FOR VALUABLE OFFERS AT **BUCADIBEPPO.COM**

f t B B ✈

Buca TO GO

"The soul is immortal and is conscious after death. It has memory." (St. Macarius the Great)

When we look at all the beauty of this created world and remember that nothing was created more beautiful, honorable, and glorious than our soul, and that God honored us above all visible things, how can we not glorify God?

Adam's soul and body were made from the ground. St. Seraphim of Sarov teaches:

"...if the Lord God had not breathed afterwards into his face the breath of life (that is, the grace of our Lord God the Holy Spirit Who proceeds from the Father and rests in the Son and is sent into the world for the Son's sake), Adam would have remained without having within him the Holy Spirit Who raises him to Godlike dignity. However perfect he had been created, and superior to all the other creatures of God as the crown of creation on earth, he would have been just like all the other creatures which, though they have a body, soul, and spirit, each according to its kind, yet have not the Holy Spirit within them. But when the Lord God breathed into Adam's face the breath of life, then, according to Moses' word, *Adam became a living soul* [Gen. 2:7], that is completely and in every way like God, and, like Him, forever immortal."[13]

A person's body grows with nourishment—food and water—whereas the soul grows with the grace of the Holy Spirit. The soul is established as a tabernacle of this Grace.

"The soul is independent, with a will and energy of its own, and it is changeable, since it is a created thing and thus has free will."[14]

"The nature of our soul involves the will to command and exercise sovereignty, and that part by nature which serves and obeys. The will, desire, sensibility—all are powers of the soul. Since we have within us that which commands, God has granted us lordship over all the earth."[15] (St. Gregory Palamas)

With the Fall of Adam and Eve, man's thoughts have become dispersed away from the love of God and focused on this world.

"All men are born and remain on earth for a limited time. At the end of this earthly life, the body succumbs to death. This earthly life is given to man by mercy of the Creator in order that man may use it for his salvation; for the restoration of himself from death to life in Jesus Christ."[16] (St. Ignatius Brianchaninov)

Fr. Seraphim Rose wrote:

"With the opening of their eyes through the transgression, Adam and Eve have already lost the life of Paradise.... From now on their eyes will be open to the lower things of this earth, and they will see only with difficulty the higher things of God...."[17]

A person can be alive in body but dead in soul. The soul dies when one begins to entirely trust one's own thinking; when one exalts one's own mind. Then man becomes the measure of all things, instead of God. He does not seek the grace of God and in the pride of his mind does not allow it to dwell there. Not thirsting wholeheartedly for God's righteousness, he is left without true enlightenment.

We should realize that the body is corruptible and short-lived, whereas the soul is immortal, and is joined to the body to be tested and deified. When we understand what the soul is, we will adjust our life to conform only to God's will; for if our body and soul are not purified, we cannot be one with Jesus Christ, now or in the future resurrection.

> When one has not seen the resurrection of his own soul, he is not able to learn exactly what the spiritual soul is. When the soul puts forth all its zeal and struggles by means of active virtues with reason and discernment, and has humbled and subjected the passions to itself, then the natural virtues surrounding, follow it, like the shadow that follows the body. They teach and guide it in what is holy, as if ascending a spiritual ladder.[18] (St. Gregory Palamas)

> Be on peaceful terms with thy soul; then heaven and earth will be on peaceful terms with thee. Be zealous to enter the treasury within; then thou wilt see that which is in heaven. For the former and the latter are one, and entering thou wilt see both. The ladder into the kingdom is hidden within thy soul. Dive into thyself, freed from sin; there thou wilt find steps along which thou canst ascend.[19] (St. Isaac the Syrian)

When the soul becomes suffused with the ineffable Uncreated Light of God, thoughts that anchor the soul to the earth are dispersed and the soul's mental activity reveals its nature to be that of Adam before the Fall, when Adam was covered by the grace of infinite light. The mind will be joined to God, and all former things will be left behind as the soul ascends to the highest, most divine things.

Then man will begin to rediscover himself as the one in whom the world is summed up, and the mediator through whom the world is offered up to God.

THE SPIRIT OF MAN

For who among men
knows the things of a man
save the spirit of the man which is in him?
Even so, the things of God no one knows but the Spirit of God.
Now we have received not the spirit of the world,
but the spirit that is from God, that we may know
the things that have been given us by God.
(I Cor. 11-12)

THE SPIRIT is the highest part of man's soul, which is formed through the grace of the Holy Spirit. It is the organ through which man apprehends God, through which man's living bond with God is established in the soul. The activity of the spirit takes place mainly in the heart, and man's conscience is the result of its action. (cf. Romans 2:15) Therefore the basic manifestations of the spirit are freedom and conscience. The organ of the spirit is the intellect.

When the Holy Spirit purifies our whole being, we become His dwelling places. *For as many as are led by the Spirit of God, they are the sons of God.* (Rom. 8:14) When a man is reborn by the Holy Spirit, he cultivates within himself the seeds of grace until he brings forth fruits of the Spirit. Through carelessness towards his spirituality, a man can descend to the level of a fleshly natural man; but when the spirit prevails, the soul has true life, gaining the ability to think and speak in accordance with the mind of God, and the desire for spiritual knowledge.

When the mind, by the grace of Christ, ascends to what is above Nature, then it is enlightened by the illumination of the Holy Spirit and splendidly reaches out into contemplation. And having come above itself, according to the measurement of grace given it by God, it clearly and purely beholds the nature of all things in accordance with its condition and order.[20] (St. Gregory Palamas)

The soul is the vehicle of the Holy Spirit, which gives it spiritual life. Guided by the Holy Spirit, the body is able through the senses to use all of creation and all of Holy Scripture to rise step by step from the seen to the unseen. Through our mind and our senses we can rise from created things to the Creator.

Come let us go up to the Mountain of the Lord, to the house of the God of Jacob; that He may teach us His ways, and that we may walk in His paths. (Isaiah 2:3)

HUMAN SOULS AND ANIMAL SOULS

IF I SAY there are other creatures made by God, some are less excellent than the soul, and some equal to it. The soul of a brute animal, for instance, is less excellent, and that of an angel equal; but nothing is better than the soul. And if at any time any of these is better, that is the result of the soul's sin, not of its nature. Still, sin does not make the human so inferior that the soul of a brute animal is to be preferred to it or even compared with it. (Blessed Augustine)[21]

The soul of brute beasts did not emerge after having been hidden in the earth, but it was called into existence at the time of God's command. (St. Basil the Great)[22]

St. Anthony the Great acknowledges that animals have souls:

Because some people impiously dare to say that plants and vegetables have a soul, I will write briefly about this for the guidance of the simple. Plants have a natural life, but they do not have a soul. Man is called an intelligent animal because he has intellect and is capable of acquiring knowledge. The other animals and the birds can make sounds because they possess breath and soul. All things that are subject to growth and decline are alive; but the fact that they live and grow does not necessarily mean that they all have souls. There are four categories of living beings. The first are immortal and have

50

souls, such as angels. The second have intellect, soul and breath, such as men. The third have breath and soul, such as animals. The fourth have only life, such as plants. The life of plants is without soul, breath, intellect or immortality. These four attributes, on the other hand, presuppose the possession of life. Every human soul is in continual movement.[23]

St. Anthony the Great

The soul has three powers: first, the power of nourishment and growth; second, that of imagination and instinct; third, that of intelligence and intellect. Plants share only in the first of these powers, animals share in the first and second only, and men share in all three. (St. Maximos the Confessor)[24]

Blessed Augustine shows that there are seven levels of the soul(paraphrased from his work *The Magnitude of thye Soul*):

Level I

—The soul is the life-force of the body, which keeps it unified and harmonious;

—it maintains nourishment, growth, and reproduction.
—This level is seen in man, animals, and plants.

Level II

—The soul seeks whatever suits the nature of the body.
—The soul has memory, remembering what it has experienced through the senses (touch, sight, smell, etc.), and what it has learned through habit.
—This level is seen in man and animals.

Level III

—The soul learns and remembers through observation (language, reading, writing, etc.), and not only through habit.
—This is the level of reason and logical thought, and of music, poetry, eloquence.
—This level bears the mark of greatness. Only humans are on this and subsequent levels.

Level IV

—The souls turns inward, seeking self-purification.
—There is recognition of the fear of death.
—The soul turns away from worldly things.
—The soul is aware of its state of purity vs. defilement.
—The battle between good and evil begins.
—The soul seeks universal love and goodness.

Level V

—The soul is free of all corruption and sin;
—it possesses utter joy and no fears;
—it advances towards God.

Level VI

—The soul focuses on God only;
—it possesses a clean heart and thoughts;

—it eliminates all attachments to corruptible things;
—it seeks the highest perfection and truth.

Level VII

—This is the dwelling-place to which the previous steps have led, everlasting peace and goodness.
—The soul truly understands the supreme reality of God's truth, how "all things under the sun are vanity of vanities."
—It apprehends the truth of the seedless incarnation of Jesus Christ, and of all the teachings of Mother Church.
—In its certainty of faith, it yearns for death as the greatest boon.

In His hand is the soul of every living thing, and the breath of all mankind. (Job 12:10)

"God knows all things, God only, Who is in all things, even the unborn offspring of the animals."[26] (St. Barsanuphius the Great)

God created animals with distinct natures and characteristics: the fox is crafty, the ox steadfast, the deer timid, the lion fearless and courageous. God endowed each animal with what it needs for its well-being and survival. Animals are said to be irrational, to lack reason. Reason is the logical faculty in man by which observation and analysis of data leads to logical conclusions. Animals were not given this ability, because they do not have free will. Instead, they have heightened sense reactions. Animals have been taught things by God which humans need a lifetime to learn. God compensated for the lack of reason in animals by endowing them with the superiority of their senses.[27]

Nothing is without order and purpose in the animal kingdom; each animal bears the wisdom of the Creator and testifies of Him. God granted man and animals many natural attributes, such as compassion, love, feelings…. "…for even dumb animals bewail the loss of one of their own."[28]

Can the love and gratitude a dog shows to his owner compare with the ungratefulness man shows to his Creator? "Fear not the wild beasts more than your own lack of faith." (St. Basil the Great)

THE HEART

THE LIFE of the soul and all its feelings are seated in the heart. The heart is the unifying organ of life. Our heart is the sacred altar where our mind meets God and where God reveals Himself to us.

When we have pride within our hearts, we believe that we are perfect and sufficient unto ourselves; that we are rich and don't need anyone or anything; that we are already blessed; that we shall be as gods. (cf. Gen 3:5)

There is much beauty and richness in our physical world, but perfect life can only be found in the spiritual realm, when we live our lives in communion with God. Therefore, we must keep constant vigilance over our heart, against all external temptations, guarding the purity of the heart. We can obtain peace of the heart by praying unceasingly the Jesus Prayer: *Lord Jesus Christ, Son of God, have mercy on me, a sinner.* Our heart is the root of all the good or all the evil that we do, because it holds the inner senses within it: "If the root is holy, so are the branches"(St. Nikodemos of the Holy Mountain).[29] The heart contains the spirit of man. Our thoughts emerge from our heart, and our words are its overflow. That is why it is so necessary for us to know Jesus Christ, and to live in Christ with all the strength of our soul.

And the Word became flesh and dwelt among us, full of grace and truth. (John 1:14)

Man does not live on bread alone, but by every word that proceeds from the mouth of the Lord. (Matt. 4:4)

In this life, we fill our mind and heart either with God's grace, or with Satan's evil. If you focus your heart on God and raise your mind to heaven through repentance, God's grace will come to you. St. Isaac the Syrian spoke with a burning heart to us, his brothers and sisters of a new generation, when he said:

> "What is a charitable heart? It is a heart that is burning with love for the whole creation, for men, for the birds, for the beasts, for all creatures. He who has such a heart cannot see or call to mind a creature without his eyes being filled with tears by reason of the immense compassion which seizes his heart; a heart which is softened and can no longer bear to see or learn from others of any suffering, even the smallest pain, being inflicted upon a creature. That is why such a man never ceases to pray also for the animals, for the enemies of truth, and for those who do him evil, that they may be preserved and purified. He will pray even for the reptiles, moved by the infinite pity which reigns in the hearts of those who are becoming united with God.[30]

THE INTELLECT OF MAN AND THE INSTINCTS OF ANIMALS

THE INTELLECT (in Greek νους—*nous,* also translated as "mind") is the highest faculty in man. Through it, as long as it is purified, man can know God and the inner essences or principles of created things. The intellect dwells in the depths of the soul and constitutes the innermost aspect of the heart.[31] With the intellect man can achieve wisdom and attain spiritual knowledge. One's life can become a spiritual pilgrimage back to the Creator.

Spiritual knowledge is a gift given us by God so that we may contemplate the world and all its beauty and grandeur and come closer to knowing Him Who created all things for man's benefit.

Man was given freedom to choose between good and evil, whether to know or not know the Lord. When we use our intellect correctly, we always choose what is good and best; we can then attain an understanding of God and His creation. The intellect that enjoys the love of God is the light of the soul. When a person has purified the intellect, he knows himself and where he is going, and he knows that life on this earth is merely transitory. He who knows himself, knows all things; he knows that all things are created by God and made for man's salvation.

Our human intellect cannot by itself ascend to divine illumination: God must draw it up to Himself and illuminate it with rays of divine light. The proper work of the intellect is to abide within the heart and maintain a vigilant watch over it.

The evil one tries to surround the heart, preventing the intellect from communicating with God. When our intellect dominates our passions, it makes our senses instruments of virtue; but when the passions dominate our intellect, our senses conform to sin.

The intellect *(nous)* must be carefully distinguished from reason *(dianoia):*

> Unlike the *dianoia* or reason ... the intellect does not function by formulating abstract concepts and then arguing on this basis to a conclusion reached through deductive reasoning, but it understands divine truth by means of immediate experience, intuition or 'simple cognition' (the term used by St. Isaac the Syrian)....
>
> The function [of reason] is to draw conclusions or formulate concepts deriving from data provided either by revelation or spiritual knowledge, or by sense observation. The knowledge of the reason is subsequently of a lower order than spiritual knowledge and does not imply any direct apprehension or perception of the inner essences or principles of created things, still less of divine truth itself. Indeed, such apprehension or perception, which is the function of the intellect, is beyond the scope of the reason.[32]

Both intellect and reason, as they are defined here, are unique to man among the earthly creation: animals do not possess them. The animals do, however, have instincts. God blessed animals with an unchangeable, simple nature, and gave them the information which He wanted them to have, and which is necessary for their nature. Animals were created with an instinct to love and protect their young. They can instinctively locate their homes (or, in the case of fish, their spawning stream) from hundreds or thousands of miles away. And unlike man, they instinctively know to seek out healing herbs when they are sick.

Animals are true to their nature. Only man forgets the dictates of his nature. Therefore St. Peter Damascene calls us to humility with these words:

> Dogs are better than man because they are true to their nature like all animals are; we are the insensitive brutes. (St. Peter Damascene)[33]

Animals, though not endowed with reason, are endowed with feelings, keenness of senses, and God-given instincts. It may be said that God "commands" the animals through their instincts.

THE NATURE OF ANIMALS:

THE SENSES

THROUGHOUT Holy Scripture and the works of the Desert Fathers, animals are referred to as irrational or dumb. These terms were never intended to be derogatory; they were used as terms of comparison between the natures of animals and men, to distinguish different unique characteristics.

The mind is the guide and counsellor of the soul. God gave man and animals a soul, but only man was given freedom of will. Animals were not given freedom, but God guides them with His mind.[34] As a rational being, man leads nature rather than being led by it. When a man has a physical desire, he has the authority either to override that desire or to follow it. Animals are irrational because they are led by their natures. They do not judge a desire, but immediately rush to action when it comes.[35]

God created the five senses of the body to serve as openings to the world around us: eyes, nose, mouth, ears, and touch. By using the eyes to see the beauty of the flowers and sky, the mind by exercising rational thought can see the wisdom, creativity, power, and glory of Him who created them. He can thus reason and say: if the sky is so beautiful, how much more beautiful is the Creator of the sky? Thus the mind climbs to the knowledge of the Creator, and it incites the heart to love Him. The senses were created so that one might marvel at the works of the Lord.

> Through this sense perception, the mind is guided through rational thought to acquire wisdom, goodness, power, grace, truth, sweetness, and perfections of the Creator that can be discerned in the creation and in the Bible. (St. Nikodemos of the Holy Mountain)

The mind rises from created things to the Creator, from the sacred Scriptures to Him Who inspired them. The mind can move with wings of thought to go beyond to the knowledge and vision of God.

> *From the greatness and beauty of created things comes a corresponding perception of the Creator.* (Wisdom 13:5)

> *Ever since the creation of the world, His invisible nature, namely, His eternal power and deity, have been clearly perceived in the things that have been made.* (Romans 1:20)

Souls aspiring to acquire the sanctifying power of the spirit direct all of their love towards Jesus Christ. They pray, think, and meditate on Christ. The soul's five senses, its understanding, spiritual knowledge, discernment, patient endurance, and compassion receive the grace and sanctification of the Spirit.[36]

THE  RACE
OF THE HOLY SPIRIT

GRACE is one of God's energies—the energy of the Divinity of the Trinity.

St. Macarius of Egypt says that the grace that comes to man from God enters him and unites with his freedom of choice in order to reveal whether man's will is in accordance with grace or not. Grace is ready to help, if man desires it.[37]

When the intellect begins to perceive the Holy Spirit with full consciousness, grace is beginning to paint the divine likeness over the divine image in us. The grace of God starts to remake the divine image in man into what it was when man was first created.

The capacity to respond to the grace of God by free will distinguishes man from animals, and from inanimate things, which are also dependent on the grace of God both for their existence and for whatever is good in them. If man allows grace to permeate his mind, body, and soul, then man will be raised to his original pure and natural state. It is grace that allows man to fulfill what is holy within him. Therefore, we must purify our hearts so that when the pure Spirit of Grace enters them, it will have a loving home.

JESUS CHRIST THE LOGOS

SINCE the transgression of Adam and Eve, man's nature has been steadily declining to the lowest depths of human existence. Man has been experiencing an internal warfare—the war the flesh wages against the soul, taking it captive by sin.

We all once lived in the passions of the flesh, following the desires of the body and mind. (Eph. 2:3)

For who shall be pure from uncleanness? Not even one, if even his life should be but one day upon the earth. (Job 14:4)

Out of love for His creation, God sent His Son, Jesus Christ, the Second Person of His Divine Essence, to the earth. Jesus Christ is God Incarnate, Who came into the world to raise up human nature into the blessed state that was originally lost through the transgression. Jesus Christ came for this reason: to change and transform and renew human nature, and to recreate this soul that had been overturned by passions. He came to unite human nature with His own Spirit of the Godhead.38

The purpose of the Incarnation was to restore Adam and Eve's humanity to the position of honor they originally had, had they kept the divine commandment. They would have grown in divinity and knowledge by having eaten of the trees of knowledge and life. They would have acquired divinity in humanity, infallible knowledge and immortal life.[39]

> *...And the Logos became flesh and dwelt among us, full of grace and truth.* (John 1:14)

Whoever approaches God and truly desires to be in Christ must be changed and transformed from his former state and attitudes (the old man) to become a good, new person.

> *Therefore, if any man be in Christ, he is a new creature: old things are passed away; behold, all things are become new.* (2 Cor. 5:17)

BAPTISM OF THE HOLY SPIRIT

TO OBTAIN the divine grace of God, we are baptized—a Sacrament of the Church. When you are baptized in Christ, you put on Christ. You are immersed in the illumination of Christ's grace. You are returning to the original state of man and woman in the Garden of Eden—a state of sinlessness, purity, and wholeness. You are redeemed and become an inheritor of the Kingdom of God. Through baptism, grace is within us and truth rules our soul. As our soul advances, this divine grace reveals itself to our intellect and encourages our soul to goodness.

Truly, truly I say to you, unless one is born of water and the spirit, he cannot enter the Kingdom of God. (John 3:5-6)

God saved us in Jesus Christ through the mystery of His will (Eph. 1:9) in order *to make all men what is the plan of the mystery hidden for all ages in God Who created all things.* (Eph. 3:9, Rom. 16:25-26, Col 1:25)

Through baptism, our soul becomes penetrated by the example of Jesus Christ, and our free will is more easily inclined towards blessedness and sanctity. We humans are the natural link joining God with all other material creatures; we join heaven with earth, things invisible with things visible, and gradually progress in our ascension back to the Creator.

We can have a foretaste of Paradise even here on earth by leading a virtuous life after having been saved by God's grace through baptism in the Holy Spirit. After baptism, we must unite our intellect's knowledge with the knowledge of our senses to attain true wisdom.

> ...He sees all things in God, first as flowing from God into existence, and second, through them, rising to God, as to the end of all moved creatures.[40]

With baptism we are given God's grace, but we have to focus our effort to keep it and not lose it through sin. We can accomplish this by using Jesus Christ as a "measuring stick" in all the decisions we have to make throughout our lives. Let us remember this beautiful poetic passage of the apocryphal text *Adam and Eve:*

VERILY I say unto thee, this darkness will pass from thee, every day I have determined for thee, until the fulfillment of My covenant; when I will save thee and bring thee back again into the garden, into the abode of light thou longest for, wherein is no darkness. I will bring thee to it—in the kingdom of Heaven."

Again said God unto Adam: "All this misery that thou hast been made to take upon thee because of thy transgression, will not free thee from the hand of Satan, and will not save thee.

"But I will. When I shall come down from heaven, and shall become flesh of thy seed, and take upon Me the infirmity from which thou sufferest, then the darkness that came upon thee in this cave shall come upon Me in the grave, when I am in the flesh of thy seed.

"And I, who am without years, shall be subject to the reckoning of years, of times, of months, and of days, and I shall be reckoned as one of the sons of men, in order to save thee."[41]

Throughout our lives we can rejoice because:

the inner essences of all things are embraced by the Logos. (St. Maximos the Confessor)[42]

Rejoice in the Lord always. Let your gentleness be evident to all. The Lord is near. Do not be anxious about anything but in everything by prayer and petition with thanksgiving, present your requests to God. And the peace of God, which transcends all understanding, will guard your hearts and your minds in Christ Jesus. (Phil. 4:4-7)

When we focus on Jesus Christ instead of "our wants and desires," we cannot but remember the truth in every situation:

God giveth to all life, and breath, and all things.... In Him we live, and move, and have our being." (Acts 17:25, 28)

God, Who is rich in mercy, out of the love with which He loved us, even when we were dead through our trespasses, made us alive together with Christ. (Eph. 2:4-5)

That at the name of Jesus Christ, every knee should bow in heaven and on earth and under the earth. (Phil. 2:10)

God is the Creator, Protector, and Owner of All Animals

THE LIVES of holy men and women have shown us that our whole life is a battle against the passions within us. Once we have eliminated these from our hearts, by God's grace we will be able to live at peace with other men and even the wild beasts.

Job confirms this: *And the beasts of the field shall be at peace with you.* (Job 5:23)

Through obedience to God's commandments, God's holy ones restored the image of God in themselves, taking unto themselves the gifts of the Lord's grace and radiating the original purity and light. Therefore the animals, sensing in man the fragrance of the original purity, became obedient to them. What power there is in love and virtue: St. Pachomius used the crocodiles of Egypt as ferry boats, and they seemed pleased enough to ship him back and forth over the Nile.[43] He was also able to sleep in a cave full of poisonous reptiles.

God is the Creator of Nature, and therefore nature helps us to truly see and understand God.

Knowest thou the time when the wild goats bring forth among the rocks, or hast thou observed the hinds when they fawn? Hast thou numbered the months of their conceiving, or knowest thou the time when they bring forth? They bow themselves to bring forth young, and they cast them, and send forth roarings. Their young are weaned and go to feed, they go forth, and return not to them. Who hath sent out the wild ass free, and who hath loosed his bonds? To whom I have given a house in the wilderness, and his dwellings in the barren land. He scorneth the multitude of the city, he heareth not the cry of the driver. He looketh round about the mountains of his pasture, and seeketh for every green thing.... (Job 39:1-8.)

Reverence for all life, kindness, love and compassion for animals and the rest of creation, are all attributes of intelligence and virtue: *A righteous man has pity for the lives of his cattle, but the bowels of the ungodly are unmerciful.* (Prov. 12:10)

Let us learn from all of creation, especially the animals:

Go to the ant, O sluggard; and see, and emulate his ways and become wiser than he. For whereas he has no husbandry, nor any one to compel him, and is under no master, he prepares food for himself in the summer and lays by abundant store in harvest.

Or go to the bee, and learn how diligent she is, and how earnestly she is engaged in her work; whose labor kings and private men use for health, and she is desired and respected by all; though weak in body, she is advanced by honoring wisdom. (Prov. 6:6-8)

Bees derive their noble descent from Paradise, and make honeycombs by the instinct of their nature.

We must always remember that the true owner of animals is God the Creator, not man.

For God, Who gives the beasts their food, and to the younglings of the ravens that call upon Him, He will provide for thee. (Ps. 146:9-10)

And wilt thou hunt prey for the lions? and satisfy the desires of the serpents? For they fear in their lairs, and lying in wait couch in the woods. And who has prepared food for the raven? for its young ones wander and cry to the Lord, in search of food.... (Job 38:39-40)

And does the hawk remain steady by thy wisdom, having spread out her wings unmoved, looking toward the region of the south? And does the eagle rise at thy command, and the vulture remain sitting over his nest, on a crag of a rock, and in a secret place? Thence he seeks food, his eyes observe from afar. And his young ones roll themselves in blood, and wherever the carcasses may be, immediately they are found. (Job 38:39-41; 39:26-30)

THE NEW CREATION

AT the final Resurrection, our world will pass away. *A new heaven and new earth* (Rev. 21:1) will be created, in which man and all animals will again live in harmony and peace. The Spirit of the Lord, the Spirit of love, will prevail in Paradise. Wild animals will become peaceful and will eat herbs and fruits again.

For there shall be a new heaven and a new earth; and they shall not at all remember the former, neither shall they at all come to their mind. But they shall find in her joy and exultation. (Is. 65: 17-18)

The enmity of man and the enmity of animals shall cease:

And the wolf shall feed with the lamb, and the leopard shall lie down with the kid; and the young calf and bull and lion shall feed together; and a little child shall lead them. And the ox and the bear shall feed together; and the lion shall eat straw like the ox. (Is. 11:6-7)

The new earth will be in harmony by the Grace of God, as it was before sin entered the world. As creation fell into corrup-

tion because of man, so together with man it will be restored to incorruption at the end of the ages:

For the eager longing of creation awaits the revelation of the sons of God. For creation was made subject to vanity, not by its own will but by reason of him who made it subject, in hope. Because creation itself also will be delivered from its slavery to corruption into the freedom of the glory of the sons of God. (Rom. 8:19-21)

St. Symeon the New Theologian comments on this:

...when man again (will) be renewed and become spiritual, incorrupt and immortal, then also the whole creation, which had been subjected by God to man to serve him, (will) be delivered from this servitude, (will) be renewed together with him, and become incorrupt and as it were spiritual. All this the All-Merciful God foreordained before the creation of the world.[44]

This would indicate that animals as a group will inhabit the transfigured new earth after the General Resurrection. However, we have no indication from Patristic writings that individual souls of animals will survive death. For we know that, among the creatures of earth, only man has been given individual, immortal souls meant to dwell with God unto the ages.

TRANSFIGURATION: OUR PILGRIMAGE BACK TO EDEN

ALL THE TRIALS and tribulations of life are necessary in order for us to transfigured and be with Jesus Christ. Our life on this earth should be one of repentance for our sins; we must pick up our cross daily and bear it. All that we bear aids in our purification; being tried in fire, we will come out bright gold.

God allows man to be tempted by Satan so that, after passing through trials of storm and fire, he may come in the end to the full enjoyment of divine blessings.

We went through fire and water, and Thou hast brought us out into a place where the soul is refreshed. (Ps. 66:12)

For it has been granted to you on behalf of Christ, not only to believe on Him, but also to suffer for Him. (Phil. 1:29-30)

We are called by God to reflect divinity, to become icons of Jesus Christ. This can only be accomplished by making the totality of our lives a constant prayer to God. Our souls must swim and float in the Scriptures. By our lives we must demonstrate the Gospels and the presence of Jesus Christ.

73

If our priorities are right, we will understand that life is not for the acquisition and accumulation of material goods, but for the acquisition of the Holy Spirit. The grace of the Holy Spirit purifies, sanctifies, and transfigures human nature, so that it is deified.[45]

When man is united with God in the Holy Spirit, he is united in brotherhood with everything that lives. When we reflect on the beauty of animals, we must remember that beauty is a manifestation of the Creator. People have a tendency to love creatures more than the Creator. We must raise our mind from the creature to the Creator and become fixed on him.

By the greatneess and beauty of the creatures, proportionately the Maker of them is seen. (Wisdom of Solomon 13:5)

We must strive to attune our souls to God. Prayer is the echo of the soul reverberating throughout eternity.

We must know the truth about where we came from before we can know where we are going. By exercising our freedom, we choose to see the light or to live in darkness.

St. Basil the Great said:

"We should think such thoughts to rise from the visible to the invisible and from the ephemeral to the eternal. If the physical sun is so great, how much more beautiful is the Sun of Righteousness? And if the loss of a blind man who cannot see the sun is so immense, how much greater is the loss for a sinner who is deprived of the true light?"

Why is it that most people have to be perishing before they want to be saved? Human nature and the passion of human pride, since the time of Adam and Eve, are responsible for man's downfall into sin. Redemption can only begin by wanting God in your life more than anything else, and by making the decision to surrender your whole life to Christ.

> If you love Me, I will ask the Father to send the Holy Spirit Who will remain with you forever. He will be the other counselor in My place. He will be the Comforter, the ennobler, and the defender at the difficult times in your life. He will guide you to the whole truth.[46]

> *I am in My Father and you are in Me, and I am in you. He who loves Me obeys My commandments is loved by My Father, and We shall come to dwell in him as friends forever.* (John 14:18-24)

The ultimate purpose of our lives on earth is to see the divine light, to see the glory of God. When we are capable of seeing this, we will be transfigured. We will have developed a "oneness of soul" where each part of the creation is a "reflection of God." We become caretakers of the creation and stewards for God. God's grace allows us to be reborn spiritually; it guides us back to God, justifying and sanctifying us, making us worthy to be heirs of the eternal kingdom of God.

We can receive eternal life with God and our families and all the material creation—the incorruptible crown. But instead we spend our lives in mediocrity and negligence. The only thing holding us back from attaining virtues and perfection is not having a pure heart, not forgiving others, and refusing to deny ourselves and let God act.

Let us cleanse ourselves from all pollution of flesh and spirit. (II Cor. 7:1)

He who remains flesh and blood is far from the realm of life. (I Cor. 15:50)

True life is life in the Spirit. We must strive to overcome every problem, using them as stepping-stones upwards in the growth of the soul. If we endure to the end, we will proceed from strength to strength and shall receive invisibly from God enlightenment of soul.

St. Maximos the Confessor said:

Man is not a being isolated from the rest of creation; by his very nature he is bound up with the whole of the universe.... In his way to union with God, man in no way leaves creatures aside, but gathers together in his love the whole cosmos disordered by sin, that it may be transfigured by grace.[48]

Do not be conformed to this world, but be transformed by the renewal of your mind, that you may prove what is the will of God, what is good and acceptable and perfect. (Rom. 12:2)

St. Maximus

There are several spiritual endeavors that harmonize the mind, body, and spirit:
—fulfilling the divine commandments;
—acquiring Christian virtues;
—reading the Holy Scriptures;
—contemplating the beauty of creation;
—contemplating the Incarnation of Jesus Christ;
—contemplating God Himself;
—partaking of the Holy Sacraments.

These endeavors are the fine-tuning that refine the mind, body, and soul internally and externally. They will enhance, beautify, strengthen, and transfigure us to a state of blessedness.

> Do not let your mind misuse its God-given freedom, precipitating it into slavery to the flesh, the world, and the devil, but nail it onto Christ as onto the cross, that your mind may be given resurrection in Christ.... Fence your mind about from all selfish imaginings, by which it becomes intoxicated and falls a prey to the devil, and hold it girded in the confines of your heart, where it can be sobered by prayer and purified by tears. In brief, it means to train the mind not to misuse freedom through its own pride towards the living and merciful God, and by the deadening of the soul by the passions.
>
> O Lord Jesus, Thou Mind of God and Wisdom of God, help us to gird up our minds, that they may ponder only on what is from Thee. (St. Nicholas Velimirovich)[49]

Remember, as it says in the book *Unseen Warfare:* "Today is in our hands, but Tomorrow is the hands of God."

SAINTS:

LIVING ICONS

THE REMAINDER of this book is dedicated to God through His Saints. These true-life stories of Saints and animals are historically documented. These stories will show you how we can reach such a state of blessedness and grace with the animals and rise to communion with God.

Throughout this book we have made use of icons as illustratons. Icons serve as "windows into heaven" and focus the believer's attention and love towards their prototypes. When we look at an icon, we sense a mystical communion between ourselves and the Saints.

These saintly men, women, and children exemplify dedication and perseverance in the love they have for Jesus Christ. They are true reflections of sanctity and righteousness and participators of heavenly grace. Their souls have received the divine inheritance—a treasury of virtues on earth leading to an insatiable spiritual yearning for the heavenly Bridegroom, Jesus Christ. The truth of Jesus Christ has illuminated their lives and made them God-bearing luminaries to the world. They have fought the good fight, making the totality of their lives a living prayer and sacrifice to God.

God so values the sweat of obedience that He counts it as the blood of martyrs.[50]

True knowledge of the first-created world and Adam is accessible only through God's Revelation and the divine vision of the Saints.[51] These holy men  and women form a visible link between our world and the Kingdom of Heaven. The grace of the Lord has flowed from

generation to generation through these holy souls.

In these chaotic, apostatized times, Christ's martyrs are a source of healing grace to all of us who draw near to the Church Triumphant in Heaven. Christianity was sustained by these martyrs' blood. Their persecuted bodies became the fruitful harvest of men's souls. The martyrs, filled with grace and abounding with love, placed themselves, like a "lighted candle upon a candlestick," so that all could see the good works of the Father and glorify Him Who is in Heaven. God tested His true servants, "as gold in the furnace" in order to finally redeem them, revealing their victory over sin.

Many of the Saints were visionaries, who knew from experience the reality of man as he was intended to be. They taught that the original state of Adam was man's natural state, and that the present state of corruption after the Fall is unnatural. The Saints during their earthly lives glimpsed that transfigured, incorruptible world for which man was created. It was precisely by becoming dispassionate through prayer and ascetic struggle that the Saints restored in themselves, while yet in a corruptible body, some measure of the "likeness" of Adam. Like him, they were shown to be impervious to the elements; like him, they were masters and stewards of creation, and all creatures obeyed them. As man was created to be in the beginning, so again he will be in the future age when he will be raised up in a body incorruptible.[52]

These blessed souls realized how difficult it is to maintain a burning zeal and spiritual fervor in daily life, because worldly needs dampen our concentrated efforts. Therefore they went to the wilderness to pursue their fervent love of God and the apostolic life.

The Saints were glad to live with the wild beasts in the wilderness, judging them less harmful than their fellow fallen men. They trusted the animals as their friends, because animals don't teach us to sin, but revere and respect holiness. Men tried to kill Daniel, but the lions saved him, preserving him; and when human justice condemned the blameless, the animals proclaimed his innocence. Whereas Daniel's holiness gave rise to strife and envy among men, among the wild animals it evoked awe and veneration. (Daniel 6:22)

Let us prepare now to enter the realm of blessedness.

It is impossible to describe in words the sensation of intimate and spiritual sweetness which is inseparable from solitude, the joy and serenity which no scepter and no honor can secure. What peace neither to see or hear or participate in worldly life, which is delusion. Nothing distracts you from the service of God; nothing prevents you from reading and meditating upon sacred books…. The virgin forest separates you from the world. All you can see is the sky above, you already live as in heaven. This proves that man was created for beatitude. If, from the contemplation of the beauty above, the eye turns to the contemplation of nature, the heart is again inflamed with love for Him Who created such beauty. The heart quickens before the marvels of His Wisdom and in thanksgiving for His goodness.[53]

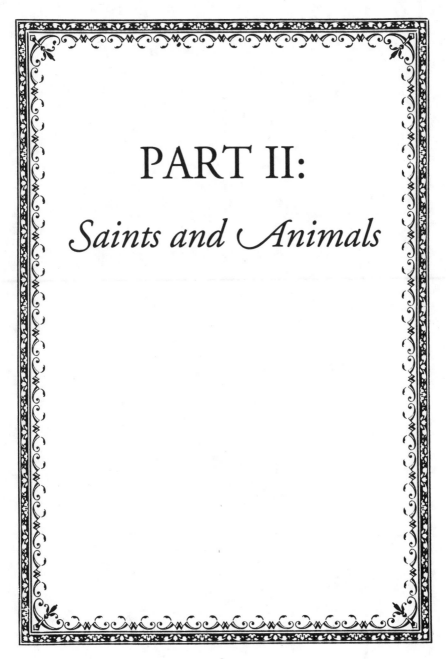

PART II:

Saints and Animals

SAINT AEMILIANUS
THE HERMIT

Commemorated February 9

EMILIANUS (†576), having left his parents and his possessions, sought solitude in the territory of Auvergne [in ancient Gaul] where, chopping down the trees, he made a little field which he cultivated and which furnished him with the food necessary for life. He also had a little garden which he watered with rainwater and from which he took vegetables which he would eat without any seasoning. He had no other consolations than those that came from God, for there were no other inhabitants than the beasts and birds, which would crowd around him every day as around a servant of God. He gave all his time to fasting and prayer, and no worldly care could turn him from them, because he sought only God.

There was at that time in the city of Clermont a man named Sigivald, bestowed with great authority, who had in his service a youth named Bracchio, which means in their language "bear cub." The man of whom I have just spoken had charged this young man with hunting wild boar; accompanied by a large pack of dogs, Bracchio went about the forest, and if he took anything, he would bring it to his master. One day, while he was pursuing an enormous boar with the dog pack, the quarry entered the enclosure around the Saint's cell. The baying pack followed it there and came to the entry of the first room, but suddenly they stopped short, not being permitted to go in after the boar.

Seeing this, Bracchio recognized with astonishment that there was something Divine there, and going toward the cell of the Saint, he noticed the boar standing before the door without

fear. The Elder came to greet Bracchio, embraced him, and invited him to sit down. When they were seated, he said to him, "I see you, beloved son, elegantly dressed and occupied with seeking things which dispose more to the loss of the soul than to its salvation. I beg you, abandon the master whom you serve here below and follow the true God, the Creator of heaven and earth, Who governs all things by His will, Who submits all things to His rule, and Whose very majesty, as you see, renders this beast fearless. May your master's authority—which is nothing—not make you vain and proud. For thus says the Apostle Paul: 'He that glorieth, let him glory in the Lord' (I Cor. 1:31), and elsewhere: 'If I yet pleased men, I should not be the servant of Christ' (Gal. 1:10). Subject yourself to the service of Him Who said, 'Come unto Me, all ye that labor and are heavy laden, and I will give you rest' (Matt. 11:30), worship of Whom gains both present things and eternal life. And thus He said, if anyone renounces all he possesses, he 'shall receive a hundredfold, and shall inherit eternal life'" (Matt. 19:29).

While the Elder was occupied with these words and others equally worthy of a man, the wild boar withdrew safe and sound into the woods. The young man departed from the Saint, not without admiration from seeing that the wild boar he had begun to hunt became, despite his natural savagery, as gentle as a lamb in sight of the Elder. Turning over in his mind various thoughts and asking himself what he should do—whether he should leave the world or continue to serve it—finally, touched by the Divine goodness and (I believe) by the prayer of Saint Aemilianus, he began to look for some secret way to come to the clerical state....

After Sigivald had died, Bracchio hastened to the aforesaid Elder, and when he had spent two or three years with him, he knew the Psalter by heart.... Later, other monks joined the Elder and himself.

Finally blessed Aemilianus fulfilled the measure of days counted for his life: he died about the ninetieth year of his age and left Bracchio as his successor. The latter, having founded a monastery, obtained from Ranichilde, Sigivald's daughter, several parcels of land which he left to this monastery. They were made up of woods from the Vindiacens estate. Having gone forth from this monastery, Bracchio came to Tours, where he built oratories and founded two monasteries....

Saint Anthony the Great

Commemorated on January 17

IS eloquent defense of the Orthodox belief in Christ as true God earned him the title of St. Anthony the Great.

Anthony was born of extremely humble parents in the year 251 A.D. in Coma in middle Egypt. He received no education and when he was orphaned at eighteen he had not yet learned to read and write. In spite of this handicap he sought to learn the meaning of his existence. One day he was greatly impressed by a sermon based on a text from St. Matthew in which Christ said: "If you would be perfect, go, sell what you possess and give to the poor, and you will have treasure in heaven; and come and follow me." Anthony then sold his meager belongings, gave the money to the poor, and went into the Egyptian desert. There he met a group of monks who took him into their care. In the desert Anthony applied himself diligently to prayer and study.

✳ ✳ ✳

A certain voice came to him from above, saying, "Anthony, where are you going, and why?" He was not distressed, but since he was accustomed to being called this way often, after he listened he answered, saying, "Since the crowds will not allow me to be alone, I want to go into the upper Thebaid because of the many annoyances of those who beset me here, and especially because they ask me for things that are beyond my power." But

the voice said to him, "Even if you go into the Thebaid, and even if, as you are contemplating, you go down to the pastures, you will have more, even twice as much, toil to endure. If you truly desire to be alone, go now into the inner mountain." Anthony said, "And who will show me the way? I have no knowledge of that." And immediately there were shown to him Saracens who were about to travel that route. Approaching them and drawing close, Anthony asked to travel with them into the desert. And as if by the command of Providence, they eagerly welcomed him. After journeying three days and three nights in their company, he came to a very high hill. Below the hill there was water—perfectly clear, sweet and quite cold, and beyond there were plains, and a few untended date palms.

Then Anthony, as if stirred by God, fell in love with the place, for this was the place the one who had spoken with him at the river bank had designated. Then, after first receiving loaves from his traveling companions, he remained on the mountain alone, no one else living with him. Looking on it as his own home, from that point forward he stayed in that place. Even the Saracens themselves, perceiving the zeal of Anthony, would make it a point to travel that way and would joyfully bring loaves to him; but he also had a little modest relief from the date palms. In time, when the brothers learned of the place, they were anxious to send things to him, like children remembering a father. But Anthony, seeing that some there were burdened and suffered hardship on account of the bread, and being considerate for the monks in this matter, took counsel with himself and asked some of those who came to him to bring him a hoe, an axe, and a little grain. When he gathered these things he inspected the land around the mountain, and finding a small, suitable place he plowed it; and having abundant water from the spring, he planted it. And by doing this every year, he had bread from then on, rejoicing because he would be annoying no one because of this, and because he kept himself from being a burden in all things. But after this, again seeing certain people coming, he also planted a few vegetables in order that the visitors might have a little relief from the rigor of that hard trip. At first, however, when the beasts in the wilderness came for water, they often would damage his crop and his planting. But gently capturing one of the beasts, he said to all of them, "Why do you hurt me, when I do you no injury? Leave, and in the name of the Lord do not come near here any longer." From then on, as if being afraid of the command, they did not come near the place.

SAINT AREDIUS
Holy Abbot of Limoges

Commemorated on November 17

N the year 591 Abbot Aredius finished his life here
below and went to heaven at the command of our
Lord. He came originally from Limoges in Gaul, a
man of free birth, descended from very important people in that
area. He was sent to King Theudebert and joined the group of
noble youths attached to the royal household. At that time
Nicetus, a man of great holiness, was bishop of the town of
Trier. He was regarded by his flock to be a remarkably eloquent
preacher, and he was famous far and wide for his good works
and his miracles. Nicetas noticed the young man in the king's
palace. Perceiving some divine quality in his face, he ordered
Aredius to follow him. Aredius left the king's palace and joined
Nicetus. Together they went to the bishop's cell and spoke of
those matters which are the concern of God. The young Aredius
asked the saintly bishop to correct him in his errors, to be his
teacher and to give him instruction in the Holy Scriptures. He
was full of flaming zeal for his studies. Having passed some time
with Bishop Nicetus, he had his head tonsured. One day when
the clergy were chanting psalms in the cathedral, a dove flew
down from the ceiling, fluttered gently around Aredius and then
alighted on his head. In my opinion, this was a clear sign that
he was filled with the grace of the Holy Spirit. Embarrassed by

what had happened, he tried to drive the dove away. It flew around for a while and then settled down again, first on his head and then on his shoulder. Not only did this happen in the cathedral, but when Aredius went off to the bishop's cell the dove went with him. Day after day this was repeated, to the great surprise of Nicetus.

Both Aredius' father and brother died, and this man of God, filled, as I have said, with the Holy Spirit, returned home to console his mother Pelagia, who had no one to look after her, save her one remaining son. By now he was devoting all his time to fasting and prayer, and he asked his mother to continue being responsible for all the household duties, to be in charge of the servants, the tilling of the fields and the culture of the vines, in order that nothing should come between him and his praying. There was but one commitment for which he wanted to remain responsible, and that was that he should have control of the building of churches. What more is there that I can say? He built churches to the glory of God's saints, collected relics for them and tonsured his own family retainers as monks. He founded a monastery in which was followed the Rule of Cassian, Basil and the other abbots who had set rules for the monastic life. His saintly mother provided food and clothing for all the monks. She did not allow this heavy burden to interrupt her prayers to God. No matter what she was doing, she continued to pray and her words ascended like fragrant incense, finding favor in the sight of God. Meanwhile, the sick began to flock from everywhere to the saintly Aredius. He restored them to health by making the sign of the Cross on each of them with his hand.

One thing I know, that no sick man ever came to him without going away healed.

ELDER ATHANASIUS

ATHER Athanasius was Abbot of Grigoriou Monastery on Mount Athos from 1924 to 1937, and reposed in 1954. This chapter is excerpted from *Contemporary Ascetics of Mount Athos* by Archimandrite Cherubim Karambelas, recently published in the English language.

* * *

A Merciful Heart

"A merciful heart," writes the wise Abba Isaac the Syrian, "is one that burns with love for all creation—for men, for the birds and animals, for the demons, for every created being. And by the recollection and sight of them the eyes of a merciful man pour forth abundant tears, from the strong and vehement mercy which grips his heart and from his great compassion, his heart is humbled and he cannot bear to hear or to see any injury or slight sorrow in creation" (Homily 81).

"A heart burning for all creation!" This is a great saying. Who can achieve it? Who is able to reach such a height of charity that he even feels compassion for the demons? To Fr. Athanasius, however, these high summits, so difficult of access, were not unknown. The lungs of his soul breathed deeply of the divine air of Eden. His sensitive nature was filled with a rare love for all creatures. There are many incidents in his life that show this clearly, and which bring to mind similar events in the lives of the great monastic saints. They especially remind us of the renowned hermit of Elikon, St. Luke (10th century), who fed birds, took care of snakes, shielded deer from hunters, tamed wild beasts, made friends with poisonous reptiles, and embraced all creation with love.

In the southeastern part of Grigoriou Monastery, a roe-deer was running like a tornado down towards the rocky shore, terrified for its life. Some laymen who worked in the Monastery, had discovered it high up the mountain and were madly pursuing it, equipped with weapons and dogs. They had encircled it so that it had no way to go but down, and the poor animal dashed down to the seaside, leaped into the water, and began to swim away from shore. The hunters, however, lost no time, but quickly ran to the dock, loosed a rowboat, and began rowing out towards the deer. They caught it, even though it managed to swim two kilometers out to sea. They couldn't wait to get it back to shore and slaughter it, roast it, and enjoy its savory meat.

Fr. Athanasius was soon informed of what had happened. Immediately he set aside all his work, as if something serious had happened, and rushed down to the dock. Why all this haste and extraordinary concern? For no other reason but to be in time to spare the captured animal's life and restore it to freedom. This is what is meant by "a heart burning for all creation."

Let us leave the roe-deer—a gentle and prized animal—and go on to the foxes. Was he equally concerned for them?

Across from the Monastery, on the side towards Simonopetra, are the vineyards of Grigoriou. There one would always find Fr. Ioannikios. He had the obedience of "vine-dresser," and he took great care to fulfill his duties well. Among other things, he had to guard the vineyard from enemies that hid in the surrounding scrub. Even the Scriptures mention these enemies: "Catch the little foxes that spoil the vine" (Song of Solomon: 2:15).

The monk was capable and energetic and he took strong, effective measures against his crafty foe, the foxes. He set special iron traps and caught them, and then killed and skinned them. And he did all of this with a quiet conscience, confident that he was fulfilling his duty in everything.

The Elder knew nothing of his disciple's exploits. As soon as he was informed, his soul reacted strongly against it. He could not accept even the thought of such harsh measures. What a terrible thing—to slaughter an animal caught in a trap! To kill it and skin it! How horrible! And the one doing this was a monk wearing the angelic schema! This could not continue. He could in no way endure such disharmony. Therefore he summoned the vine-dresser in order to give him some suitable advice.

"My child," he said, "you must think of other ways to deal with the foxes. Hang tin cans around and bang them, or whatever else you want. Don't use any more traps. Monks are not allowed to use such cruel and torturous methods."

Now and then, Fr. Athanasius would pay a visit to Voultista, a metochion of Grigoriou. It is in a beautiful location! It sits on a high promontory, and the eye can see as far as the plain of Thessaly and the sparkling waters of the Axios and Alikmonos rivers.

"Elder," the workers of the metochion told him at one of his visits, "we have a surprise for you. We're going to show you a rare sight."

"What surprise is that?"

"Well, we found two little wolf cubs in the forest. We thought we wouldn't kill them immediately, so we could show them to your holiness."

In a little while, the Elder was looking at the two wild animals. Indeed, he had never seen anything like them before. He carefully examined the beautiful design of their bodies, their long legs, necks, muzzles, their alert ears.... They were frightened at being in such strange surroundings. He felt great sympathy and affection for the wolves. He thought of how their mother was suffering. Finally, he told the workmen something they had not expected: "Listen! Don't hurt them or kill them. Let them return to their den. Their mother is sad and looking for them now."

The affection Fr. Athanasius showed to wild animals was reciprocated. They were meek and gentle with him, and even obeyed him, as we shall see in the following narrative.

In the Monastery cemetery, which Fr. Athanasius often visited, there prowled a large snake. It wasn't long before a

friendship developed between them. Neither of them was disturbed by the presence of the other. This did not hold true, however, for the other monks, such as Hierodeacon Pachomius, who had to go to the cemetery now and then to light the lampadas. He happened to be fearful by nature, and whenever he saw the snake he would not only be frightened, but would even give way to disorderly flight. He was truly to be pitied.

When he told the Elder of his sad state, Fr. Athanasius soothed him and calmed him down, assuring him that the unwanted reptile would soon go away permanently from the cemetery.

And truly, it happened as he said. Fr. Pachomius never saw the snake again, to his great joy. Only one doubt, one unanswered question, remained in him: By what means did the Elder expel the snake? Did he pray? No one knew. It was enough that it had disappeared, although no one knew how or why.

The close intimate bond between the saints and creatures— even wild beasts and reptiles—underlies a great truth: that in their souls resides the Creator. When there are bonds of love between a soul and the Creator, there are also with creatures. "The first is a proof of the second," as the holy author of the *Ladder* would say.

SAINT ATHENOGENES
Bishop and Martyr

Commemorated on July 16

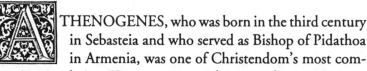THENOGENES, who was born in the third century in Sebasteia and who served as Bishop of Pidathoa in Armenia, was one of Christendom's most compassionate clerics. He was a man whose gentle sincerity was evident throughout a lifetime of service to God and mankind in an outpouring of love and understanding meriting the plaudits of his people and St. Basil. His short life was a fulfillment of a pledge to Jesus Christ when he was quite young, and his death in flames was a sacrifice which was made with the joy of the Holy Spirit in his heart.

Athenogenes has been immortalized in the hymns of the noted hymnographer Joseph who attests in liturgy to the quiet courage and enduring faith of one of Christianity's most noble martyrs. Athenogenes is said to have gone to his death chanting the evening vesper hymn entitled "Fos Hilaron" (Joyful Light). The hymn he chose to chant as he was about to die has been sung for centuries in vespers. Although sometimes chanted too methodically, the hymn has an added glow when we recall that one of the sweetest of martyrs voiced it with his dying breath.

Athenogenes would rather be known for his pious work while alive, but he is best remembered for his courageous tribute to the Lord in his final moments. The entire hymn bears

96

quotation even though it lacks the solemnity of the chant. Its words are: "Joyful light of the Holy Glory of the Immortal Father, the Heavenly, the Holy, the Blessed Jesus Christ, we have come to the setting of the sun and beholding the evening light, praise God, Father, Son and Holy Spirit. It is meet at all times that thou shouldst be hymned with auspicious voices. Son of God, Giver of Life; wherefore the world glorifieth thee."

Of Athenogenes the great St. Basil had this to say: "the people use these ancient words, and no one accuses them of blasphemy for singing 'We praise Father, Son and God's Holy Spirit.' If you are familiar with the hymn of Athenogenes, which he left as a gift to his disciples as he went to his martyrdom by fire, then you know what the martyrs think concerning the Spirit" (Basil, *On the Holy Spirit*, Chapter 29).

When Athenogenes was arrested, the form of death prescribed for him was fire. But the fiery consummation is subordinated to the fact that he approached this ghastly end with a joyous chant praising Jesus Christ for whom he gave his life on July 16. Athenogenes was laid to rest in the Chapel of St. George in Kyparissia in the remote mountain region of Asia Minor. What ensued after his death was a departure from the expected creation of a shrine. In fact, it was a highly unusual phenomenon that started when he was still alive.

It is said that when Athenogenes received prior knowledge of his death sentence, he went to warn his followers in a monastery which he found empty. As he was leaving, a young deer emerged from the woods and Athenogenes, surprised that the timid creature did not bolt as he approached, stroked the animal and blessed it as he left.

On the first anniversary of his death, a Liturgy in his memory was being offered in the Chapel of St. George when a young fawn walked into the church and stood stock still as though in reverence of the Saint. It was assumed the creature happened to stray into the church, but that is not the habit of timid deer. When it occurred again the following July 16 and on subsequent anniversaries, it was a certainty that this was not an accident, but a divine sign which can be interpreted only as an act of God.

HESYCHAST BENJAMIN

From a conversation with Hieromonk Cassian
of Sihăstria Monastery, Romania, in 1984

HEN I was little and went with my parents to Vorona Monastery, I heard about a great hesychast named Benjamin, who came from Botosani County. He was a schemamonk and struggled in the hesychastic skete of Vorona, which is four kilometers from the monastery. The older monks said that this hesychast had the grace of God in him so abundantly that even the wild animals accompanied him and honored him. He walked barefoot, winter and summer, his whole life. He ate greens and dry bread once a day after the setting of the sun, and performed mental prayer unceasingly. One winter night he came barefoot through the forest from the skete to the monastery, and the wolves walked next to him up to the entrance of the monastery. There the  wolves waited for him. The holy hermit went in, spoke with the abbot, received dry bread and wine for Holy Communion, and returned to the skete. At the gate the wild animals of the forest joined him again and accompanied him to his hut. This hesychast even performed miracles, healing many sick people by his prayers. It seems to me that he died in 1915.

St. David of Garesja

Commemorated on May 27

From *Lives and Legends of the Georgian Saints*

T HE homeland of this worthy and marvel-working Father was the Mesopotamian valley of Assyria, from which there has stemmed such a host of excellent and saintly men fertilized by the Holy Spirit and made into a spring-sown field of spiritual grace. But I could not discover when the Saint was born, nor who were the parents from whom he received fleshly birth and upbringing, though we may assume that this noble branch sprang from excellent roots. As the good tree brings forth good fruit, so did the Saint by his fruit make known the quality of his forebears.

Although I am ignorant of the names of his corporeal parents, his spiritual father is well known to all, namely the wondrous and noble John Zedazneli. This blessed Father John was from the borders of Antioch in the land of Mesopotamia. And by the guidance of the Holy Spirit, he arrived in this country of Georgia nearby the sacred capital city of Mtskheta. He longed for a hermit's life, and said to his disciples, "My sons, why do you stand idle? Do you not know that the Lord Jesus Christ has sent and guided us here for the benefit of this country? For this is a virgin land. Now it is time for you to go away separately and strengthen our brethren to walk in Christ's ways."

So our holy father David departed to dwell in desolate and waterless places, so that by an ascetic way of life in this transitory world, he might win for himself eternal bliss and rest everlasting. He therefore chose to live outside in the wilderness, and for this reason his desert abode is called Garesja. He took with him one disciple, Lucian by name.

When they had arrived in this uninhabited and waterless place they became very thirsty. Then they found a little rainwater which had collected in a crack in a rock, so they drank some of it and lay down to rest in the shadow of the rock. Afterwards they walked this way and that, and found a cave in the crag and settled down in it. Whenever it became sultry or rained they rested in the cave. For food they collected roots and grass, as it was spring time, and plenty of nourishment for the flesh was to be found. So they collected provisions and glorified God, the giver of all good things.

After some days had passed, the meadows became withered and burnt up because summer had arrived. Suddenly there came three deer, followed by their fawns, and stood before them like peaceable sheep. Father David said, "Brother Lucian, take a dish and milk these deer." And he got up and milked them. When the dish was full he took it up to the hermit. And he made the sign of the Cross and it turned into curds, and they ate them and were filled and glorified God. After that  the deer came every day, except for Wednesdays and Fridays, and brought their fawns with them, so that they were contented in body and joyful in spirit.

But underneath, close by the cave where the Saints resided, there was another cave, in which was a large and fearsome dragon with bloodshot eyes and a horn growing out of his forehead, and a great mane on his neck. One day the deer were

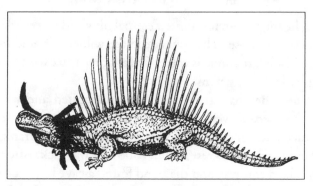

going by the entrance to the cave when the dragon attacked them and seized a fawn and swallowed it. The terrified deer ran to the hermit and trembled. When Lucian saw them shivering with fright he said to St. David, "Holy Father, these deer have come flying to us and are shaking with terror, and they have left one of their fawns behind." So the hermit went out with his staff in his hand. When he had reached the place past which the deer had come, he saw the dragon and said, "Evil dragon, why have you harmed our deer, which God has given us to comfort our weak flesh? Now depart from here and go far away into the desert. If you do not obey me, then by the power of our Lord Jesus Christ I will rip open your stomach with this staff of mine and turn you into food for the mice."

But the dragon exclaimed, "Do not be angry, O servant of God Almighty! If you want me to go away from here, lead me up to the top of that mountain, and promise that you will not take your eyes off me until I have reached the river which flows on the south side of the hills, because I am afraid of thunderbolts and cannot endure them." St. David gave his promise, and the dragon set out with St. David escorting him and reciting a psalm. And the rocks of that place wobbled from the tread of the dragon.

When Lucian saw this, he was afraid, and fell on his face and lay as if dead. And St. David led the dragon up as far as the top of the mountain, and the dragon began to scramble up to the peak. When the dragon had left the plain, St. David set off back towards his desert abode keeping his eye on the dragon. But the angel of the Lord spoke from behind him and said, "David!" So he looked around, and as he turned the dragon was struck by a thunderbolt and completely burnt up.

When St. David saw this he was very sorry and said, "O Lord, King of Glory, why didst Thou kill this dragon which put its trust in me, in spite of which Thou hast relentlessly destroyed him?" Then the angel of the Lord said to him, "Why are you sorry, O virtuous follower of our Lord Jesus Christ? For if the dragon had entered the river waters, he would have passed on into the sea. By eating the fish there, he would have grown enormous in size, and have overturned many ships in the ocean and destroyed many living souls in the seas. So do not grieve because the Lord has shown His mercy in this way, but go to your cavern, because your disciple Lucian has fallen on his face and is lying terror-stricken from fear of the dragon. Stretch out your hand and raise him up and strengthen and fortify him, and both together glorify God who has freed you from the fear of that detestable monster of a dragon."

On this the angel departed. David went and found Lucian quaking with fear, lying on the earth, and he stretched out his hand and raised him up and said, "Brother Lucian, why were you frightened of a worm, which God has shrivelled up with fire in an instant? Now do not be afraid, for the might of God is with us, and God's grace protects all that fear Him." So Lucian was cheered by the hermit's words and gave thanks to the Lord.

Then several days went by, after which some huntsmen arrived from the borders of Kakheti, for in that wilderness, even up to the present day, there is abundance of game, including deer and wild goats and a countless variety of other sorts of game. When the hunters came they spied this way and that and caught sight of the hermit's deer going into the cave in the rock. Then the hunters hastily turned aside to trap them in the cave in the rock. As they reached the hermit's cavern they saw the deer

standing while St. Lucian milked them. When the men saw this, they were stricken with fear and ran in and fell at the feet of the holy hermit and said to him, "How is it, holy Father, that these deer, wild animals of the field, are so tame as to be more peaceable than sheep brought up in a domestic farmyard?"

He said to them, "Why are you astonished at the glories of God? Do you not know that He tamed lions for Daniel, and saved the three children unharmed from the fiery furnace? So what is so wonderful about these deer? Now go and hunt other game, for these animals are granted by God for our feeble flesh."

The holy father David came out every day to the caves in the cliff and there peacefully offered up sacred prayers, and with his sweat and tears watered those places as with a spring. One day when he was praying thus, there arrived a certain man belonging to a tribe of barbarians from the district of Rustavi, and he was hunting game. Now his hawk brought down a partridge near the place where St. David was praying, and the partridge took refuge by the hermit and perched by his feet, and the hawk perched close by. This was by divine intent, so that this hunter should himself be hunted by the grace of God. Then the barbarian hurried up to take the partridge from the hawk.

When he saw the Saint standing in prayer, and the partridge sitting by his feet, the barbarian was amazed, and said, "Who are you?" David replied in the Armenian language, "I am a sinful man, a servant of our Lord Jesus Christ, and I am imploring His mercy, to forgive me all my sins, so that I may leave this transitory life in peace and quietness." Then he asked again, "Who looks after you and feeds you here?" David replied, "He whom I believe in and worship looks after and feeds all His creatures, to whom He has given birth. By Him are brought up all men and all animals and all plants, the birds of the sky and

the fishes of the sea. Behold, this partridge which was fleeing from your hawk has taken refuge with me, the sinful servant of God. Now go away and hunt other game, for today it has found a haven with me, so that it may be saved from death."

The barbarian replied, "I intend to kill you, so how do you expect to save the partridge from death?" But St. David said, "You can kill neither me nor the partridge, for my God is with me and He is powerful to protect."

At this word of the Saint the barbarian, who was on horseback, drew his sword to strike St. David on the neck. When he raised his arm, suddenly it withered away and became like wood. Then the barbarian realized his wickedness and got down from his horse and fell at the hermit's feet, and begged him with tears to rescue him from the error of his ways.

Then St. David had pity on him and besought the Lord, saying, "Lord Jesus Christ, our God, who didst come down to give life to the human race, Kind and Merciful One who didst cure the hand that was withered up—likewise, O Heavenly King, just as Thou didst see fit to do this, so cure the arm of this barbarian, that he may understand and recognize Thee and glorify Thy name." Then the Saint took his hand, and when he touched it, in an instant it was healed by the grace of God.

DESERT ANCHORITES

HERE have been a large number of men called anchorites who inhabited the desert without any huts to cover them. They lived on the roots of herbs, and, out of fear of frequent visitors, they never remained fixed in any one spot. Wherever night found them, that was their dwelling.

Included below are several stories written by Sulpicius Severus (363-420) about his travels to the Egyptian desert and some of the anchorites who lived there.

* * *

I had now come into the first stretches of the desert, about twelve miles from the Nile. As a guide, I had one of the brothers who had a good knowledge of the region. We arrived at the dwelling of an old man who lived at the foot of a mountain. Here we found something that is very rare in those parts, a well.

The old man owned an ox, whose work consisted entirely in turning a wheel for drawing water. The garden there was full of vegetables, contrary to what is usually the case in the desert. There, everything is parched, burned by the heat of the sun. Nowhere

can the least root of any plant draw nourishment. That holy man owed his crop to the joint labor of himself and the ox and to his own diligence. What gave fertility to the sands was the repeated irrigation. As we saw, this caused the vegetables in that garden to be remarkably vigorous and fruitful. These were what the ox, along with master, lived on, and from this same abundant supply the holy man gave us dinner. I saw there something you Gauls will perhaps not believe: the pot was filled with the vegetables that were being prepared for dinner and was boiling without any fire. The sun's heat is so great that there is no cook who would not find it sufficient even for preparing Gallic specialties.

After dinner, when evening was coming on, our host invited us to go and see a palm tree, whose fruit he would eat from time to time. It was about two miles away. In the desert, palms are the only trees, and these are rare. Was it the industry of antiquity which provided them, or do they come about from the force of the sun? I do not know. Perhaps God foresaw that the desert was one day to be inhabited by His saints and provided these trees in advance for His servants. Of the people who have settled in those solitudes where there are no other plants, the greater part feed themselves on palm fruit.

When we came to the tree to which our kind host was leading us, we met a lion there. My guide and I trembled at the sight of him, but the old man approached without hesitation. In spite of our fear, we followed him. The beast discreetly withdrew a short distance, as if under orders from  God. He stopped while the old man picked the fruit that hung from the lower branches. He held out a handful of dates. The beast came running up and took the fruit more gently than any domestic animal. When he had eaten, he went away. As we watched this, still trembling, it was not hard for us to measure the great strength of the old man's faith and the extreme weakness of our own.

We saw another man equally remarkable. He lived in a tiny hut not big enough for more than one. It was told of him that

a she-wolf regularly attended him at dinner. The beast almost never failed to come running up at the regular mealtime. She would wait outside the door until the hermit would hand out whatever bread was left over from his meal. She would lick his hand and, as if having performed the proper courtesies and extended her greetings, would go away.

It once happened that the holy man had had a brother visit him and was accompanying him on his way home. In consequence, he was away some little while and failed to return until nightfall. Meanwhile, the beast had presented herself at the customary mealtime. She sensed that the cell was empty and that her familiar patron was not at home. She went in, making a careful search where the master could be. By chance, a palm-leaf basket hung near by, containing five loaves of bread. The wolf took one of these and devoured it. After perpetrating this crime, she went away. On his return, the hermit saw that the basket was disarranged and did not contain the proper number of loaves. He realized there had been a theft from his supply and near the threshold found fragments of the loaf that had been eaten. He then had no uncertainty about the identity of the thief. In the following days, the beast did not come as

usual. She was, no doubt, conscious of her presumptuous deed
and was refraining from visiting the victim of her wrong-doing.
On his part, the hermit was distressed at losing the comfort of
the guest and companion of his meals. After seven days, recalled
by the hermit's prayers, the wolf was there again, as before, for
dinner. The embarrassment of the penitent was easy to see. The
wolf did not presume to come close. In deep shame, she would
not lift her eyes from the ground. It was plain that she was
imploring some act of pardon. The hermit had pity on her
confusion. He ordered her to come near and with a caressing
hand stroked her sorrowful head. Then he refreshed the culprit
with a double ration of bread. The wolf had received her pardon.
She put her grief aside and renewed her habitual visits.

I ask you to consider this very special aspect of Christ's
charity. Through His grace even the brute is intelligent, even
the savage beast is gentle. A wolf does acts of courtesy, a wolf
recognizes the sin of theft, a wolf feels guilt and is ashamed.
When summoned, she comes, she offers her head and perceives
that forgiveness has been granted, just as before she had carried
the shame of wrong-doing. This is the power, O Christ, of Thy
charity; these, O Christ, are Thy miracles. For, whatever Thy
servants do in Thy name, these things are Thine. And for this,
indeed, do we grieve: that savage beasts perceive Thy majesty
when men do not revere it.

If anyone happens to find the foregoing story incredible, I
have still greater marvels to tell. Faith in Christ is my witness
that I am not inventing anything. I shall tell nothing that has
been circulated from uncertain sources, and I shall confine
myself to what I have learned through trustworthy men.

There was a man following the anchoritic mode and rule of
life whom two monks of Nitria set out to find. They were,
indeed, coming from a distant region, but they had once been
the object of his special affection, when they all lived in a

monastery, and they had heard subsequently of his miracles. After a long and intensive search, they finally found him in the seventh month, living on the very edge of the desert, near Memphis. It was said he had been inhabiting those solitudes for twelve years. In spite of his desire to avoid any meeting with man, he did not flee from the visitors when he recognized them. He even devoted himself for three days to their friendly demands. On the fourth day, when they left, he went forward a short distance to accompany them. Suddenly, they saw a lioness of remarkable size coming toward them. The beast, though confronted with three men, had no hesitation as to which she would approach. She lay down at the feet of the anchorite. Lying there, she whimpered and whined and gave signs of grieving and at the same time of asking for something. All three men were moved, especially the anchorite, since the request was directed to him. The lioness went ahead and they followed. She stopped from time to time, and from time to time looked back, making it quite clear that what she wanted was that the anchorite should follow where she was leading. Why lengthen the tale? They came to the beast's cave. Here, the unfortunate mother nourished five cubs now well grown, who were born with closed eyes and had been blind ever since. One by one the mother brought them

from the cave and laid them at the feet of the anchorite. At last, the Saint saw what the beast was asking for. He called on God's name and with his hand touched the closed eyes of the cubs. At once, the darkness was dispelled, the beasts' eyes were opened, and the light long denied them shone in.

This done, the brothers returned. They had visited the anchorite they were eager to see and had received a very rich reward for their toil. They had become witnesses of a great miracle. As well as the Saint's faith, they had seen Christ's glory, to which they were called on to testify. The story embraces still another miracle. After five days, the lioness returned to her benefactor, bringing him as a gift the skin of a rare animal. The Saint would frequently wear this as a mantle, not declining to receive from the beast a gift he believed to have quite another source.

Another anchorite of that region was very renowned. He lived in the part of the desert near Syene. When he first came to the desert, where he intended to live on the roots of herbs (which grow in the sand and are sometimes very sweet and of an exquisite flavor), he was not skilled in distinguishing among plants and often gathered harmful ones. Nor was it easy to distinguish the nature of the roots by their taste. All were equally sweet, but many contained a hidden, poisonous liquid. As the anchorite was eating, he felt violent torture: all his vitals were racked by horrible pains; he vomited frequently from a stomach weakened to exhaustion. His sufferings were unendurable and threatened his very life. In dread of anything that was edible, he ate nothing for seven days. When his life's breath was failing, a wild

beast approached him, an ibex. As it stood near, the anchorite threw it a bunch of herbs he had collected but had not dared to eat. The beast used its muzzle to put to one side the herbs that were poisonous and choose out those it knew were harmless. This example taught the anchorite what he should eat and what he should reject. He could now avoid poisonous herbs and thus escape the danger of hunger.

* * *

PALLADIUS (363-425), a native of Galatia, was a monk first in Jerusalem, then in Egypt. He later became Bishop of Helenopolis in Bithynia, and was a good friend of St. John Chrysostom. He wrote in 420 the Lausaic History *of the Egyptian Thebaid, from which the following two accounts are taken, having spent the greater part of his life among the solitaries of whom he wrote.*

The History of Dorotheos Of Thebes

NOW the life of Dorotheos was one of exceedingly hard toil, and the manner thereof was severe, and his food was meager and wretched, for he lived on dry bread. And he used to go round about in the desert by the side of the sea the whole day long in the heat of the noonday sun and collect stones with which he built cells, which he used to give unto the brethren who were unable to build [cells for themselves]; and he used to finish one cell each year. One day I said unto the holy man, "Father, why workest thou thus in thine old age? for thou wilt kill thy body in all this heat." And he said to me, "I kill it lest it should kill me." He used to eat one small bread cake, which weighed about six ounces, each day, and a little bundle of green herbs; and he drank water by measure. What then? I know not. As God is my witness I never saw this man stretch out [his legs] and lie down as [men are] wont [to do]; and he never slept upon a bed of palm leaves, or upon anything else, but he used to work the whole night long weaving baskets made of palm leaves to provide himself with the daily bread which he required for food. Now I imagined at first that he used to work in this manner because I was present, and then I thought, "Peradventure it is only for my sake, and to show me how to perform such severe labors, that [he doeth this]." So I made enquiries of many of those who had been his disciples and who were then living by themselves and were emulating his spiritual excellencies, and I also asked others of his disciples who were living by his side if in very truth he always labored in this wise, and they said unto me, "He hath held to this practice from his youth up, and he hath never been in the habit of sleeping according to what is right. In the daytime he never sleepeth willingly, but [sometimes] when he is working with his hands, or when he is eating, he closeth his eyes and is snatched away by slumber. As he sitteth working he eateth, and unless slumber overcame him [suddenly] he would never sleep at all...." And when from time to time I used to urge him to sit down, or to throw himself upon a mat of palm leaves and to rest a little, he would answer and say unto me in a grievous manner, "If thou art able to persuade the angels to sleep, then thou wilt be able to persuade me."

One day, towards the ninth hour, Dorotheos sent me to the fountain from which he drank water to fetch him some water, so that he might eat his meal, for he used to eat about this time, and when I had gone there I chanced to see a viper going down the well; and because of [my] fear I was unable to fill [the pitcher] with water, and I went back to him, and said unto him, "O father, we shall die, for I have seen a viper [going] down into the water." Now when he heard [these words] he laughed reverently, and constrained himself, and he lifted up his face and looked at me not a little time, and he shook his head, and said unto me, "If it were to happen that Satan had the power to show thee in every fountain an asp, or again to cast into them vipers, or serpents, or tortoises, or any other kind of venomous reptiles, wouldst thou be able to do without drinking water entirely?" And when he had said these words unto me, he went forth and departed [to the fountain] and drew water, and brought [it back], and having made the sign of the Cross over it he straightway drank therefrom before he ate anything. And he constrained me to drink and said unto me, "Where the seal (or sign) of the Cross is, the wickedness of Satan hath no power to do harm."

Of Sabas, the Layman of Jericho

AND there was a certain layman from Jericho whose name was Sabas, and he had a wife, and this man loved the monks so much that during the night season he used to go round about in the desert, and pass by the cells of the solitary monks therein, and outside the cell and habitation of each one of them he would set down a bushel of dates and vegetables, which would be sufficient for his wants, for the monks who lived by the side of the Jordan did not eat bread, and thus this man Sabas supplied the wants of the monks. One day as he was carrying along a load [of food] for the usual needs of the monks, through the operation of the Evil One who is the Adversary of the monks, a lion met him, which terrified him, and wished to make him cease from his ministrations to those holy men, and schemed to prevent him from performing his benevolent intent for their

comfort. And the lion having overtaken him about a mile from the place where the monks were, and having seized him by his hand in order to turn him aside from his business, He Who by the hand of Daniel shut the mouth[s] of the lions (Dan. 6:22; Heb. 11:33), shut the mouth of this lion also, and the beast did this lover of alms no harm whatsoever; and although the lion was exceedingly hungry he only took a very little of the things which Sabas was carrying for the old men, and then he departed. And it is manifest that He Who gave this man his life also satisfied the hunger of the lion.

* * *

ST. JEROME in the 4th century also wrote histories of the monks who lived in the Egyptian desert. *"...Inasmuch as I have been requested, earnestly and frequently, on several occasions, by the brotherhood of blessed men who had their habitation in the Mount of Olives, to write an account of the lives and deeds of the blessed men, and of the solitary dwellers who were in Egypt, according to what I myself have seen of their abundant love, and their patient endurance, and their vexatious toil for God's sake, I have then put my trust in their prayers, and have been so bold as to narrate the following history, and to set it down in writings, so that I myself may gain a fair and abundant reward, and so that those who hearken unto the same may be benefitted [thereby], and may emulate such beautiful deeds, and may depart from the world in a state of perfection, and may enjoy peace and rest through the excellent long-suffering of their toil. For in very truth I have observed and seen the treasure of Christ which is hidden under human garments, and I have not buried it for the advantage of many, but have brought it forward that it may be for the good of every one. And I am sure that for me to give this benefit to the blessed brethren will be noble merchandise for me, for they will pray for the redemption of my soul...."*

From The Triumph of the Blessed Apollo

ONE of the brothers of the monastery of the Blessed Apollo related to me this story:

"In the times which are past a certain holy man, whose name was Ammon, used to dwell in this monastery, and he it was who converted me, and the thieves used to vex him, for they stole his apparel and his food, and by reason of their vexatious attacks he went forth and departed into the desert; and he brought two great serpents and commanded them to guard the door of his abode, and when the thieves came according to their custom, they saw the serpents and marvelled, and, by reason of their fear, they fell down on their faces upon the ground. Then, having gone forth and seen the thieves, the blessed man spake unto them, and reviled them, saying, 'Observe how much worse ye are than the serpents! These creatures are, for God's sake, obedient to our command, but ye are neither afraid of God, nor do ye hold His servants in reverence'; and he took them into his dwelling, and fed them, and admonished them, and told [them] that they ought to change their mode of life. And straightway they repented and took up their habitation in a monastery, and they excelled more than many in spiritual works, until at length they also were able to work miracles."

The Triumphs of Abba Apellen

AND we saw also another Abba whose name was Apellen, and he had persevered in the sternest and most austere ascetic labors with the brethren who were by his side, from his youth up....

And from time to time he used to visit the brethren who lived near him in the desert, and he admonished them frequently. On one occasion he was very anxious to go to his own desert, and to carry there such things as were necessary for him of the blessings (i.e., the gifts) which the brethren had given him, and as he was going along the way he saw some wild goats feeding and he said unto them, "In the Name of Jesus Christ, let one of you carry this load"; and straightway one of them came, and he placed his hands upon [its back], and bowed himself, and sat upon it, and he arrived at his cave in one day....

And on another occasion he went to certain monks on the first day of the week, and he saw that they were ceasing to perform the service of the Holy Mysteries, and he blamed them, saying, "Why do ye not perform your service?" And they said unto him, "Because no priest hath come unto us from over the river"; and he said unto them, "I will go after him, and call him." Then they made answer unto him, saying, "It is impossible for any man to cross the river, both on account of its depth, and because of the crocodiles which destroy human beings"; but he went a little distance and came to the place where the river was usually crossed, and he seated himself fearlessly on the back of a crocodile, and passed over [to the other side]. And having gone and found the priest, he entreated him not to neglect the brethren, and when the priest saw that Apellen was dressed in old and ragged garments, he marvelled at his humility, and at the poorness of his apparel; and he clung to him, and followed him to the cave. Now when they came [to the river] and found no boat to take them over, the blessed man Apellen cried out with a loud voice to that crocodile, which straightway heard him and came to him, and it made ready its back before the holy man to sit upon; and the blessed man  entreated the priest to sit with him and pass over to the other side, but when the priest saw the crocodile, he was afraid, and he returned to his own place. And the brethren, who were dwelling in the mountain on the other side of the river, feared when they saw the blessed man sitting in the water on the back of the crocodile; and as soon as he had crossed over on to dry land, and had come up [out of the water], he slew the crocodile, saying, "Death is better for thee than punishment for the souls which thou hast already slain, and wouldst slay"; and the animal died straightway.

And Apellen remained with the brethren three days, and he sat and taught them the commandments, and the thoughts which one of them had secretly he made clear and plain before them, saying, "This man is vexed by lust, and this man by love of vainglory, and this by evil dislike, and this by pride, and this by arrogance, and this by envy, and this by boasting, and this by anger, and this by greediness, and this by avarice; and this man is humble, and this man is straight, and these men are praiseworthy and good, and these are bad and rebellious." And he admonished [them] and showed forth [these things], and when the brethren heard them they marvelled, for in very truth it was even as [he had said].

SAINT ELEUTHERIUS

Commemorated on December 15

IN the reign of Adrian in the second century, we have records of an extraordinary scene in the Coliseum [of Rome]. We have given the title of "young bishop" to our present notice, for our hero was but twenty years of age when he wore the mitre. He was a noble Roman youth of consular rank: he had a saintly mother, who was a convert of the great Apostle St. Paul, and afterwards suffered martyrdom with her son. He was called Eleutherius. Brought up under the care of his pious mother and the holy Pope Anaclete, he made rapid progress in the science of the saints. So great was his piety and innocence of life, that, at the age of sixteen, he was made a deacon; at eighteen he was ordained priest, and was consecrated by the hands of the Pope himself for the see of Aquileia (Venice) at the age of twenty.

The preaching and miracles of the youthful Bishop were reaping a fruitful harvest of souls, and his name was carried on the wings of fame to the ears of Adrian. The hypocritical policy of the emperor was to show his piety to the gods by persecuting the most noted amongst the Christians. Having heard of Eleutherius on his return for the last time from the East, he sent one of his generals named Felix, with two hundred men, to seize the Bishop and bring him to Rome. When Felix arrived with his soldiers, he found Eleutherius in his church, preaching to a great concourse of people. He drew up his soldiers in guard around the church, whilst he and a few of the most trusty entered to seize the Saint. No sooner had Felix entered the church than the grace of God entered his heart. He was struck with the solemnity of the scene. The silence and devotion of the Christians assembled in the temple of the Most High, the heavenly light that shone round the Bishop, the unction and eloquence with which he spoke, made the pagan soldier stand riveted to the ground in awe and reverence. He waited till the sermon was over; but instead of rushing on the defenseless servant of Christ to drag him to martyrdom, he was seen kneeling in the center of the church, praying to the true God. The people were surprised, and the soldiers looked at each other in amazement. The first to rouse him from his thoughts was the Bishop, who touched him on the shoulder, and said to him: "Rise, Felix; I know what brought thee hither: it is the will of God that I should go with thee to glorify His name." The general awoke, as if from a beautiful dream, and proclaimed his belief in the God of the Christians.

On the journey to Rome, when they came up to a large river (probably the Po), they halted at a shady place on its banks. Eleutherius, whose heart burned with zeal and love, seized every opportunity of preaching the gospel and saving souls. Gathering the little band around him, he spoke at great length of the Christian faith. His fervor and eloquence not only convinced them, but drew tears from many of the rough and benighted soldiers who heard him; and, when he had ceased speaking, Felix cried out aloud: "I will not eat until I am baptized." The holy Bishop having further instructed him, baptized him and some of the soldiers before they left the banks of the river.

When they arrived in Rome, the emperor ordered Eleutherius to be brought before him. He was led to one of the halls in the palace on the Palatine, where Adrian had his throne erected. When the Martyr stood before him, Adrian was struck with his beauty and modesty; a peculiar sweetness of countenance, blended with nobility and majesty, forced the pagan persecutors to look on the servant of Christ with a feeling almost amounting to reverential awe. The emperor was well aware that the father of Eleutherius had thrice borne the consular dignity under his own reign, and he saw in the victim before him every inducement to mercy and compassion that wealth, rank and talent could offer. He addressed him mildly at first, and seemed rather to conciliate and bribe him with the promise of his friendship and a position in the imperial palace; but finding the noble youth immovable in his profession of Christianity, he gave vent to all the rage that pride and the devil could raise in his soul. The Acts of the Martyr give a portion of the conversation that passed at this interview; it is so beautiful and touching we will translate it.

"The emperor said: 'How is it that you, such an illustrious man, could give yourself to such a foolish superstition as to believe in a God who was crucified by men?'

"Eleutherius was silent. Again the emperor addressed him, and said, 'Answer the question I ask you; why do you give yourself to the slavery of superstition, and serve a man that is dead, and who died the miserable death of a criminal?'

"Eleutherius, looking up toward heaven, and making the sign of the Cross, said, *True liberty* is only to be found in the service of the Creator of heaven and earth.'

"Adrian in a milder tone said, 'Obey my commands, and I will give you a post of honor in my own palace.'

"'Thy words,' said Eleutherius, 'are poisoned with deceit and bitterness.'"

Adrian was enraged at this answer, and ordered the copper bed to be prepared for the servant of God. This was an instrument of torture greatly in use at this period of persecution. It may be better understood by calling it a large gridiron. It consisted of several cross bars of brass or copper, supported by feet about nine inches from the ground; underneath was placed fire to consume the Martyrs. It is a strange fact, however, that Almighty God permitted very few Martyrs to meet death by this terrible instrument. Eleutherius will not be its victim.

It was ordained by the laws of Augustus, that the execution of criminals and malefactors should be public, and that a crier should announce to the people the crimes which brought the offender to his miserable end. This law, which was wisely destined to deter others from the perpetration of similar crimes, was in practice in the time of Adrian. Although it became arbitrary in its application under the rule of some of the tyrants who were permitted to disgrace the throne of Augustus, yet in the case of Christians it was enforced even beyond the limits of its requirements. Christianity was the greatest crime against the state; a man might be accused of murder, conspiracy, or robbery, and he would escape with a light punishment, or be condemned to fight for his life with the gladiators in the Coliseum; but it seems to have been only against Christians that all the horrors of pagan cruelty were directed.

In consequence of this law, a crier was sent through the city to announce the sentence pronounced by the emperor on the Bishop Eleutherius. An immense crowd assembled. The Acts say the whole people of Rome hastened to witness the execution. The great God whom they knew not was inviting them to recognize His power, and serve Him instead of idols. When the fire was kindled, and was blazing furiously round the copper bed, the Martyr was stripped and lifted by the rough hands of the soldiers to his bed of torture. Never did the footsore pilgrim cast his wearied limbs in repose on the mossy bank with more ease and refreshment, than Eleutherius did on his bed of fire: the elements of nature are the creatures of God—they obey when He commands. After the lapse of an hour, during which he remained chained to the gridiron, unburnt, and without even a hair of his head being singed, he was liberated; seizing the favorable moment, he raised his voice and preached an eloquent sermon to the Romans whom curiosity had gathered around. "Romans," cried out the Martyr, "listen to me. Great and true is the Omnipotent God. There is no other God than He who was preached to you by the Apostles Peter and Paul, through whom so many cures and miracles were worked amongst you, through whom was defeated the impious Simon Magus, and through whom were broken to pieces the deaf and dumb idols such as your emperor adores."

Adrian, who was listening, foamed with rage, and ordered another and still more terrible instrument of torture to be prepared for Eleutherius. This was an enormous frying pan filled with oil and pitch and placed over an immense fire. Whilst the composition in the cauldron was foaming and seething with heat, the emperor said once more to the holy youth: "Now, at least, take pity on your youth and nobility, and do not any longer incur the anger of the gods, or you will soon be like that burning oil."

Eleutherius laughed at the threat of the emperor. "I wonder," he said to him, "that you, who know so much, have never heard of the three young men cast into the fiery furnace of Babylon. The flames of the fire rose to forty-seven cubits, in the midst of this fire they sang and rejoiced, for there walked in the midst of them the Son of the God whom I adore, whose unworthy priest I am, who has never abandoned me from my infancy."

Having said this, he made the sign of the Cross, and sprang towards the boiling pan. The moment he placed his hand on it, the fire was extinguished, and the foaming mass of oil and pitch became cold and solid; the holy Martyr, turning towards the emperor, said, "Now where are your threats? Your fire, your gridiron and your frying pan have become like a bed of roses to me, and have no power to hurt me. O Adrian! thine eyes are darkened with incredulity, so that thou dost not see the things of God; recognize thy folly, do penance for thy misdeeds, and weep over thy misfortune that thou hast not hitherto known the only great and true Ruler of heaven and earth and all things."

Adrian was not converted by this extraordinary miracle, although it is certain he relaxed the rigor of his persecution against the Christians after the death of Eleutherius. He must have been astounded at what he saw; the extraordinary miracles which were worked by almost every Christian who was brought before him, the inefficacy of the most dreadful torments he could devise, and the attractive sweetness of innocence and virtue which shines even in the external deportment of a true Christian must have opened his eyes and raised a doubt in his mind respecting the truth of paganism. Hence it is reported of him by some historians, that shortly before his death he had resolved to erect a temple to the God of the Christians.

When Eleutherius had worked the extraordinary miracle just mentioned, and addressed him in the sublime and fearless language of reproof for his folly, Adrian was not able to speak for confusion, and bit his lip with rage. There stood near one of the sycophants of the palace, who was the prefect of the city; seeing the perplexity and defeat of the emperor, he said: "Great emperor! the whole world, from east to west, is under your control, and every one trembles at your word except this insolent young man. Let your Majesty order him to be taken to prison; I will prepare an instrument in which you will see he will not insult you much longer. Tomorrow you will see your triumph in my amphitheater before the whole Roman people."

These words brought relief to the baffled emperor, and he immediately gave orders that Eleutherius should be handed over to the prefect, Corribonus, to be treated according to his wish.

But the servant of God heard what was said, and, filled with a divine inspiration, cried out, in the hearing of the emperor, as the soldiers were leading him away: "Yes, Corribonus, tomorrow you will witness my triumph, which will be the triumph of my Lord Jesus Christ."

...Corribonus left nothing undone to ensure the success of his undertaking. As the public games were not going on at this time, criers were sent through the city to announce a special entertainment for the morrow. The fame of the invulnerable Christian had spread far and wide; the grief of the baffled emperor, and the promise of Corribonus to prepare a new and terrible machine that was sure to destroy the Christians, roused the interest of the people, and on the following morning they flocked in thousands to the Coliseum. This was arranged by the providence of God, that not only the Romans, but the world and future ages, might recognize His power and glorify His name. Corribonus spent some time in devising an instrument of torture. The emperor and the people expected something terrible.... But the issue of his labors was an instrument that expressed indeed brutality and ignorance, but no novelty or art. We are tempted to smile when we read of the machine he invented to baffle the power of the Most High. It was nothing more than an immense boiler with a lid. In it was to be placed oil, pitch, resin, and some nauseous poisonous ingredients; and then, when a terrible fire had heated the mixture to scalding temperature, the Martyr was to be thrown in, and thus consumed, as he thought, in a moment.

The sun is already high in the heavens, and the deafening shouts from the Coliseum tell us the benches are filled with the impatient mob. The immense cauldron is placed in the middle of the arena, and the burning faggots are blazing around it; the air is impregnated with the fumes of the heterogeneous mass, and the thick dark smoke of the fetid composition rises slowly to a cloudless sky. Two or three men, half-naked, and of dark, fiendish looks, are supplying the fire with faggots, and at intervals stirring up the seething and crackling contents of the boiler. The picture was like the vision often given to the saints of the horrors of hell. Around, the demons were calling aloud for the death of the Christians. There was fire, torment, and hatred of God; what more is there in hell save its eternal curse!

The emperor and prefect arrived, and some games of gladiators and bestiaries were witnessed with the usual excitement and delight. But the great attraction of that day's amusement was the smoking cauldron in the arena. After each contest between the gladiators and the beasts, loud shrill voices would ring from the upper benches calling for the Christian. The emperor and prefect cheerfully yielded to the importunities of the people; and "at the third hour," say the Acts, Eleutherius was brought into the arena. He looked young, beautiful, and cheerful as he moved, with heavy chains on his hands and feet, towards the tribunal of the emperor and prefect. When he was brought under the throne of the emperor, Corribonus commanded silence with his hand and spoke thus aloud:

"All nations obey the power of our great emperor—you alone, young man, despise his wishes; wherefore either obey his orders and worship the gods and goddesses whom he adores, or by Jupiter you will be cast into the boiling cauldron."

Those latter words he pronounced with great emphasis, and pointed towards the dreadful cauldron. He had calculated on a certain victory over the Martyr, and thought he had only to use the threats with which he was accustomed to terrify his cowardly slaves. Eleutherius, without showing any signs of fear or trouble, quietly answered the prefect in this manner: "Corribonus, listen to me: you have your king who made you prefect; I have my King who made me Bishop. Now, one of these two must conquer, and he who is the conqueror should be adored by you and me. If your cauldron overcome my faith, then I must serve your king; but if your cauldron be overcome by my King, you must adore the Lord Jesus Christ."

Then the lictors seized him and tore off his garments. Whilst they were leading him towards the boiler, he prayed thus aloud: "O Lord Jesus Christ, Thou art the joy and light of all souls who believe in Thee! Thou knowest that all sufferings are pleasing to me on account of Thy name; but to show that the very elements resist those who oppose Thee, do not permit me, Thy servant, to be consumed in this cauldron."

He was flung into the burning mass, and the great lid was drawn over.

All was as silent as death in the amphitheater. The people bent forward in breathless suspense; they expected something extraordinary. Another minute passed in silence—the fire still raged and the cauldron was not dashed to pieces; the Martyr must be dead. The emperor smiled, and Corribonus rubbed his hands in complacent glee at his imagined triumph. After a few minutes of suspense, the emperor ordered the lid to be removed to see if anything remained of the Martyr. But all honor and glory to the eternal God! He laughs at His enemies, and sets their machinations at naught. Eleutherius was unhurt—not a hair was touched—not a fibre in his body was contracted—not a movement in his features showed a sensation of pain; but calm, beautiful and collected, he seemed rather to be going through his daily devotions in his own little episcopal chapel, than floating in a terrible cauldron of burning oil before tens of thousands of the Roman populace. When he stood erect in the arena, a murmur of surprise ran through the amphitheater. Adrian was fixed to the ground in wonder; he looked at Corribonus with anger flashing in his eyes. But at that moment the grace of God entered the heart of Corribonus, and rushing towards the emperor, he addressed him with vehemence: "O great emperor! let us believe in the God who protects His servants in this manner. This youth is indeed a priest of the true God. If one of our priests of Jupiter, of Juno, or Hercules were cast into this cauldron, would their gods save them thus?"

The words of the prefect fell like a thunderclap on the ears of Adrian. Unconverted in his superstition and hardened in his impiety, the sudden change which grace had wrought in the heart of Corribonus roused his indignation to the highest pitch.

"What!" he cried out, after a moment's pause; "is it you, Corribonus, that dare speak thus? Has the mother of this wretch bribed you to betray me? I have made you prefect; I have given you gold and silver; and now you turn against me to take part with this hated Christian! Seize him, lictors, and let the caitiff's blood mingle with the burning oil of the cauldron."

"Hear me for a moment, great emperor!" cried out Corribonus. "The honors and favors you have conferred on me have been short-lived and temporal. Whilst I was in error I could not see the truth which now shines resplendent before me. If you wish to scoff at the great God of the Christians, and remain a victim of the follies of your impiety, look you to it. I, from this moment, believe Christ to be the true God. I deny your idols to be gods, and I believe in Him, alone great and powerful, whom Eleutherius preaches."

Adrian stomped the ground with passion, and made a sign to the lictors to lead him at once to the arena to be executed.

When the lictors had taken him to the arena, he flung himself on his knees before Eleutherius, and thus addressed him: "Man of God! pray for me, I beseech thee, to that God Whom today I have confessed to be alone great; give me that saving sign thou didst give Felix the general, that I may brave the torments of the emperor."

Eleutherius shed tears of joy. He thanked God in his heart for the conversion of Corribonus, and prayed to the Almighty to strengthen him to sustain the torments he was about to suffer. The prefect was cast into the very instrument that he had prepared to destroy Eleutherius; the lid was closed over him, and he was left in the terrible instrument for several minutes. When the cauldron was uncovered, he was still alive, unhurt, and without pain; he was singing the praises of the true God, Whose power and divinity he no longer doubted; and, although ten minutes had not passed since he was a pagan, yet his faith was as immovable as a mountain. The emperor, seeing that he too escaped the destructive power of the burning cauldron, ordered the gladiators to dispatch him in the sight of all the people. The noble prefect fell in the arena of the Coliseum under the eyes and blessing of Eleutherius. His prompt and generous response to the calls of grace merited for him the peerless crown of martyrdom. The great sacrifice was momentary, yet worth a thousand years of penance. Wealth, friends, family were abandoned without a murmur or a farewell, and torments and death cheerfully accepted. What faith—what confidence—what love is expressed in the neophyte's declaration of Christianity! Happy the exchange he made! Would that we, born in the faith and grown old in it could come near him in the brilliant mansions of everlasting joy!

When we contemplate the wonderful works of God, how must not our mind expand and our heart warm and be elevated! Some have said that our reason alone can comprehend everything within the confines of the vast creation, and account for all that is not beyond the sky; but foolish and absurd the man that does not recognize the all-present influence of the great God. There are mysteries and wonders in nature and grace at every moment passing around us that no human intellect can perceive or explain. Strange it is that men who are ready to acknowledge the power and wonders of God in the material creation, deny Him the glory He demands for similar works in the spiritual order. There are many in every position of life, amongst Christians and unbelievers, amongst the educated, the rich and the poor, who are unconsciously prejudiced against God in the manifestation of His power through men. He may cause wonders in the revolving orbits of the heavens; the brute animals, and the very stones of inanimate nature, may become the instruments of the most marvelous effects; but the moment the ordinary laws of nature are suspended in favor of our fellow creatures—in favor of the rational being, the highest of the works of God—then there is doubt, misgiving, some unaccountable reluctance to believe. The most manifest interpositions of the divine power are explained away by chance, by hallucinations, by skill; and where eyewitness testimony does not prove, the fact is immediately denied. This is the case with all the strange things that are recorded in history. When we read of a miracle in the lives of the saints we are prepared immediately to doubt; perhaps the records that surprise us are but inventions to amuse us. Thus some of the most consoling and beautiful traits of the paternal providence of God for His suffering creatures are cast to the winds as incredible as the myths of paganism. Is there not some taint of the corrupt spirit of the world and the devil in the proud feeling of contempt and incredulity with which we treat the works of God?

...After the death of Corribonus, Eleutherius was sent to prison. Adrian tore his purple robe in anger, and retired to his imperial saloons to give vent to this impotent rage. He summoned his courtiers, and offered a great reward to any of them who would suggest how he could get rid of the troublesome Christian. The plans suggested were numerous and cruel, but Adrian selected one which would cause less excitement among the people and which seemed to render death inevitable. It was to leave him shut up in a loathsome prison, deprived of food and light, until the exhausted frame could no longer perform the vital functions. He commanded the prison doors to be locked, and the keys to be brought to his own palace, making sure that no bribery or treason would rob him of his victim. But stone walls and prison bars cannot keep out the Spirit of God.

His prison was a dark, subterranean cell below the level of the city. The only light or air that could come into it was through a small hole about the size of a brick in one of the angles of the roof. The accumulation of dirt, the fetid air, and the horrid darkness make the imagination recoil from the contemplation of the terrible lot of being condemned to pass days and nights and weeks in prisons such as served for the cruelty and justice of pagan Rome. History teems with harrowing scenes of madness, despair and death which terminated the career of the victims of these dreary dungeons.... But these gloomy cells were homes of peace and light to the servants of God. Solitude, darkness and confinement were sources of supernatural joy that ravished their souls to pure delights, which are the foretaste of the bliss of heaven.

When the heavy iron doors of the prison were closed on Eleutherius, his soul was filled with celestial joy. The Spirit of God not only went down with him into the pit, but sent him food every day. Each morning of his confinement, a beautiful little dove would come through the narrow crevice that served for light and air, and drop some delicate refreshment at the feet of the Martyr. When fifteen days had passed—days that were happy and cheerful to the servant of Christ—the emperor sent down the keys of the prison to see if death had rid him of Eleutherius. When it was reported to Adrian that he was still alive, and seemed happy and contented with his vile prison, the emperor was once more seized with rage and passion. He had Eleutherius brought before him. He expected to find the holy youth worn away to a skeleton, and humbled and terrified like the wretched pagan victims who had been flung into these prisons but for a few hours. What must have been his surprise to find Eleutherius more comely and beautiful than ever— *"in flore primae juventutis velut angelus fulgens"*—still immovable in his resolve to worship Christ alone, fearlessly confronting the tyrant, and reproving him for his impiety.

Adrian now ordered the Martyr to be tied to a wild horse, that he might be dragged over the massive pavements of the

Roman roads, and thus be bruised and broken to pieces. The sentence was executed; but the moment the horse was let free, an angel loosened the bonds of Eleutherius and, lifting him up, placed him on the back of the horse. Away the animal flew across the Campagna, bearing its precious burden on its back, and never stopping until it had reached the summit of one of the highest and bleakest mountains of the Sabine range of the Apennines. The liberty of the mountain side, the beautiful fresh breeze that bore around him the odors of a thousand flowers, and the exquisite view of the green valleys, formed a great contrast with the horrors of the prison he had just left.

Whilst he was pouring forth the acknowledgements of his grateful heart to the true God, the wild animals gathered round him, as if to express their welcome to the holy man who was sent to live amongst them. Eleutherius spent some weeks in happy solitude on the mountain, feeding on roots and fruits, and singing the praises of God. He longed to come to the everlasting gardens of heaven, which he saw faintly reflected in the beautiful world around him; but Almighty God had still some greater triumphs and trials for his faithful servant.

One day some hunters from Rome were passing over the Sabine hills in search of game. They saw at some distance a man kneeling in the midst of wild animals. They hurried back to the city to tell of the strange sight; and from the description they

gave, the people knew it was the immortal Eleutherius, who had escaped once more from the dreadful fate destined for him by the cruel emperor. If a thunderbolt had split the earth in two, and placed Adrian on the brink of the yawning gulf, he could not have been more startled than when he heard that his victim was still alive. He ordered a commander of the army and a

thousand men to march at once to the mountains to seize Eleutherius.

When the soldiers arrived at the spot pointed out by the hunters, they found the Saint surrounded by an immense troop of wild animals, which seemed to form a bodyguard around him, and to be defying the soldiers to come near. The Roman soldiers were brave and fought desperately in battle against their fellow men, but there was something supernatural in the scene before them that unnerved them and made them cowards. After much exhortation and

intimidation from their general, some of them advanced to seize the Saint, but they would have been instantly torn to pieces by the wolves had not Eleutherius ordered them in a loud voice to desist. The animals obeyed him instantly, and came crouching at his feet as if afraid of chastisement. He then ordered them to retire to their home in the mountains, and thanked them in the name of their common God for the services they had rendered him. The troop of wild beasts moved away, and left Eleutherius alone with the soldiers. These he gathered around him, and addressed in beautiful and powerful language. He called on them to recognize the power of the true God, whom the very beasts of the desert obeyed. He showed them their folly in adoring a piece of carved marble or painted wood, and how He Who reigns above can alone give eternal life and happiness. Before the sun set on that auspicious day, six hundred and eight sturdy warriors from the Roman garrison were regenerated in the waters of baptism. Amongst the converted there were some captains of noble families and favorites of the emperor. They offered to let Eleutherius remain free, and to return to Rome without him; but the holy Bishop knew they would only bring the indignation of Adrian on themselves, and that thus their families would have to suffer a persecution their young faith might not be able to endure. Moreover, he was longing to receive the crown of martyrdom, which he knew by inspiration was to come in the end; he therefore cheerfully accompanied them, to appear once more before the hardhearted and cruel emperor.

The excitement in the city when Eleutherius was brought back again was beyond description. Not one of the extraordinary scenes we have just described was private; they took place before thousands of the populace. They were discussed and talked over in every triclinium, and the loungers of the Forum were in constant conversation about the wonderful Christian. The cause of the emperor became their own. There were many amongst the people more wicked and cruel than Adrian, and who vied with him in their hatred of Christianity. It was not sympathy, but curiosity and indignation, that made them flock round the Martyr of Jesus Christ. Adrian knew well what were the feelings of the mob, and wished to pander to them, and

hence felt himself obliged to condemn Eleutherius once more
to a public execution; yet he felt himself subdued. His mind was
changed towards the Christians; and although the holy and
youthful Bishop of Aquileia suffered under him, he was his last
victim. The order issued, the people were to assemble again in
the Coliseum to witness the execution of Eleutherius. The
events that passed in the amphitheater on this occasion were
strange and terrible, and form a grand tragic finale to the wonder
of this marvelous history.

The morning of the 18th of April, A.D. 138, must ever be
memorable in the annals of the great city, not only for the
passion of one of the greatest of the martyrs, but for the death
of thousands of people who came to an untimely end on this
day within the walls of the Coliseum. The demons were let loose
for an hour in the amphitheater, and they left the indelible stain
of their presence in the records of blasphemy, cruelty and
bloodshed. Doubtless the evil spirits were more annoyed than
the pagan emperor at the constancy of Eleutherius. His miracles
and prayers were daily swelling the ranks of Christianity, and
thousands were beginning to fear the name of the true God. The
tortures and public executions which were intended as intimi-
dations to the people were the fruitful source of conversions.
They gave them evidence of the divinity of Christianity—the
power and sublimity of its faith, which raised men above passion
and fear and enabled them to smile with the independence of
martyrdom on the most terrible of all the catastrophes known
to the pagan—the separation of the soul from the body. The
blood of the martyrs fructified the soil of the Church, and for
one that fell, thousands were gained.

On the day that Eleutherius fell under the sword of the
executioner in the arena of the Coliseum, different emotions
animated the crowd which witnessed the terrible scene. Some
were excited by curiosity at the extraordinary miracles which

were worked in behalf of the holy youth, whilst others raged like the furies of hell for the blood of the Christians. There were Christians, too, amongst them, glad and proud of the champion, who conferred so much honor on the Church and gave so much glory to God. Doubtless there were mixed up in the motley crowd some of the poor soldiers whom Eleutherius had baptized a few days before at the foot of the Sabine hills. How the tears of grateful sympathy must have trickled down the sunburnt cheek of the hardy warrior as he saw the angelic youth roughly treated by the menials of the emperor. Christianity softens the heart the moment it enters; it changes the brutal tendencies of the most ferocious nature into mildness, simplicity and love: the pagan who yesterday could bend with delight over scenes of bloodshed and cruelty, today turns away in horror and disgust.

The sun is now high in the heavens, and pouring its meridian rays in burning splendor over the city. The people are hurrying in crowds from every side to their favorite amphitheater. Most of them were present a few days before when Eleutherius was cast into the cauldron of Corribonus, and hoped to see some similar scenes of excitement and wonder on the present occasion. They will not be disappointed.

The emperor arrives with all his court. He looks sad and anxious. Old age and much travelling have told on his robust frame; he enters feebly and heavily to his crimson couch under the royal dais. He justly fears a repetition of his former defeats in contending with the angel of God, whom his own cruel heart and the voice of the mob bring once more into the arena.

Elevated by pride to absurd ideas of power, and too weak-minded to brook disappointment, he would have given half the Empire to get rid of Eleutherius.

Hark, the trumpets have sounded—the games are commenced. A few gladiators pass in procession round the arena and salute the emperor with the usual words—"Hail, Caesar! Those who are going to die salute thee." Some lions and tigers are exhibited, and allowed to frisk about for a few moments. The poor captive brutes appreciated the light and pure air of heaven when set free from the dark and fetid keeps of the Coliseum. Then the trumpet was sounded again, and the gladiators fought—

some blood was shed—a captive from Thrace has fallen.

Loud and shrill was the call of the excited spectators for the execution of Eleutherius. The order was given, and behold the

holy youth brought in in chains! His lovely, angelic features shone more beautifully than ever. He looked cheerfully round the crowded benches. Terrific yells were succeeded by breathless silence as he moved with a firm step towards the center. A crier went before him, announcing, in a loud voice, "This is Eleutherius, the Christian." A messenger was sent from the emperor to know whether he will sacrifice to the god Jupiter; but a severe, cutting answer about the demons that represented Jupiter proved the Martyr was as fearless and invincible as ever. Adrian ordered some wild beasts to be let out on him to devour him.

One of the subterranean passages was opened, and a hyena was sent into the arena. The animal seemed frightened and ran quickly from side to side; coming gently towards the spot where Eleutherius was kneeling, it lay down, seeming to be afraid to

approach the servant of God. Then the keeper, who knew the indignation and disappointment of the emperor, let loose a hungry lion, whose terrific roars terrified the people. The king of the forest rushed toward Eleutherius, not to tear his tender flesh with his horrid claws, but to reverence him and caress him. The noble animal crouched before the Martyr, and wept like a human being. "When the lion was set loose," say the Acts, "he ran to the blessed Eleutherius and wept like a father who had not seen his son after a long separation, before the whole people, and licked his hands and his feet."

A thrilling scene followed. Some people cried out that he was a magician, but the lightning of heaven struck them, and they were killed in their seats. Others called for his liberty; whilst more, in the enthusiasm of the moment, cried out: "Great is the God of the Christians!" The evil spirit had entered into the worst of the pagans, and, in maddened frenzy, they fell on those who cried out that the God of the Christians was great, and murdered them. They were attacked in turn by the friends of their victims, and a horrid scene of bloodshed ensued. The whole amphitheater was in commotion, and nothing was heard but the shouts of the infuriated populace, who were tearing each other to pieces, mingled with the screams of terrified women and the groans of the dying. The emperor had the trumpet-blast sounded shrill and clear to command attention, but to no effect; the carnage went on, and the blood was already flowing from tier to tier. The emperor at length ordered the soldiers to clear the upper benches; with much difficulty, and even loss of men, they succeeded in quelling the fatal quarrel.

Eleutherius was all this time on his knees in the arena. Many of the people had leaped over the safeguards of the amphitheater, and had gathered round him for protection. The wild animals dared not touch them. But the holy Martyr prayed to the great God to remove him from such revolting and dreadful scenes. His prayer was heard. Almighty God revealed to him by an interior voice that He would allow him to be martyred by the sword. In a rapture of joy he told some of the persons who had gathered round him, that if the emperor would command him to be put to death by the sword, he would succeed. The message was taken immediately to Adrian, who, in a paroxysm of rage, cried out: 'Let him die then by the sword; he is the cause of all this tumult!' The trumpets were once more sounded, and, in the midst of confusion and terror, all became silent as the grave; the spectators bent forward with breathless anxiety to see if the lictor would succeed. He wields the mighty ax—it falls— Eleutherius is no more! His blood flows on the arena—the earth shook, and thunder was heard in a cloudless sky. A loud voice rang through the vault of heaven, calling Eleutherius to eternal bliss.

Yet he was not the last victim of that terrible day. There was another mother of the Machabees in the crowd of spectators—it was the mother of Eleutherius. She had watched with the joy of a true Christian mother all the scenes that her brave son had passed through; and when she saw him at length passing triumphantly to his crown, her heart was bursting within her with the natural feelings of maternal sympathy and religious joy; she almost forgot she was in the Coliseum, and in the midst of a pagan crowd, and rushing frantically to the arena, she threw herself on the bleeding corpse of her son. A murmur of surprise and pity roused the attention of the emperor, who had not yet left the Coliseum. He sent to know who she was, and why she came to embrace the body of the Martyr. When it was reported that she was his mother, and a Christian, who wished to die with her son, the cruel and enraged emperor ordered her to be executed. The same axe that brought the crown of martyrdom to the son drank the blood of the mother. She was executed while embracing the dead body of Eleutherius, and their virtuous souls were united in the blissful world where separation shall be no more.

During the night their bodies were stolen by some Christians, and buried in a private vineyard outside the Porta Salara; they were kept there for some days, and then taken to the city of Rieti, where a magnificent church was erected in their honor in the reign of Constantine. Innumerable miracles were performed by these sacred relics. The holy Bishop Eleutherius was more formidable to the devils after death than before; and, during the lapse of seventeen centuries, the poor people who had first the honor of his remains amongst them, never lost their devotion nor called on him in vain. The relics of the holy Bishop were subsequently removed to Rome, to be distributed amongst several churches that were constantly applying for relics.

The marvelous history of this Saint was written by two brothers, who were eyewitnesses to most of its extraordinary facts. They conclude their report in these words: "These things we, the brothers Eulogius and Theodulus, who have been ordained for that purpose, have written; and being ever assisted by his holy admonitions, we have persevered with him, and we have made mention of those things which our eyes have seen or our ears have heard."

✠

PROPHET ELIAS AND
THE RAVEN

Commemorated on July 20

OME call him Elias and others Elijah. If you had seen him when he was living in the Holy Land you would have taken him for one of these hermits that this book is so interested in. To begin with, there was his appearance. His only garment was a goat-skin fastened with a leather belt, while his bare feet were so tough that he was able to skim over the ground and climb the rocks like a deer. His manner of life, too, was that of a solitary. For food he depended on the fruits and herbs of the earth, and when he was thirsty he drank from a mountain torrent. For all these reasons, Elias is known as the Hermit of the Old Law; and the Christians belonging to the Greek Church invoke him as the Patron Saint of the Mountains.

Whenever he felt that it was his duty to do so, Elias quitted the wilderness and came into the cities. Then he would reproach the people of Israel, and even the king, for the wrong things they were doing. So strongly worded were these reproaches of his that they were compared to a burning torch. Those that listened to him felt that they were being set on fire. He was a wonder-worker as well. For three whole years not a drop of rain fell in Israel, so that the land was parched and barren. But Elias prayed, and the drought ceased with a heavy downpour. A remarkable man he was altogether. There is a very fine composition by

СВ. ПРОРОКЪ ИЛІА

Mendelssohn which tells the story of Elijah's doings to the accompaniment of powerful music.

There were times when Elias found it difficult to get anything to eat, especially during the famine. On one such occasion, he knocked at the door of a poor woman's house. In spite of her poverty, she made him welcome. "Give me," he said, "a little water that I may drink. And, while you are about it, let me have a morsel of bread as well."

"But I have no bread. There is nothing left in my kitchen except a handful of meal and a little oil."

But Elias told her to fetch the meal and the oil. Then he prayed and worked a miracle; for although the meal and the oil were eaten and eaten, there was always plenty left over for another time.

The king of Israel got so annoyed with Elias that in the end he threatened to take his life. The prophet, therefore, fled into the wilderness, and was so famished that he thought he was going to die. He was fed again; this time by an angel who brought him bread and water. This food was so nourishing that, in the strength of it, he walked for forty days and forty nights without stopping, until he came to the top of Mount Horeb.

Elias resembled these other hermits because, like so many of them, he once depended entirely upon the services of the animals. It was at the time when no food was to be had on account of the scarcity which ravaged the countryside. God told him to go and hide himself in a mountain-cleft near a certain waterfall. Elias did as he was told, although he knew that if he stayed there for any length of time he would die of hunger. Water he had plenty of, but that was all. But God promised to take care of him, and He kept His promise. After a long climb, the prophet reached the appointed hiding-place, a sort of cave hollowed out of the rock within sound of the tumbling water.

He was hungry enough by this time; but he was too tired, and very soon he was fast asleep.

When he awakened, it was broad daylight. From his perch he could see the country for miles around, with the river Jordan winding its way among the fields like a huge serpent. But Elias was in no mood for admiring the scenery. He had not broken his fast for forty-eight hours and had hardly strength enough to stand on his feet. Yet he never doubted that God would keep the promise He had made.

By and by in the far distance he spied two black specks moving towards him across the valley. When they were closer, he saw that they were a pair of ravens, and each one was carrying something in its beak. Straight to the edge of the cave they came, bringing their cargo safely to land. This was the prophet's morning meal, a loaf of bread and a piece of meat. The ravens returned again just before nightfall, and this went on as long as Elias was in his hiding-hole.

Saint Eustachius

Commemorated on September 20

AINT Eustachius or Placidus (by which name he was more generally known) was one of the great generals of the Roman army at the commencement of the second century. His influence and name were as great amongst the soldiers on account of his virtues as for his triumphs and military skill. He was admired by all for his mildness, love of justice and charity. He was the father of his soldiers, and treated them with leniency and justice; virtues unknown to the barbarian soldier, but loved the moment their benign influence was felt. He was generous and charitable to the unfortunate, and although a pagan, he was eminently chaste. True greatness is incompatible with the indulgence of the brutal propensities of man. The virtues and exalted position of Placidus rendered him the most conspicuous man of the time, like the solitary star shining through the dark masses of cloud on a stormy night....

One day Placidus went out according to his custom to hunt. He proceeded with some officers of the cavalry division over which he had the command to the brow of the Sabine hills, and fell in with a troop of beautiful stags. Amongst them there was one larger and more beautiful than the rest, and Placidus immediately pursued it with all the ardor of the chase. In the excitement which huntsmen alone know, he was soon separated from his companions, and passed over hills and rapid rivers and on the edges of the most terrible precipices. He knew no danger;

he was not accustomed to defeat. On he went, over mountains and through valleys, until he came up with his magnificent prize in a wild and lonely ravine, not far from the spot where now stands the picturesque village of Guadagnolo. This was the moment and place in which the providence of God destined to illumine the mind of the great general with the light of Christianity. The stag stood on the ledge of a rock just over him, and between its beautiful and branching horns there was a dazzling light; in the midst of an aureole of splendor he saw an image of the crucifixion. Struck with wonder and amazement, he heard a voice saying to him, "Placidus, why dost thou follow Me?

Behold I have taken this form to speak to thee; I am the Christ, whom thou servest without knowing. Thy charity and deeds of benevolence to the poor have stood before Me, and have made Me follow thee with My mercy. The just man, dear to me on account of his works, must not serve devils and false gods, who cannot give life or reward."

Placidus dismounted in terror and confusion. He could not remove his eyes from the beautiful vision that shone more brilliantly than the sun between the horns of the stag, and although he heard he did not understand the voice that spoke to him. At length gaining courage, he cried out in an excited and tremulous tone:

"What voice is this? Who speaks?—reveal Thyself that I may know Thee."

Again the heavenly sounds fell on his ears, and he heard these words:

"I am Jesus Christ, Who created heaven and earth out of nothing, Who threw all matter into shape, and made the light spring from the chaos of darkness. I am He Who created the moon and the stars, and caused the day and the night; Who created man from the dust of the earth, and for his redemption appeared in human flesh, was crucified, and rose the third day from the dead. Go, Placidus, to the city, and seek the chief pastor of the Christians and be baptized."

A ray—the last ray of the brilliant light which had dazzled his eyes—had entered his heart, and he understood all. He remained for hours on his knees, in his first warm and grateful prayer to the true God. When he awoke from his deep reverie of adoration and prayer, he found all was dark and silent. The sun had disappeared behind the mountains, and his faithful and wearied horse and dog slept beside him. He rose, like the Apostle Paul on the road to Damascus, with the courage of a lion, to proclaim the truth of the Christian religion, and the wonderful mercy of God. He roused his horse, and returned slowly through the bleak passes of the mountain towards the city.

In the meantime, alarms for the safety of Placidus were increasing at his residence in the city. He was gifted with a noble and amiable spouse; their union had been strengthened by long years of peace. In the similar and moral tendencies of their virtuous souls their home presented a scene of domestic bliss rarely found in pagan circles. The unusual absence of the general gave her immense anxiety; all night she sat up watching for his well-known tread on the threshold, but the gray dawn was breaking on the horizon and still no sign of Placidus.

Starting from the momentary repose of a delusive dream, she found her slave awaiting her return to consciousness to deliver a message.

"Most noble lady, Rufus, who had accompanied the general this morning to the hunt, has returned and prays an audience."

"Quick, quick, Sylvia, bring him to my presence."

She sprang from her seat, met the veteran soldier at the door, and trembling with excitement, she addressed him:

"Say Rufus, knowest thou aught of the general; thou wert ever a true soldier, and kept by his side in the darkest hour. How came you to be separated from him? Speak, I fear thy silence."

The veteran leaned on his halberd; after a moment's pause, he spoke in a deep, solemn voice.

"Noble lady, I am loath to fan thy misgivings to darker anticipations of ill, but we fear for the safety of the general."

"I conjure thee, Rufus, tell me all," she cried frantically; "has his trusty steed fallen and cast him down the awful precipice? Have ravenous wolves fed on his mangled corpse?"

"None of these calamities, noble lady, have befallen our brave commander," interrupted Rufus. "We believe he has but lost his way in the mountains, and shall be here before noon. This morning I was by his side when a large stag started from the copse; the dogs gave chase, and our steeds flew over the rugged mountainside. The stag was the largest ever seen in these hills, and the chase the fleetest ever run. Our inferior horses soon fell back, and we saw the glittering helmet of our commander rushing like a ball of fire through the woods; he was soon lost from our sight near the ravines of Marino. We halted under the shade of a fig tree, hoping each moment to see our gallant commander return with the spoils of his brilliant chase. The hours passed slowly on; anxiously we listened for the echoes of his horn; no dog returned with blood-stained mouth to tell of victory; each moment of anxiety made the hammer of life beat with a heavier throb. We searched the mountain side, and called louder and louder the name of our general; there was no response save the mournful echoes that broke the stillness of the olive groves. Trembling for his safety, I hurried back to head-quarters to ask a detachment of horses to scour the mountain. Behold, noble lady, how I am separated from the general. The life stream of my heart's blood is not dearer than the safety of thy lord—Rufus shall serve under no other commander but Placidus."

Whilst Rufus was yet speaking a bustle was heard outside, and some excited slaves rushed in, announcing the general had come. Wearied and covered with dust, he dismounted. In silence he embraced his wife, and having made a sign for all to leave the room, he addressed his spouse.

"Stella, I have a strange tale to tell thee. Thou knowest the terrors of war and the crash of empires have ever been my ambition. Heretofore I feared nothing, and I knew no God but my sword, but since last I sat under the shadow of these ancestral towers and the beams of thy loving smile, a change has come over my dream of ambition. Like the sunrise bursting from a thick bank of clouds, a vision from the invisible world passed before these eyes—a Deity greater than the gods of this Empire manifested Himself to me. Stella, I am a Christian!"

With many tears he described his vision—the miraculous interposition of Divine Providence to call him to the light of faith. That day he arranged his affairs to abandon himself generously to the call of divine grace. Messengers were secured to guide him to the Catacombs, where the Christian Bishop ruled the Church of God. In spite of the remonstrance of his timid spouse, who dreaded the awful consequences involved in the profession of Christianity in these days of terror, he hastened the first hour after nightfall to the crypts on the Salarian Way....

It is probable that the terrible persecution of Domitian was but subsiding at this time. The Christians were obliged to seek shelter in the Catacombs from the fury of the storm; and whilst Almighty God permitted that they could not preach the law of grace and redemption publicly to the world, He supplied the ministry by the interior operations of grace, and gave to His suffering and banished Apostles the consolation of a more fruitful harvest. If, as we imagine, the martyrdom of Eustachius did not take place until about sixteen years after his baptism, the holy Pope Anacletus (according to Baronius) must have been sitting in the chair of St. Peter. Trajan was at this time emperor.

The holy Pope had taken shelter from the storms of persecution in a crypt in the Catacombs of St. Priscilla on the Via Salara. God vouchsafed to inform him in a vision of the conversion of Placidus. He was kneeling before a rude cross placed on the marble slab that covered a martyr's tomb, and constituted the altar of the dread sacrifice of the mass. A small oil lamp cast a dim flickering light on the sepulchral slabs; the silence of those corridors of the dead was only broken by the gentle murmur of prayer, or the faint echo of the hammer and axe of the fossores. Suddenly the holy father saw the walls of the archisolium fade before his view, and in their stead a charming scene in the

Appenines. On the ledge of a rock he saw a majestic stag bearing in his horns, amidst a sun of light, the sacred sign of redemption, and prostrate in prayer lay the Roman General. The vision faded away again, and the holy father, who understood the mercy God had shown to a noble soul, remained long wrapt in grateful prayer.

When night had enveloped the city a mysterious party, thickly veiled and concealed under large cloaks, passed through the Salarian Gate. No questions were asked, for the military cloak of Placidus was a guarantee of protection. Two little children of three and five years held with childish fear their mother's garments, and their quick little steps pattered musically on the massive pavement with the solemn strides of their military father. In silence they passed by the stately villas that adorned either side of the road, and soon reached the gentle declivity known to the ancient Christians as the *Clivum Cuumeris*. The guide brought them down through the long narrow corridors and introduced them to the presence of the holy pontiff, who rose and embraced Placidus as if he had known and loved him in years gone by.

We can imagine with what joy the holy Pope baptized the Roman general and his family. It was on this occasion he received the name of Eustachius; his wife was called Theopista, and the two children Agapius and Theopiston, all names derived from the Greek, expressing favor with God. The parting words of the venerable Pontiff to the neophyte family were to take up their cross manfully, and bear it, like their crucified Master, to the very utmost of human endurance; they were called to glorify the Church in the days of its trouble. The Christian must be tried in the furnace of affliction: "through many tribulations we must enter the kingdom of heaven." He seemed to speak with a prophetic spirit.

God tries those whom He loves. Having chosen Placidus for a vessel of election, he proved him by a series of afflictions.... He whom he had now taken for his Master and Model was ever in sorrow and affliction; the disciple is not to be better than the Master. A life of ease, a bed of down, silken garments, and ornaments of jewels and gold, are not the armor which distinguishes the soldiers of a naked and crucified God. When we suffer the slight and passing sorrows of life, we should remember they are tokens of God's predilection and sanctification for our souls.

After his baptism and reception into the Church, Placidus returned to the memorable spot in the Sabine hills where he had beheld the wonderful vision, to give thanks to God. The Most High was pleased with his prompt and generous response to the call of grace, and vouchsafed to give him again other and consoling visions, and to forewarn him of the trials that were awaiting him.

He had no sooner reached his home after his pilgrimage, than the terrible storm of sorrow broke on him and crushed him to the very earth. The sad tale of his trial would excite pity in the hardest heart. In a few days he lost all his horses and cattle, and every living thing about his house; even his servants and domestics were swept away by a virulent pestilence. The awful gloom that death had spread around, the stench of unburied carcasses, and the unhealthy state of the corrupted atmosphere, obliged him to leave his home for awhile; but this was a source of new affliction. During his absence thieves entered his house and removed everything he had; he was reduced to absolute beggary. At this time the whole city was rejoicing and celebrating the triumph of the Roman armies over the Persians. Placidus could not join in these festivities, and, overcome with grief, disappointment and shame, he agreed with his wife to flee to some unknown country, where at least they could bear their sufferings and their poverty without the cruel taunts of proud and unfeeling friends.

They made their way to Ostia, and found a vessel about to start for Egypt. They had no money to pay for a passage; but the captain, who was a cruel and bad man, seeing the youth and beauty of Theopista, felt an impure passion spring up in his heart, and thought that by permitting them on board he might be able to gratify his wicked desires. But he knew nothing of the beauty, the sublimity, the inviolability of the virtue of chastity in the Christian female; and when he found himself treated with the scorn of indignant virtue at even the whispered suggestion of infidelity, he writhed under his disappointment and meditated revenge. The devil suggested a plan. Arrived at the shores of Africa, the captain again demanded the fee for the passage, and intimated to Placidus if it were not paid he would keep Theopista as a hostage. He was sent on shore with his two helpless little children, and his beautiful and faithful spouse was forcibly detained on board; they immediately set sail for another port.

Poor Placidus felt the warm tears steal down his cheek as he saw the sails of the little bark filled with a fair wind, and waft from him the greatest treasure he possessed in this world. He saw himself on a barren and inhospitable shore, exiled, poor, and widowed. Did his faithful legions but know of his sad fate, how their trusty swords would flash in vindication of their injured general! Looking on his little ones, robbed of their mother and protector, he drew them near his breaking heart, and pointing, with a trembling finger, to the white speck the little vessel had now made on the blue horizon, he cried out: "Your mother is given to a stranger." Striking his forehead with his hand, he bent down and wept bitterly. There is no pang in human sorrow so galling as blighted affection, and this is more keenly felt when the object of our love is handed over, not to death, to bloodshed, or want, but to infamy and dishonor.

But "better is the patient man than the brave." The man who can bear trials and misfortune is greater than the hero of the battlefield. Remembering his promise to God in the ravine of the Apennines, he instantly checked his grief; and rising up, with an ejaculation like holy Job, and taking his two little children by the hand, he moved towards the interior of the country with a brave and resigned heart. But God had other trials to prove him yet more.

He had not gone far when he came up to a river much swollen by some late rains; it was fordable, but Placidus saw it would be dangerous to take his two children over together, so he determined to take one first  the other. Leaving one on the bank, he entered into the stream with the younger. He had scarcely reached the opposite bank when the screams of the other child attracted his attention, and looking around, he beheld an enormous lion taking the child in his mouth and carrying it away to devour it. Placidus left the infant in his arms on the bank, and, reckless of fear or danger, plunged once more into the rushing torrent. Grief must be terrible when it can make an unarmed man believe

 he can chase and fight the king of the forest. He was scarcely out of the stream when his other child was seized by a wolf. This last afflicting sight paralysed his courage, and he could not move another step. He fell

on his knees, and appealed to the great God Who he knew had arranged all; with the fervor of his young faith and the natural sorrow of a bereaved father, he prayed for patience that no blasphemy might escape from his lips—that no misgivings might undermine the confidence of his worship. He remained for some time in prayer, and felt the balm of heavenly consolation gradually creeping over his troubled soul. Faith alone can break the barriers of time and waft the soul in anticipation to the union that immortality must bring. Placidus committed his family to God, and knew they were happy; and as for himself, he determined to bear manfully the few days of trouble which Providence had yet allotted to him. He arose once more from his prayer, strengthened and consoled, more detached from every human consolation, more united to God. He soon left the vicinity of these sad and sorrowful scenes, and fled to another part of the country.

We next find Placidus as a poor laborer in a farm called Bardyssa. But this is the last part of the dark night of his trial, the twilight that precedes a glorious sunrise. Almighty God had now proved His servant by the severest adversity which can befall a man: in a whirlwind of affliction all his temporal comforts, his domestic felicity and paternal affection were taken; and the neophyte vessel of election was found faithful, and now comes the sunshine of his crown. Some years had passed since he lost his wife and children, and he had spent all that time unknown, in labor, prayer, and solitude, mounting higher and higher on the ladder of perfection, and in union with God; but the time of his reward is at hand, and by one grand stroke of that all-directing Providence which knows no chance, he was restored to all his former honor and comfort....

The great capital of the Roman Empire was all in commotion. News had been brought from the East that the Persians and other nations had broken over the frontier and were devastating everything before them. Preparations were made for war on every side. Old veterans were brushing up their swords, and armies of young men were pouring in from the provinces. Fresh rumors of the advancing foe gave new impulse to the excitement, and an expedition of more than usual magnitude and importance was speedily equipped. The haughty soul of Trajan, who still sat on the throne of the Caesars, could not brook for a moment the slightest infringement on the Empire, or the diminution of his own glory; and he lost no time and spared no expense in striking quickly and heavily on the daring enemy. But to whom will he commit his warlike legions and the very fate of the Empire? There were none but young and inexperienced men around him. He thought of Placidus, who had carried the tide of victory in years gone by to the farthest limits of the Empire, the great general who was the idol of the army and the terror of every foe. Rumor said he was still alive, but retired from public life. Trajan seized the rumor with all the avidity of a man whose hopes had been blasted and was risking everything on a last chance. He offered immense rewards to anyone who would discover the retreat of Placidus, and bring him once more to be the head of the legions of the Empire. In burning anxiety and doubt he delayed the departure of the expedition from day to day, hoping that some tidings would come of his favorite general. He was not disappointed, for Placidus was found.

Two veterans, named Antiochus and Acacius, started off towards the Egyptian provinces in search of Placidus. Their wanderings and unceasing inquiries seemed fruitless, when one morning as they were giving up the search and were about to return to the seashore, they came up to a beautiful and well-kept farm; and a short distance from them they beheld a poor laboring man at work. They went towards him, and made inquiries if a Roman citizen named Placidus lived in those regions. The two solders thought they saw something in the old man which reminded them of their general; the nobility of his appearance and bearing seemed to tell of one who had seen better days. They even thought they saw in his worn features, browned by the sun and wrinkled by grief and care, some traces of the amiable features of Placidus; yet, it could not be—their general an exile, a laborer in this miserable place! What reverse of fortune could have reduced him to this change? How could so great a man be cast from such honor and glory to such obscurity and poverty? But he who stood before them in the tattered garments of a poor laborer had already recognized two of the bravest veterans of his legions. The memory of the wars and battles and victories of other days flashed across his mind; the very places these two men took in the defeat of the enemy, their bravery by his side in the field of battle, and the scars they received in the bloody fight—all rushed on him in a moment, and roused every great and brave feeling of his soul. He was about to run towards his companions in arms and embrace them, but prudence held him back, and by an act of self-control he suppressed his excited feeling. Drawing himself up majestically with a sigh, which alone told of the struggle that passed within, he asked: "Why seek you Placidus?" Whilst Antiochus was recounting how the enemies of the Empire had once more declared war in the East, and the emperor wished to entrust to that general alone the care of the expedition and had sent the soldiers who served under him to all parts to seek him, Placidus could no longer contain his feelings; and opening the rude garment that covered the scars on his breast, he showed them to the astonished veterans and told them that he was the general they sought. Another moment and they were hanging round his neck, and shedding tears of joy.

Placidus was received with the universal joy of the people— the confidence of the army was restored, and new life appeared in all the troops—battles and triumphs were anticipated and declared before they were fought or won. The emperor was filled with delight; he embraced his former master of the horse, listened with interest to the history of the vicissitudes of his loss and grief, and, placing around his waist the golden belt of consular command, begged of him to draw his sword once more in the cause of the Empire. The holy man had already recognized, in the humility and prayer of his heart, the great change that had come over his circumstances so strangely and so suddenly, as the disposition of the loving providence of God, and prepared, even in his old age, to mingle again in the din of arms and fatigues of war. During the days of his trial and resignation in the lonely vineyards of Egypt, the Divine Spirit had revealed to him that a day of restoration to all he had lost in this world would soon dawn on his gloomy path.

Whilst Placidus is casting his rough army into shape, and exercising his soldiers in the terrible science of bloodshed and war, we must retrace our steps for a moment, and take a glance at the poor, wretched Theopista, whom we left in the bark of the tyrant captain who cruelly tore her from her husband and her children.

Doubtless, in the sympathy of his pious heart, the reader has pitied her in her affliction, and hoped that some fortunate circumstance may have saved her. But has Almighty God ever abandoned His servants when the angelical virtue was threatened? Who is more powerful before Him than the innocent defenseless female? In the history of the past no virtue has had more visible protection from Heaven than chastity; no vice has caused more terrible vengeance than impurity. The prayer of the virgin for the protection of her innocence not only pierced the clouds, but drew from them the electric bolt that struck the oppressor with judgment. Fear not for the virtuous and faithful Theopista; God is her shield, and who can prevail against the

Most High? The means He adopted to protect His servant were silent, consoling, and merciful. He did not strike the impious captain with a sudden and terrible blow of merited retribution, but breathed on his heart a sentiment of tenderness and pity that made him blush for his cruelty and impiety towards the young mother. Scarcely had the fair wind wafted the little ship out of sight of Theopista's husband and children, than the sobs which grief was pressing from her breaking heart struck a fiber of pity in the feelings of the pagan captain. At the same moment Almighty God removed the stimulus of the flesh, and made him love and admire in his captive a virtue he never knew before. The virtuous soul is like the fruit tree in blossom, that gives fragrance to every breeze, and spreads a delicious odor on the atmosphere around. The sublimity of virtue that shone in the fidelity of the Christian matron, the patience and forgiveness of that suffering child of misfortune, so completely won the pagan, that, from being her enemy and oppressor, he became her protector and guardian. He landed Theopista at the next port he touched at, and gave her money and goods to maintain her for some time. She, too, had her share of trial, and fifteen long years of suffering and exile proved her worthy of the joy and crown that were awaiting her.

Everything was ready, and the expedition started for the East. The spirit of joy and bravery which animated the soldiers was the harbinger of the greatest triumphs. They poured in thousands through the eastern gates of the city; and, whilst the morning sun was reflected from their burnished battle-axes and spears, the tombs of their mighty dead, which lined the Appian Way, were made to echo once more with the war songs of the irresistible legions of the Empire. The octogenarian leader—the Christian Placidus—brought up the rear of the march, and was drawn in a chariot by two beautiful Arab horses.

We need not tarry long over the oft-told tale of Roman triumph. The legions poured like Alpine avalanches into the country of the enemy, crushing in their course everything that was opposed to them. Not only were the rebellious subjects reduced to submission, but the conquering eagle spread its wings over new dominions, and new provinces were added to the boundless territory of the Caesars.

The meekness and skill of Placidus knew how to turn everything to profit; few of his conquests were purchased with unnecessary bloodshed and carnage. He pardoned freely, and never retributed the resistance of a brave people by the retaliation so terrible in the annals of pagan warfare.

Every army has its heroes. The campaign of Placidus was nearly at an end before its real soldiers were known. Where the conquest was easy all were brave, but a moment of danger and trial came, and the laurels of fame fell to those who won them. The army was surprised in an ambuscade, but was saved by the prompt action of two youths belonging to the Numidian corps. They were the two brave young men who had met each other for the first time in the ranks and become friends. They were strolling outside of the camp when the cry "To arms" was heard. They rushed like startled lions to the front and cheered on their companions; they fought together against fearful odds, but their battle-axes were wielded rapidly and skillfully, and dealt destruction on every side. With a few brave companions they withstood the progress of the enemy until their own army had come up to the rescue; such brave and unexpected resistance sent a panic through the enemy, and they fled with terrible massacre. Some thousands were slain, and the army of opposition was so completely destroyed that it never stood in the field of battle again.

The general had seen what had passed, and when the battle was over, he sent for the young heroes who had saved the army, raised them to the rank of captain, and bestowed on them the honor of his intimate friendship.

The army had passed on from triumph to triumph, and we must now open the scene of our tale on a wild plain on the coast of Arabia, where they were encamped before the return to the great capital. There were a few little huts of fishermen on the seashore, and here and there, along the banks of a fertile stream, some pretty little houses surrounded by gardens and vineyards. Amongst them there was one more beautiful than the rest, and sitting on a gentle slope towards the river. It belonged to a poor widow, who lived by the fruits of her little garden and the labor of her own hands. Here the old general, wearied and fatigued from the hardships and privations of the campaign, pitched his tent and arranged to remain some time before undertaking the fatiguing journey of return. Near him he had the two young captains, whom he had made his confidents, and treated as if they were his adopted children. Doubtless the old man saw in the youth and beauty of the young men what his own sons would have been if they had been spared to him. Some invisible attraction made him love them tenderly, and he could not bear them to be absent from his side. They, too, grew in the deepest friendship with each other; a similarity of feeling and disposition, a secret love for virtue, and a certain trait of nobility in every thought and action, not only knit them together in inseparable bonds of harmony, but enhanced them in the love and esteem of all who knew them.

One day, as was their custom, they strolled together along the banks of the little stream. Everything was fresh and beautiful around them; the birds sang in the trees; and the flowers, that grew in great abundance in the vicinity of the stream, spread a thousand odors on the gentle breeze that rippled the waters. The young soldiers sat down under the shade of a fig tree and entered into an animated conversation. The elder was a tall, handsome young man of about eighteen years, and seemed about two years older than his companion. He was of a gentle, silent disposition, and often seemed rapt in thought as if some cloud hung over him. His younger companion noticed this to be particularly the case on the day in question, and during their conversation he would frequently pause and look abstractedly on the little stream, which was rapidly rising and swelling up to its banks from a heavy shower which had fallen in the neighboring mountains. In that familiarity which their tried friendship permitted, he affectionately asked his companion the cause of his trouble.

"It is now some time since you and I first met," the young officer said, "and I have all along thought you had some secrets locked up in your heart which it would console and interest me to hear. Do tell me your history, that I may participate in your sorrow. You know I am your friend."

The other looking on him with kindness, and as if reading his countenance to see if he were in earnest, grasped his hand, and turning his eyes towards heaven, gave a sigh; then drawing his companion nearer to him, he said, in an excited manner: "Yes, I will tell you a strange story, but you must not betray my secret. I am a Roman citizen and a Christian."

The young man started up as if a clap of thunder had burst over him, but the other, preventing him from saying a word, and calling him by his name, continued in a kind and majestic tone: "Although I enlisted in the Roman army in the same province as yourself, I was not born there. My father was a Roman general and a man of great esteem. I remember when I was but five years of age, one day he went to hunt, as was his custom, and did not return until an early hour the next morning. He came home in an excited state, and said things that made my mother weep. The following night, when all was dark and still, they took me and my little brother, who was only three years old, to a dark cave in the earth; and after we had passed some winding and gloomy corridors, we entered a little room beautifully lit up. There was an aged man sitting on a stone chair, and he wore a beautiful stole around his neck. The walls of the little room were covered with beautiful paintings of men in rich garments of fishes and lambs, and I remember the picture of a man nailed to a cross. The venerable old man spoke to my father and mother for a long time. I do not remember all he said, but he spoke of the true God whom the pagans did not know, and all the good things God had done for man—how He loved him, how He died for him, how He promised him eternal happiness hereafter. My parents were very much affected, and I remember my father wept again, as if he had done something wrong. Then the aged man baptized us, and called us all by different names; my name was Agapius. I knew by all this that I was made a Christian and a child of the great God he spoke of. After this many prayers were said, and when leaving that strange place, my father and mother seemed very much rejoiced.

"Soon after my father suffered the loss of all his property; his cattle and horses died of a terrible disease; even our slaves and servants also died; and we left the house and went to a vineyard outside the Nomentan Gate. While away, my father was robbed of all he had, and was reduced to poverty. Then one night, taking my brother and myself and mother, he led us to the seashore, and we got into a ship and were fifteen days on the rough sea. When we came to land, my father and my little brother and myself were sent on shore, but not my mother, and the little ship went away with her immediately. Oh! I shall never forget the grief of my poor father on that occasion."

He buried his face in his hands and wept for some time, and a tear stole down the cheek of his young companion. Looking up again, he continued his tale amidst tears and deep sighs.

"Then rising suddenly, he took my little brother in his arms and me by the hand, and we went into the country. We came to a river that was running very rapidly, and as my father could not take us both over together, he bade me remain on the bank whilst he took my little brother over first, promising to come back for me. But while my father was crossing the stream—oh! I shall never forget it!—a terrible lion came out of the woods

and seized me." A shudder passed over his companion; he seemed all excitement, and cried out—

"How strange! But tell me how you were saved."

He seemed much agitated; some words had come to his lips, but he repressed them and listened with motionless anxiety to the remainder of his companion's story.

"Well," continued the young captain, "I screamed for help, but it was too late. The lion caught me in his mouth—I have still the marks of his teeth on my body—and carried me towards the forest. Fortunately there were some shepherds passing by, and when they saw me they set their dogs after the lion. One of the dogs caught hold of me and was pulling me from him, when the lion let me fall and seized the dog and went away with it. The shepherds carried me to their little house, and a good woman put me to bed and took care of me. I recovered, and grew up in that house; but I never saw my father or my brother since then." Seizing his companion by the arm, and his eyes suffused with tears, he said: "Wonder not, my friend, that I am sad; this stream, those trees, and this wild plain in which we are encamped, remind me of those terrible scenes of my youth. Can I ever forget that day on which I lost father, mother, brother, all?" He could say no more, but buried his face in his hands again and wept bitterly.

He remarked, during the recital of his story, that his young friend was getting more and more excited; and from time to time gave expression to incoherent sentences and ejaculations of surprise. "Strange! It must be! Oh, joy!" was all the young man could say. After a moment's silence, he cried out, with energy and excitement: "Agapius, I believe I am thy brother."

The other started. "How! Speak! Say why thou thinkest so—or dost thou trifle with my sorrow?"

The young man replied quickly, and with agitation: "I too lost my parents in my youth. The people who brought me up told me they saved me from a wolf near the stream of Chobar; that I was of a noble Roman family, for I had around my neck this golden ornament."

Whilst he was putting his hand into his breast to look for the ornament, the other sprang to his feet in excitement and cried out: "Show it! Has it got on it the name of *Theophistus* and the *Ides of March?*"—"Yes, here it is." Agapius, recognizing the amulet his mother had put round his neck on the morning after their baptism, caught the young man in his arms, and cried out: "My brother, my brother!"

Further explanation placed the fact beyond doubt, and the two brothers remained for hours together, every now and then embracing each other with tears of affection. They told each other all the particulars of their after-lives. Theophistus was saved from the wolf by some ploughmen, who saw the child in its mouth and, rescuing him, brought him up as one of their own children. They were reared some miles apart from each other and did not know it; but God, whose ways are inscrutable, brought them together in the Roman army that he might restore them to their lost father and mother, as the reward of their patience and virtue....

When the excitement of the first moments of recognition had subsided, they agreed to repair to their general to inform him of the extraordinary discovery they had made. They found the old man in his tent, sitting at a rude table; his face was covered with his hands, and he seemed rapt in meditation and thought.

The eldest rushed towards him and told him he had strange and joyful glad news to tell him. The old man raised his head; his eyes were moist, and a cloud of gloom mantled his brow. Looking with a parental smile on the cheerful youth, he said to him:

"Speak, then, my child, for thy joy shall be mine; the happiness of others makes us forget our own sorrows, thy words will come like sunshine breaking through the gloom of my heart. Alas! This day has sad reminiscences for me. It is the anniversary of a series of misfortunes which deprived me of my wife and my children."

He paused for a moment, and raising his eyes, dimmed with the filling tears, towards heaven, exclaimed: "But it was the will of Him who reigns above; He gave, and He took away: blessed be His holy name!"

The young captain was astonished. It was the first time his old general prayed to the true God before him. A thousand thoughts rushed into his mind; he knew not whether he should first declare that he too was a Christian, or relate the discovery of his brother. He loved the old man as a father, and his softened heart melted once more to see his veteran chief in sorrow. A few hasty explanations sufficed to reveal the truth that he was talking to his own father. Another moment, and the young men were hanging round his neck, and the old chief was pressing his brave sons to his heart....

Whilst the events we have recorded were taking place, there was a great commotion in the camp. A courier had arrived in great haste. He announced the death of Trajan in Selinonte (a town of Cilicia), and the election of Adrian by the army. This election had been confirmed by the Senate, and the army of Placidus was ordered to return immediately to join in the triumph accorded by universal acclamation to the ashes of the deceased emperor. The soldiers under Placidus had been nearly two years absent, and were wearied with the fatigues and privations of war. They hailed with delight the news of their return. Deafening shouts that announced the glad tidings had reached the tent of Placidus before the courier could be brought before him. The messenger, foot-sore and covered with dust, handed the general a parchment roll, on which was written—

"It has pleased the gods to raise us to the throne of the Empire. We decree a triumph for the army of Placidus, and command our brave general to return forthwith to the Capital.

Adrian."

The general held the parchment for a few moments in his hands. He became distracted; raising his eyes slowly towards heaven, he said: "Thou art setting, thou brilliant sun of my hopes—those grand destinies foreshadowed in prophetic whispers are fast gliding into realities. Aye! to Rome!—to triumph!—to martyrdom!"

He then gave orders to strike the tents and prepare for general march on the morrow. Dismissing all from his tent he remained alone to commune with God in gratitude for the felicity of that day. He paced his tent rapidly; the vision of his future martyrdom passed before him. We hear, in fancy, the majestic tones of his fervent soliloquy:

"Aye! to triumph!—to step from the golden chariot to the tomb—to climb the glittering heights of the Capitol amid the shouts that rend the heavens with blasphemies against my God—to kindle the fires of impure sacrifice to the demons of idolatry! Rather shall Placidus be cast on the burning pile, and be himself the victim.

"My children! Will ye drink of my cup? Will you ride in the same chariot, and drink a chalice of earthly joy till you reach the atrium of the temple of Jupiter, then be bound to the same stake; the flames of our funeral pyre shall send our freed spirits to the land of eternal triumph, where the shout of real joy shall ring out the congratulation of Heaven's choirs for our Christian victory!

"Poor Theopista! Thy noble soul is still wanting to complete the holocaust! Art thou pining away in some villain's home?"

He was interrupted by a servant announcing that the poor woman who owned the garden on which his tent was pitched wished to see him. Placidus was not a proud, austere man, who left the business of the poor to be transacted by a cruel and heartless official. He was accessible to the roughest soldier in his camp, as well as to the highest of his officers. By a sign of his hand, he signified assent to have her brought before him.

She seemed advanced in years, and the victim of much sorrow. Her attenuated frame, and the meanness of her dress, told of want and poverty; yet her bearing was noble. Her eyes were bloodshot, and showed signs of much weeping; tears had traced their own channels down her cheeks. But her countenance still, in all its tender expression of care and grief, showed evident traces of beauty, nobility, and innocence. Having entered the tent, she fell on her knees before Placidus, and said:

"Great chief and leader of the armies of Rome! I beseech thee to commiserate the sorrows of a poor unfortunate woman. I am a Roman citizen. Some years ago I was separated from my husband and children, and brought here by force for unlawful purposes; but I pledge my word, before thee and before Heaven, I never lost my fidelity to my husband and my children. I am here an exile, in sorrow and misery. I ask thee, by the love thou

bearest to thy own spouse and children, to take me back to
Rome—to my friends—to my—"

She could say no more. In her excitement she sprang to her
feet—she clasped her hands—and looking fixedly at Placidus,
she recognized her husband. At the moment she appealed to
him for the love he bore his spouse, the aged general raised his
hand to his forehead to hide the ever-ready tell-tale tear of his
afflicted heart. In turning his head he exposed a large scar on
the back of his ear; the quick eye of the matron recognized the
wound her husband received in the Judaic wars, and one steady
look at the worn and changed features of Placidus convinced
her. She rushed towards him, and with sobs that choked every
word:

"Tell me, I beseech thee, art thou Placidus—the master of
the Roman horse—whom the true God spoke to in the mountains of Italy—who was baptized—called Eustachius—lost his
wife—"

"Yes! Yes!" interrupted Placidus. "Knowest thou of her?
Speak!—Does she still live?"

The poor creature made an effort to throw herself into his
arms, but, overcome by emotion, fell to the ground, crying out,
"I am Theopista!"

The weakened frame of Theopista could not bear the shock
of the sudden discovery. When motion returned, she was still
delirious, and seemed like one who saw a beautiful dream
passing before her. At times her reason returned, and she would
ask, "Is it true? Does the evil spirit create phantasms to deceive
me? Oh; how good is God!"

Another hour, and the little tent of Placidus was the scene
of joy seldom felt on this side of the grave. Four widowed and
bleeding hearts were healed; the husband and the spouse, the
parents and the children, after years of separation and trial, were
thrown together and recognized in the space of a few hours.

Almighty God had never abandoned them for a moment from the time He decreed the vicissitudes which were to try them; finding them faithful, He knew how to reward. The flood of joy which He pours on the faithful hearts of His servants is but as a stray rivulet of the mighty stream of ineffable delight that inundates the souls of the beatified. If Christians would remember that God watches with a special providence over the afflicted—that the troubles and trials of life are often directly sent by Him—how many a pang would lose its sting, how many a bitter loss and disappointment would become, not only supportable, but the source of interior peace! The troubled soul humbly kneeling before the Cross is the type of the true Christian. If the strange history of Placidus should fall into the hands of any one in trouble, let him, like that brave and generous soul, await the dispositions of Providence without blasphemy, suppressing even a reproachful thought towards God, and every murmur of impatience; as sure as the hour of trial and affliction is long and dark, so shall the hour of reward come quickly, brilliantly, and unclouded.

Greater joy than the soul can long bear in its earthly tenement is prepared by God for this happy family. Their union here is to last but for a few weeks. When the camp was struck, and the army on the march to Rome, Placidus knew, by inspiration, that he was going to the last and most severe struggle which God had in store for him—his triumph in death over self, the world, and the powers of darkness. He gave all his time to prayer and the instruction of his sons in the sublime morality and doctrine of the Christian faith. He asked a favor from God, which was granted—that as He had deigned, in His mercy, to bring him again to the embraces of his family, the happiness of their union might never again be clouded by separation; that if the testimony of his blood were demanded for the defense of the faith and the glory of the Church, his spouse and children might partake in the same last crowning favor of the Divine mercy....

Adrian entered Rome in the borrowed glory of the deceased emperor; the shouts of triumph resounded through the city. He deified Trajan from the tomb of Augustus, and sent the eagle of his 'spirit' to the liberty of the skies; he dedicated the superb column erected to the conqueror, and the arena of the Coliseum was once more reeking with the blood of gladiators and victims. During these games more than two hundred lions were slaughtered, and an immense number of captives and slaves were put to death.

It was one evening during these celebrations that word was brought to the city that the army of Placidus had arrived, and was already on the Appian Way. A new impulse was given to the rejoicings, and a new triumph and procession were prepared for the victorious army. There is nothing so calculated to excite a people's enthusiasm as the return of its armies from a triumphant campaign. According to custom the emperor went out to meet the general, and embraced him. As the evening was far advanced and the sun was already sinking beneath the blue Mediterranean, the emperor gave orders that the army should encamp outside the walls for the night, in order to enter the city in triumph next morning. Placidus and his family returned with the emperor to the Palatine, and were entertained at a sumptuous banquet. He gave the emperor the history of his campaign, and spoke until a late hour of his battles, the bravery of his two sons, and the extraordinary discovery of his wife and family.

Loud, shrill and cheerful were the trumpet blasts that roused the sleeping army on the following morning. The cup of joy for these poor creatures was full to the brim. They knew of no greater reward for years of hardship and trial, for the scars and wounds which disabled them for life, than the shouts of a brutal and barbarous mob, who hailed them along the road of triumph.

As they poured in through the gates, each of them received a laurel crown, whose freshness and beauty contrasted deeply with the sunburnt features and tattered garments of the veterans. Round their necks and about their persons they carried a profusion of tinsel trinkets, which they took from the conquered people as ornaments for their wives and children. There were wagons drawn by oxen laden with spoils, that made the massive pavements of the Appian Way creak; armor, gold and brass ornaments, wild animals in cages, and everything that could show the habits and manners of the conquered people. The general, together with his wife and two sons, was in a gilt chariot, drawn by four white horses, in the rear of his army. None of the pride and flush of drunken joy that characterized the pagan conqueror was to be seen in the meek countenance of Placidus. All this rejoicing and gorgeous display was to him and his Christian family the funeral pomp that led them to their tomb. The king who, on his death-bed, had himself invested with his crown and royal robes to meet death as a monarch, was a picture of Placidus led in triumph to martyrdom—a tale of the emptiness and instability of human greatness. He was silent and collected; not even the deafening peals of applause from crowds of idle spectators, who made his name ring through the palaces and tombs that bend over the streets from the Capena gate to the Forum, induced him to look up with the smile of joyful approbation. He was well aware that in a few moments his belief in Christianity would be declared, for he could not sacrifice to the gods.

Whilst the procession was moving along, a murmur passed through the crowd. They asked one another where were the victims?—where the captive chiefs?—where the slaves usually dragged at the chariot wheels of the conqueror?—where the wailing matrons and daughters of the conquered race to sound the mournful music of triumph? Arrived at the Forum, the procession halted as usual, and the executioners and keepers of the Mamertine prison looked in vain for their victims; it was the first time in the annals of triumph that their axes had not been steeped in the blood of heroes, whose only crime was that they fought bravely for their homes and their countries. They knew nothing of the sublime morality that can forgive an enemy. Placidus pardoned the moment he had conquered, and instead of dragging helpless victims from their country and family, to be immolated to the demons of Rome, he left his name in the traces of his march in love and benediction.

But now the procession arrived at the entrance to the temple of Jupiter. The priests were waiting in their robes, and snow-white oxen, with gilded horns and crowns of flowers, were held by the altar. Immense faggots were blazing in the heart of the temple to consume the victims, and fragrant incense was burning in golden vessels. Placidus and his family descended from their chariot and stepped on one side; they refused to enter— they would not sacrifice.

If an earthquake had shaken the temple to its foundations, or a sudden eclipse had darkened the sun, there could not have been given a greater shock or surprise to the assembled thousands. The news ran like fire in a train of powder through the vast crowd. A deep heavy murmur, like the swell of the troubled deep breaking on its boundaries, rose from the multitudes in the Forum. Indignation and fury were the passions that swayed the mob. The demon of paganism reigned in their hearts; pity, justice, and liberty were virtues unknown. From shouts of applause with which they hailed Placidus as the conqueror, the glory of the Empire, and the beloved of the martial god, they now hooted him with groans and hisses; and loudly from the gilded temples of the Capital were echoed the terrible cries of "Death to the Christians!"—"Away with the Christians!" But the hour of another and grander triumph had come for our hero.

The noble general and his family were brought before the emperor. Was Adrian glad to have Placidus brought before him as a criminal? Doubtless he looked with a jealous eye on the glory, popularity and real triumph of one who, a few months before, was his equal as a commander of the army, and his acknowledged superior in skill and attainments, whilst his own triumph was but a mockery—the borrowed plumes of a deceased hero, whose panegyric he reluctantly preached from the chariot of triumph.... When asked by the haughty Adrian why he would not sacrifice to the gods, Placidus answered, bravely and fearlessly, "I am a Christian, and adore only the true God."

"Whence comes this infatuation?" asked the emperor, quickly. "Why lose all the glory of the triumph, and bring thy gray hairs to shame? Dost thou not know that I have power to put thee to a miserable death?"

Placidus meekly replied: "My body is in your power, but my soul belongs to Him Who created it. Never shall I forget the mercy He has shown me in calling me to the knowledge of Himself, and I rejoice to be able to suffer for Him. You may command me to lead your legions against the enemies of the Empire, but never will I offer sacrifice to any other god than the One great and powerful God Who created all things, stretched out the heavens in their glory, decked the earth in its beauty, and created man to serve Him. He alone is worthy of sacrifice; all other gods are but demons who deceive men."

So also answered his wife and two sons. They bantered the emperor himself for his folly in worshipping senseless pieces of marble and wood. In vain did Adrian try promises and threats, and all the silly arguments which were used in the defense of paganism. The faithful family was inflexible; the eloquence of Placidus was simple, but powerful and earnest. The palpable defeat of Adrian in his attempt to reason with one gifted with the eloquence of faith promised to those dragged before earthly tribunals, roused his pride and his cruelty, and the desire for revenge. The Coliseum stood but a few paces from them; the games were going on; the criminals and slaves of the Empire were the daily victims of its amusements. The condemnation of Placidus would be a stroke of policy to enhance the prosperity of his reign; it was the fullest gratification of the cruel passions of jealousy and revenge which the demon had stirred up in his heart. He ordered the Christian general and his family to be exposed to the wild beasts in the amphitheater....

It was not in an amphitheater, stained with the blood of wild beasts and gladiators and filled with an excited and unfeeling crowd, that the voice of pity or reason could be heard; the impatient clamors of the multitude denounced the Christians as the enemies of the gods and men, and the public condemnation of the Christian general had already rung loudly and repeatedly through the benches of the Coliseum. The coming of the emperor was announced, the buzz of conversation was hushed, and all eyes were turned towards the entrance on the side of the Esquiline, which was specially reserved for the royal cortége. As soon as he entered the amphitheater, all rose; the lictors lowered their fasces, and the senators and vestals bowed profoundly. Shouts of "great," "immortal," "divine," resounded from every seat. The crowd of spectators was nothing more than an assembly of miscreant slaves, who trembled at the beck of their rulers. Although the spectators of the Coliseum frequently hated the emperor as an oppressor and a tyrant, yet, in the wild frenzy of fear, they cried out with lying tongues that he alone was great and powerful. He carried a scepter of ivory, surmounted with a golden eagle, and a slave followed, bearing over his head a crown of solid gold and precious stones. As soon as he was seated, the shrill blast of a trumpet called for silence and the commencement of the games. After the procession of the unfortunate wretches who were to take part in the cruel sport of that day's program and the sham fight of the gladiators, it was usual to commence with sports of agility and skill, but on this day the order was changed. The crowd called for the condemnation of the Christians, and the emperor gave the order that Placidus and his family be exposed to the wild beasts.

They were led into the arena in chains. They were silent and rapt in prayer. The editor of the games asked them again to sacrifice to the gods; they refused. The keepers were told to let in some wild beasts to devour them. A death-like stillness reigned around. Everyone was struck with their fortitude; no screams of terror, no trembling, no supplications for mercy, no heart-rending and frantic farewells. All was calm and tranquil; they awaited on bended knees with majestic resignation their awful doom. The iron doors of the subterranean keeps grated on their hinges; two lions and four bears rushed into the arena.

They would not touch the Martyrs but gamboled around them. One of the lions endeavored to get his head under the foot of Placidus; the Saint permitted it, and a more beautiful or thrilling sight was never seen in the arena of the Coliseum. The king of the forest voluntarily put himself under the foot of  the unarmed old man, and crouched down as if with fear and reverence. "Goad the animals!" shouted the enraged emperor to the keepers. "Goad them on!" "Make them devour!" rang from every tier, from the senators, the vestals, and the maddened populace of the upper circles; but the animals turned on their keepers, and drove them from the

arena. Other animals were called for, but they only served to enhance the scene of triumph, and respectfully licked the feet of their intended victims. He Who made use of an animal to bring Placidus to the light of faith, and afterwards to be the instruments of the trial and his sorrow, now made them declare His love and protection over His servants.

The indignation and shame of the pagan emperor was roused to the highest pitch; his impotent rage and natural cruelty broke forth, and to gratify his brutal passion, he commanded the Martyrs to be placed in the bronze bull, and to be consumed by a slow fire. This was a horrible instrument of torture and execution used for the persecution of the Christians. It was made in the shape of a bull, and could hold several persons at the same time in its hollow womb; when fire was applied beneath, it became an oven, and it is not difficult to imagine the excruciating torture a slow fire must have caused to its living victims.

In this way Placidus and their family received their crown. Almighty God wished to show it was His will, and not the commands of the emperor, or the instruments of torture that deprived his servants of life, by performing a great miracle. After three days the bodies of the Saints were taken out in the presence of the emperor; no trace of fire was to be seen upon them; they exhaled a beautiful odor, and seemed to be lying in a sweet sleep. Their relics were laid on the ground for several days, and the whole city rushed to see the wonder. As Almighty God does nothing in vain, many were converted by this miracle, and became fervent Christians. The bodies of the glorious Martyrs were stolen by the Christians, and were afterwards buried, together with the brazen bull in which they suffered, on the spot where their martyrdom took place. A beautiful church sprang up in the very earliest ages of Christianity over the shrine of Eustachius and his family.

ELDER GABRIEL
OF PSKOV AND KAZAN

SCHEMA-Archimandrite Gabriel was born on the 14th of March, 1844, in Irbit County in the Perm Province of Russia, to the pious and wealthy peasant family of Theodore and Eudocia Ziryanov. His parents were literate, and on feast days, after returning from church two miles away in the nearby village, they would spend the day reading the Lives of Saints, the Gospel and the Psalter. Their little Ganya (Ganya is endearing for Gabriel), their only son, was taught to read by means of the Psalter, which was taught to him by his older sisters Eugenia and Anna (later nuns Eustolia and Agnia). These readings made a deep impression on the entire family: They all acknowledged the sinfulness of their own lives and became inspired to emulate the lives of the God-pleasers in accordance with the commandments of Christ. They were very close, loved to work, and never knew material want. The children were shown affection wisely and were never severely punished. In addition to mere verbal rebuke, their mother chose as her principal means of instructing the children to "complain" to God.

When Ganya first spoke of going to a monastery, his mother and sisters began to cry. His father became dreamy and grave and then cut short and screamed out:

"I won't allow you to go!" He felt sorry for Ganya's mother, who so dearly loved her son; and how would he be able to manage at his age without the help of such a meek and extraordinary son in his household?

But Ganya persisted. After a short time elapsed he would say again: "Bless me to go to a monastery."

A year went by. Ganya had greatly changed his way of life, modeling it after the manner of a monk's, but his father would not let him go. Finally, he was overcome with such a terrible anger on account of Ganya's persistent entreaties that, in place of an answer, he went out into the yard, came back in with a belt, grabbed Ganya by the hair, held his head between his legs, and proceeded to whip him. His mother covered her eyes with her hands, not even daring to breathe, and his sisters began to scream. "Shut up, all of you...." Everyone became still; only the swishing of the belt through the air and his father's deep breathing could be heard. And Ganya? He felt the blows on his back, but they did not hurt. He was struck by this fact and concluded:

"This must be God's will so that I may be freed to go to a monastery." As soon as his tired, sweating father tossed the belt aside and let him go, he bowed before his father and said:

"Bless me, my dearest father, to go to a monastery!" His father burst out sobbing, for Ganya's meekness itself pierced his heart.

"To whom will you entrust us? I am getting old and your mother is frail. Who will feed us?"

"Do not fear, Father; the Lord will not forget you." His father was at a loss for words.... Ganya still persisted in his entreaties that they would be doing a good deed by letting him go before God, in the same way as they light candles in church.

His parents finally consented to let him go. They slowly began to gather together necessary clothes and linens, and his father went to the provincial officials for a passport. They accomplished everything as planned, except that Theodore did not give him any money for the journey.... It didn't matter to Ganya; he didn't need any.

In the meantime all Ganya's relatives learned of his departure. They came to say farewell and to ask for his prayers, and to give him a little money.

On the appointed day they all prayed to God. Ganya bowed down to each of those present, and even said farewell to the  horses and cows, which also wept, particularly his own horse. What can be said of his family? His father fainted and was carried away. His mother, sisters and the rest of the townsfolk went with him to the outskirts of their land, watering the road with their tears.

Ganya left on his horse with courage. It was hard, of course, to depart from this place of many joys and tears where God had shown him His mercy, but he was leaving to serve God. On this account his sorrow was mixed with a joyous solemnity. He was a monk at heart and did not belong to this world....

Fr. Gabriel, throughout his life in service to the Lord, treated many people and animals with homeopathic remedies to restore them to health. During the last days of his life, when he was nearing death, the following occurred.

Father Gabriel continued to be very weak in body. One night was especially difficult for him, and it appeared that he was going to die.... Father Gabriel closed his eyes from exhaustion and fell asleep for a minute, and at that moment he felt some strange breeze refresh his face and fill the room with a

wonderful fragrance. Without opening his eyes, Father Gabriel
began to breathe this air with delight, and at the same time to
feel the breeze moving throughout his entire being, sending ever
so slight and pleasant shivers throughout his body.... Then,
opening his eyes, he saw something completely unexpected: a
snowy white dove was in the air a yard from his face, beating
his silvery wings over Father Gabriel's face like a fan and
hovering in the same place. Father Gabriel, without realizing
why, began for some reason immediately to sing mentally:
"Without leaving the bosom of the Father, Thou, O Christ our
God, hast come down upon earth. I have heard the mystery of
Thy dispensation and have glorified Thee Who alone lovest
mankind." At that moment the clock struck one o'clock in the
morning. He continued to sing. He sang the Great Doxology,
the 50th Psalm, the Akathist to the Savior, and many other
prayers which he knew by heart, chanting and singing until 3:30
in the morning. All this time he breathlessly observed the dove,
and, delighting in the fragrant air, he felt as if his whole organism
was refreshed and rested. Downstairs he could now hear the
cooks moving around; the monk who awakens the brothers
passed through the corridor, and the dove became like a dim
shadow and faded away....

Father Gabriel was sad to part with the dove, and he tried
to force himself to see it again. He shut his eyes and again
mentally sang prayers. Then he opened his eyes again, but the
little dove was no longer there. But the wonderful aroma
lingered for a long time in the room, and the brothers, visiting
the Elder, also smelled it with bewilderment. Several even
judged Father Gabriel that he allowed his cell-attendant to use
such expensive cologne. Father Gabriel, breathing in the fragrance, began to sense in himself an increase in his strength,
and, in general, he began to improve....

Saint Gerasim and the Lion

Commemorated on March 4

SAINT GERASIM (†475) was first a monk in the Egyptian desert, then later moved close to the Jordan River, gathering a community of about seventy monks, who lived by a strict ascetic rule, seeking to live for God and His Kingdom.

✳ ✳ ✳

Once while walking along the hilly bank of the River Jordan, Abba Gerasim met a lion which let out a terrifying roar from pain in its paw. A sharp, slender reed had pierced his paw, and it had become infected. Seeing the Elder, the lion approached him and showed him his paw, injured by the puncture, and, as if weeping, asked for his assistance. The Elder, seeing the lion in such a plight, sat down, took his paw and, uncovering the wound, extracted the splinter and forced out the pus, then washed it and bound it with linen. The lion, having received help, would not forsake the Elder, but like a devoted disciple followed him wherever he went, so that the Elder marveled greatly at the devotion of the lion. The Elder began to feed him, throwing him bread and fresh beans.

At the lavra there was a donkey which carried water for the needs of the Elder, for they took water from the Jordan. The lavra stood a mile from the holy river. It came to pass that the Elder entrusted the care of the donkey to the lion that he might guard the donkey at the bank of the Jordan. Once while grazing, the donkey walked a great distance away from the lion, and at that time some camel drivers from Arabia passed by who took the donkey and departed. The lion, having lost the donkey, returned sullen and, as it were, ashamed to Abba Gerasim. The Abba supposed that he had devoured the donkey. "Where is the donkey?" he asked the lion. The latter like a man stood silent and lowered his eyes. "Didst thou eat the donkey? Blessed be the Lord! Henceforth thou must perform the duties of the donkey." So from that time forth at the command of the Elder the lion carried the vessel, which filled four buckets, and brought the water.

Once a soldier came for prayer to the Elder. Seeing the lion, grown weary carrying water, and learning the reason, he pitied him. Taking three pieces of money, he handed them to the Elder that they might buy a donkey to carry the water and free the lion from this obligation. A little time elapsed after the liberation of the lion from his work. The camel driver who had led away the donkey returned to ask for bread in the holy city, and the donkey was with him. Crossing through the Jordan with two other drivers, he chanced upon the lion. Seeing the lion, the donkey left the caravan and fled; but the lion, recognizing the donkey, leaped towards him and, grabbing him as he always had by the halter, he brought the donkey away from the camel drivers. Growling from joy that he had found the lost donkey, he returned to the Elder. The Elder, being of the opinion that the lion had devoured the donkey, only now learned that he had chastened the lion in vain. The Elder named the lion Jordan. Afterward the lion lived at the lavra for about five more years, never leaving the Elder.

At the time that Abba Gerasim departed to the Lord and the fathers buried him, by God's design the lion was not at the monastery. A short time passed, the lion returned and began to seek the Elder. A disciple of the Elder and Abba Sabbatius, seeing the lion, said, "Jordan, our Elder has left us orphans and has departed to the Lord, so go and eat!" The lion didn't want to eat, but looked about everywhere for the Elder. Not seeing him, he began to roar. Abba Sabbatius and the rest of the fathers patted him on the back and said, "The Elder has departed to the Lord, abandoning us." But speaking in this way they were unable to stop the lion's roaring and groans; on the contrary, the more they worried over him and tried to console him with words, the louder his roar grew and the greater his sorrow. His voice and eyes clearly reflected how he longed for the Elder.

Then Fr. Sabbatius said to him, "Well, follow me, if you don't believe us. I will show you where the Elder lies." And taking the lion he walked with him to the Elder's grave. It was located about half a mile from the Church. Standing over the grave of Abba Gerasim, Abba Sabbatius said to the lion, "Here is where our Elder is." And Abba Sabbatius knelt down. Seeing him bending over the earth, the lion with unusual strength smote his head upon the grave and, letting out a roar, died upon the Elder's grave.

This took place, not because the lion possessed a reasoning soul, but by the will of God, Who glorifies them that glorify Him, not only during their life but also after their death, and has shown us in what consists the obedience of even creatures to Adam before he transgressed the commandment of God and was cast out of the paradise of delight.

SAINT HERMAN OF ALASKA

Commemorated on December 12

AINT HERMAN of Alaska is the first American Saint to be formally canonized by the Orthodox Church. In 1794 he came to America from the glorious monastery on Valaam Island in northwestern Russia. On Spruce Island, Alaska, which he named "New Valaam," he sought ascetic solitude, for his soul since childhood had been dedicated to desert living. In addition to his prayerful ascetic struggles, St. Herman labored as a missionary and a protector of orphans. Before his repose in 1836, he attained to such a degree of holiness that he was granted the gifts of miracle-working and prophecy.

From Canticle V of the Service to St. Herman:

> *By many sorrows, prayers, and vigils didst thou purify thy soul and vest it in the primal beauty, becoming like to first-created Adam, and forest beasts obeyed thee, sensing in thee paradise and the Kingdom.*

In the midst of Spruce Island, a small spring runs down from the mountain into the sea, the mouth of which is always covered by logs and seaweed brought in by the high tide. During the spring, when the river fish would appear, the Elder would dig away the sand at the mouth of the river so that the fish could pass by, and the first group of fish would run into the river. His Aleut disciple, Ignatius Aliaga, recalls the following: "At times,

Apa (Father Herman) would say, 'Go and fetch fish from the river.' With dried fish he would feed the birds, and they would fly around his cell in great multitudes. Under his cell there lived ermines. These little animals, when angered, are ferocious and cannot be approached, but the Elder fed them with his own hands. 'Wasn't it a miracle that we saw,' his disciple Ignatius would say."

They also saw how Fr. Herman would feed the bears. With the death of the Elder, both the birds and the animals disappeared. Even his garden yields no crop when someone plants there of their own will, Ignatius testified.

Following the Apostle's word,* to give place to God's anger,* thou didst flee the hardheartedness of the lovers of this world* and withdraw to Spruce Island,* finding there a New Valaam,* preferring to live* with forest birds and beasts,* conversing with God and angels,* illuminated by visions from above,* and now, dwelling in heaven above,* pray for our souls.

SAINT HILARION AND THE CAMEL

Commemorated on October 21

AINT HILARION was born about the year 297 in Tabatha, a village near Gaza, in the south of Palestine. His parents being idolaters, he was like a rose borne by a thorn bush. They sent him to a grammar school in Alexandria, where, considering his tender age, he gave remarkable evidence of mental power and moral worth. He soon gained the love of all, and acquired skill in the art of speaking. What is more than all these, he believed in the Lord, and took no pleasure in the riots of the circus, the bloodshed of the gladiatorial shows, or in the luxurious scenes of the theater. All his pleasures lay in the meetings of the Church.

Hearing then the fame of Anthony, which had spread through Egypt, he went to the desert with an eager desire to see him. When he saw him, he forthwith laid aside his ordinary dress, and stayed with him nearly two months, contemplating the order of his life and the gravity of his manners—how often he prayed—how humbly he received the brethren—how severely he rebuked—how warmly he exhorted—how no weakness could break his continence or the harshness of his diet—and how unwillingly he bore the multitudes who flocked to him for relief from various afflictions and the assaults of

demons, esteeming it unfit that he should endure in the desert
the populousness of a city.

Thus Hilarion deemed it incumbent on himself to begin,
as Anthony had done, to strive like a brave soldier for the rewards
of victory.... From his sixteenth year to his twentieth year, he
sheltered himself against heat and rain by a little hut, which he
had covered with rushes and sedge grass. Afterwards he built
himself a little cell, five feet high (less than his own stature), and
of somewhat greater length. This cell, which yet remains, received his body more like a tomb than a habitation....

He toiled ascetically for years in the desert, healed men and
worked wonders. But to cure men was a small matter with him.
Brute animals, raging with madness, were brought to him every
day; among the rest a huge Bactrian camel, which had trodden
down and bruised many, was hauled to him by more than thirty
men, with ropes stretched out on all sides. The beast's eyes were
bloodshot; he foamed at the mouth; his lolling tongue was
swollen; and above all, his wild roaring was terrible. Then the
Saint told them to let him loose. Instantly every man, both those
who brought him and those who were about the Elder, took to
his heels and ran away. Then Hilarion walked up to him, and
said in Syriac—"You are not going to frighten me, Mr. Devil,
big as you are. You are the same to me whether you take the
body of a little fox, or of a huge camel." Meanwhile he stood
with outstretched hand. The monstrous beast came up, as if he

would devour him; but in-
stantly fell down and lay
with his head to the
ground. All that were near,
wondered to see such
tameness follow such fe-
rocity. But the old man
taught them that the devil,

in order to afflict men, often took possession of their beasts, and that he had such a burning hatred against them, that he desired to destroy not only themselves but their property, as he had destroyed Job's goods before he attacked his person. Nor should anyone (he said) be disturbed, because by the Lord's command two thousand swine had been killed by demons, for this was the only way by which the spectators could be convinced that so great a multitude of demons had gone out of the demoniac....

It had not rained for three years, since the death of St. Anthony, and it was a common saying that even the elements were mourning for his death. The people of that place were not ignorant of Hilarion's fame. Both males and females, with gloomy countenances and bodies attenuated by hunger, prayed earnestly for rain to the servant of Christ, as the blessed Anthony's successor. When he saw these suppliants, he was wonderfully sorry for them. Raising his eyes to heaven and stretching forth his hands, he prayed for rain, and it came immediately. But behold the dry and sandy region, after it had been refreshed by rains, suddenly produced such a multitude of

serpents and other creatures with poisonous bites and stings, that great numbers were bitten, and would have perished immediately if they had not run to Hilarion. All the husbandmen and shepherds, by touching their wounds with oil which he had consecrated, were cured infallibly....

SAINT IGNATIUS

Commemorated on December 20

FTER the glorious transfiguration of our Blessed Lord on Tabor, He retired with his disciples to Galilee. Having foretold His passion and death, and prepared them for the awful scenes that were to come to pass in a few days, He commenced His last and memorable journey to Jerusalem. His disciples followed Him at a short distance. On the road to Capernaum they entered into conversation with each other, and disputed among themselves which of them should be the greatest. Their minds were not yet illumined by the light of the Holy Spirit, and they were yet ignorant of the sublime virtues of Christian morality.

But Jesus knew what was passing amongst them. When they arrived at Capernaum he entered a house and made the disciples sit around Him, and He commenced to teach them those beautiful lessons of humility which are the foundations of all true greatness. With love and kindness beaming in His countenance He asked them: "What did you treat of in the way?" But they held their peace.

A ray of light had penetrated their hearts as the words of Jesus entered their ears, and a blush was the acknowledgment of their pride. Near our Blessed Lord there stood a beautiful child—a bright-eyed little boy of four or five years of age, with golden hair falling in ringlets on his shoulders. He was the type of everything innocent and beautiful. Jesus called the child towards Him, and having impressed a kiss on his little forehead, He placed him before His disciples, and in the sweet tones of His heavenly voice said to them: "Amen I say to you, unless you be converted, and become as little children, you shall not enter the kingdom of heaven. Whosoever therefore shall humble himself as this little child, he is the greater in the kingdom of heaven" (Matt. 18:3).

That child was Ignatius! That infant that was embraced by Jesus Christ, and proposed in its innocence as a model of everything that was truly great, was in after years the great Bishop of Antioch, who was devoured by the wild beasts in the Coliseum.

We know nothing else of the early life of St. Ignatius. He appears on the page of history as the Bishop of Antioch. St. Peter had first established his see in this city, which was at that time one of the largest in the Roman Empire, and here ruled the infant Church of Christ for six years. In the year 44 he came to Rome. In the very heart and center of paganism he erected the episcopal throne of the Church, which is to last until the end of time. St. Evodius succeeded him in the see of Antioch, and after him came Ignatius. Our Saint was a disciple of the glorious Apostle himself and of St. John. He had learned from these able masters the sublime science of the love of God, which made him one of the pillars and ornaments of the early Church. After the Apostles themselves, he was one of the most remarkable men in the Church; his contemporaries and the fathers who lived in the three succeeding centuries mention his name with the greatest reverence. St. Polycarp and St. Chrysostom have made him the subject of their most eloquent laudations. After a life of more than fifty years in the episcopate of Antioch, the Almighty was pleased to call him to his crown, by a death that should be a glory and a model to the Church. The history of his labors and his virtues is not written, but all the particulars of his death were recorded by eyewitnesses, and distributed through the various churches; hence his Acts are the most authentic in the history of the past. The original document, written in Greek, is still preserved, and was published by Ruinart in Paris in 1690.

The scene of his martyrdom opens, according to the best authority, in the year of our Lord 107. Trajan held the scepter of the Caesars and St. Evaristus sat in the chair of Peter. The storm that attacked the Church during the reign of Domitian was subsiding. Historians tell us that Trajan did not naturally love bloodshed, and had a nobler sentiment of humanity than any emperor who had preceded him, but he was a coward and a slave to public opinion. He stifled his own feelings to pander to the brutal tastes of the mob; to gain popularity, and under pretence of devotion to the gods of the Empire, he continued from time to time the horrible scenes of persecution against the unoffending Christians. St. Ignatius was one of his victims.

In the eighth year of his reign Trajan had gained a glorious victory over Decebalus, the king of the Dacians, and annexed all his territory to the Roman Empire. The following year he set out on an expedition against the Parthians and Armenians, the allies of the conquered Dacians. Having arrived at Antioch, he threatened with the severest penalties all who would not sacrifice to the gods. The labors and preaching of the venerable bishop of this city were so crowned with success, that the Church was flourishing, and was no longer a despicable community of a few individuals. The pagans saw the Christians increase around them with an evil eye, and availed themselves of the presence of the emperor to call for their extermination. "The magnanimous champion of Jesus Christ," says the Acts of the Saint, "fearful lest his Church should become a scene of horrible slaughter, voluntarily gave himself into their hands, that they might satiate their fury on him, but save his flock."

He was immediately brought before the emperor and accused of being the head and promoter of Christianity in the city. Trajan, assuming a haughty and contemptuous tone, addressed the aged bishop, who stood fearlessly before him, in these words: "Who are you, impious and evil spirit, that dare not only to transgress our orders, but exert yourself to bring others with you to a miserable end?"

The Saint meekly replied, "Impious and wicked spirits belong to hell; they have nothing to do with the Christians. You cannot call me impious and wicked whilst I carry the true God in my heart; the demons tremble at the very presence of the servants of the God whom we adore. I possess Jesus Christ, Who is the universal and celestial Lord, and King of all things; by His grace I can trample on all the power of the infernal spirits."

"And who is he," asked Trajan, "who possesses and carries his God in his heart?"

"Everyone who believes in Jesus Christ and serves Him faithfully," replied the Saint.

"Do you not believe then that we also carry our immortal gods within us? Do you not see how they favor us with their aid, and what great and glorious victories we have gained over our enemies?"

"You are deceived," replied Ignatius, majestically, "in calling those things that you adore gods; they are accursed spirits, they are the demons of hell. The true God is only One, and it was He that created the heavens, the earth, and the sea, and everything that exists; and One only is Jesus Christ, the only begotten Son of the most High, and Him I humbly pray to bring me one day to the possession of His everlasting kingdom."

"Who is this Jesus Christ thou has named? Is it He Who was put to death by Pontius Pilate?"

"It is of Him I speak," replied Ignatius; "He Who was nailed to the cross, Who destroyed my sin and the inventor of sin, and by His death places under the feet of those who devoutly carry Him in their hearts all the power and malice of the demon."

"Do you then carry within you this crucified Jesus?" asked the emperor, with a sarcastic smile.

"It is so," answered Ignatius, "for He tells us in His holy Scripture, *I will dwell in them, and walk among them* (II Cor. 6:16).

For a moment Trajan was silent, conflicting thoughts passing through his mind. He was urged by curiosity to hear more of the religion of the Christians, and, struck by the venerable appearance of the servant of Christ, he could have almost sent him back to his people with a slight reprimand; but the demon of pride and infidelity sprang up in his heart, and reminded him that any partiality towards the hated sect would be a sign of weakness, a loss of popularity, and a want of piety to the gods. Further hesitation would betray the false zeal of his hypocritical heart, and standing on his throne he pronounced this sentence against the holy bishop:

"We command that Ignatius, who says he carries with him the crucified Jesus, be brought in chains to the great city of Rome, and amidst the games of the amphitheater, as a pleasing spectacle to the Roman people, be made the food of wild beasts."

When Ignatius heard this sentence he threw himself on his knees, and, stretching his arms towards heaven, cried out in an ecstasy of joy: "O Lord, I thank Thee that Thou hast deigned to honor me with the most precious sign of Thy charity, and hast permitted that I should be chained for Thy love as was the Apostle Paul." He remained in the same position, his arms lifted up, his eyes fixed on heaven. He seemed to catch a glimpse of those ineffable joys he so ardently desired and which he was soon to enjoy. He was startled from his reverie by the rough grasp of one of the soldiers, who seized his feeble hands and placed them in the manacles of a criminal. His crime was, "He carried within him Jesus crucified." He made no resistance; but full of joy and praying for his poor flock, he moved away with his guards to one of the cells of the public prisons, to wait his departure for Rome. A crowd of people had gathered around the courtyard of the governor's palace, in which the emperor resided; when they saw the venerable Bishop chained and condemned to death, a murmur of pity broke from every lip. Amongst them there was many a wet eye and a suppressed sob; they were from Christians who saw their beloved Bishop and Father rudely dragged away to an ignominious death....

During St. Ignatius' journey to Rome, his happiness and peace of mind were beyond description. Every day his desire for martyrdom increased. He was taken from Antioch to Seleucia, and there embarked for Smyrna. They landed safely after a long and painful voyage, and St. Ignatius endeavored immediately on landing to have an interview with the holy Bishop St. Polycarp, who was his fellow disciple under the great Apostle St. John. By the exertions of the Christians who accompanied him and who probably bribed his guards, this privilege was given, and he spent some days with St. Polycarp.

From the abode of St. Polycarp, St. Ignatius wrote some beautiful letters, begging the Christians in the different churches, especially at Rome, not to prevent his martyrdom. Not that the Christians were accustomed to rescue the martyrs from the hands of the tyrants by physical force, but Ignatius well knew they had weapons more powerful than armies set in battle array—it was the invisible, the irresistible, the all-powerful weapon of prayer. By this the rage of the tyrants was baffled and death itself defied; and Ignatius besought them with all the fervor of his heart to let him have his crown, and pass away now in his old age from a weary life of trial to the ineffable bliss of the celestial kingdom. The Christians consented, and the Martyr won his crown.

"I have at length gained from Almighty God," he writes in his letter to the Romans, "that which I have so long desired, to come and see you who are the true servants of God; and more than this I hope to gain from His mercy. I come to you chained for the love of Jesus Christ, and so chained, I hope to arrive soon in your city to receive your embraces and my long-sighed-for end. Things have commenced auspiciously, and I sincerely pray to the Lord to remove every impediment or delay to the glorious end He seems to have destined for me; but alas! a terrible fear damps my hopes, and you, my brethren, are the cause of this fear—I fear your charity will stand between me and my crown. If you wish to prevent me from receiving the crown of martyrdom, it will be easy for you to do it, but sad and painful to me will be that kindness which will deprive me of an opportunity of thus laying down my life, which may never come again. In permitting me to go quietly to my end, you aid me in that which is most dear to me; but, if, in your misguided charity, you wish to save me, you will stand like the most cruel enemies in the very portals of heaven, and fling me back into the deep and tempestuous sea of life, to be tossed again on its billows of sorrow. If you love me with true charity you will allow me to mount the altar of sacrifice; you yourselves will gather around and sing hymns of thanksgiving to the Eternal Father, and to Jesus Christ, that He has brought, from the East to the West, from Smyrna to Rome, the Bishop of Antioch, to make him the confessor of His great name, His victim and His holocaust. Oh! how happy and blessed our lot, to die to this world, to live eternally in God!"

In another portion of his letter he uses these sublime and touching words: "Let me be the food of the beasts; let me come thus to the possession of God. I am the wheat of Jesus Christ; I must therefore be ground and broken by the teeth of wild beasts, that I may become His pure and spotless bread. Caress those animals that will soon be my honored sepulchre. I desire and pray God that they may not leave anything of me on the earth, that, when my spirit will have flown to eternal rest, my body may not be an inconvenience to any one. Then shall I be a true disciple of Jesus Christ, when the world can see no more of me. Oh! pray to Him that this may be the case, that I may be consumed by the beasts and be the victim of His love…" (See Acta Sincera, Ruinart, vol. i.).

That St. Ignatius suffered much in his long and tedious journey to Rome, there can be no doubt. That journey must have lasted more than six months; his letter from Smyrna is dated the 24th of August, and he was not martyred until the 20th of December. Having arrived in Greece, they crossed overland through Macedonia and set sail again from Epidamus for Italy. They crossed the Adriatic and came round the southern shores of Italy to the western coast…. They arrived at Ostia just before the termination of the annual games of the kalends of January. These games were called *sigillaria,* and were the most popular and best attended. The soldiers, wishing to arrive in Rome before their termination, hurried on from Ostia without any delay. Many of the Christians heard of his arrival, and went to meet him somewhere near the spot where now stands the Church of St. Paul. He was hailed with mingled sentiments of joy and sorrow; some were delighted to see the venerable confessor of the Church and receive his last blessing, whilst others wept aloud that so great a man was to be taken from them by an ignominious death. He consoled them by the joy of his own heart, and begged of them again not to prevent his sacrifice by their prayers. Having arrived near the gates, they fell on their knees and received his last solemn benediction.

It was the morning of the 20th of December, A.D. 107. The sun had already risen high in the heavens and was pouring its golden flood of splendor over the city. The body of soldiers and the aged bishop in chains entered that gate through which had often rolled the stream of triumph, and through which had been dragged many a poor captive from the East, to be slaughtered on the Capitol as the climax to the glory of barbarian triumph. Ignatius had longed from his childhood to see the great metropolis of the Empire, and now it burst on him with dazzling splendor; it was a forest of temples and tombs and mansions, of snowy whiteness that seemed imperishable. But his eyes were dimmed with tears; his heart was crushed with sorrow at the awful darkness that brooded over the mighty city. The splendor and magnificence of its monuments of marble and gold were but the decorations of a mighty tomb. With his arms folded on his breast he prayed that the sun of eternal justice might one day rise over that benighted city, that the blood of so many martyrs spilled on its soil might fructify into saints, the fruit of that blood which was not shed in vain on Calvary. While Ignatius was rapt in prayer, a short turn in the road brought them in sight of the mighty Coliseum, the gorgeous remnant of the gilded palace of Nero which crowned the Palatine, and in the distance the lofty temples of the Capitol. At the same moment they heard the thunder of some thousands of voices, mingled with the roar of lions and wild beasts. Some gladiator had fallen in the amphitheater, and the brutal populace was cheering the fatal stroke that felled him. The animals were startled in their dungeons, and the earth seemed to tremble under the horrible chorus of men and beasts. A few moments and Ignatius had arrived under the massive walls of the Coliseum....

Casting one glance around the great amphitheater, it would take volumes to describe all we see. Immensity and art, beauty and comfort, mingle with the rays of light that bring the first impressions—the motley thousands that fill every available seat, the rainbow of colors, softened by the purple awning, enriched by the brilliant mail of the soldiers, and everything that gold and silver can lend to dazzle the eye. The emperor's throne is on a raised dais, with crimson canopy, and is gorgeously conspicuous. He himself is away in the hardships of the camp, but his place is filled by the prefect of the city, a worthless wretch, whose god is the will of his master....

The confusion of the voices in the amphitheater is like the murmur of the mighty deep. A rumor has passed through them that one of the heads of the Christians has been brought from Syria and condemned by orders of the emperor to be exposed to the beasts. A wild frenzy starts from bench to bench; the whole amphitheater rises and sends forth a universal shout for the Christians to be cast to the lions....

Suddenly a dead calm reigns over the living mass; every eye is fixed on the eastern gate—the soldiers are leading a feeble old man into the arena. His silvery locks have been whitened with the snows of over a hundred winters. His gait is firm, his aspect cheerful; never was a more venerable victim dragged across the sand of that blood-stained arena. He is conducted to the foot of the imperial gallery. The president, having heard of his long journey from the East and struck with his venerable appearance and age, seemed to feel a sentiment of pity, and addressed him in these words: "I wonder you are still alive after all the hunger and sufferings you have already endured. Now, at least consent to offer sacrifice to the gods, that you may be delivered from the dreadful death that threatens you, and save us from the sorrow of having to condemn you."

Ignatius, drawing himself up with majesty and casting a look of scorn on the representative of the emperor, said:

"By your bland words you wish to deceive and destroy me. Know that this mortal life has no attraction for me; I wish to go to Jesus, Who is the Bread of immortality and the Drink of eternal life. I live entirely for Him, and my soul yearns for Him.

I despise all your torments, and I cast at your feet your proffered liberty."

The president, enraged at the bold language of the Saint, said in a haughty tone: "Since this old man is so proud and contemptuous, let him be bound, and let loose two lions to devour him."

Ignatius smiled with joy. Having made an act of thanksgiving in his heart and breathed an ejaculation for strength, he addressed the assembly in these words: "Romans who witness my death, do not think I am condemned on account of any crime or bad action. It is permitted that I may come to God, Whom I desire with an insatiable desire; I am His corn, and must be ground under the teeth of the beasts to become for Him a pure and white bread." Having said this, he fell on his knees and crossed his arms on his breast, and with eyes raised to heaven he waited calmly and resignedly the moment that should set him free from the troubles of life and send his soul on its flight to eternity. Another moment and the small gates of the subterranean passages are opened and two lions bound into the arena.

A terrible silence reigns over the amphitheater—they advance—but enough, let the imagination fill up the harrowing details. The Martyr is gone to his crown. We can but transcribe the brief touching words of his Acts: "His prayer was heard; the lions left nothing but the harder bones of his body."

Night has crept over the city, and the Coliseum is as silent as a tomb. By the faint light of the moon we see three men stealing cautiously under the shadow of the mighty arches; they move hurriedly across the arena. Near the center, and on the side of the emperor's seat, they go on their knees and, spreading a white napkin, put into it some sand stained with blood and some bones. They take them away with them and disappear in the darkness of the night. They are the Christians Carus, Philon

Ο ΔΓΙΟς ΙΓΝΑΤΙΟς
Ο ΘΕΟΦΟΡΟΣ
✝

SAINT IGNATIUS
THE GODBEARER
OF ANTIOCH

and Agathophus, who have accompanied Ignatius from Antioch, and are securing the relics of their beloved bishop.

Near the Coliseum there was a house much venerated and frequented by the Christians. It was the house of Clement, one of the Flavian family, a disciple of St. Peter and his third successor. Here they bring the relics of the Martyr, and according to the custom, they made a temporary altar in one of the most spacious rooms and left the sacred deposit exposed the whole night amidst burning torches. The Christians, many of whom were present at his martyrdom in the amphitheater, gathered from every side of the city and passed the night in prayer. During the night the Saint appeared to them. "A gentle sleep seemed to steal over us," say the above-named Christians, who wrote his Acts, "and suddenly we saw the holy Martyr, who lovingly embraced us. He seemed to be praying for us, and was covered with sweat as if he had just come from a great battle, and then he passed into the glory of the Lord, where he will rest for ever. When we saw this consoling vision our joy was ineffable, and having awakened we spoke over the vision which we all saw, and gave thanks without end to God, the great Giver of all good gifts, Who brought to eternal happiness the glorious martyr Ignatius" (Ruinart, Vol. i., chap. 10).

His relics were brought from the house of Clement to Antioch, and were placed in a beautiful shrine outside the Porta Daphnitica; but in the arrangement of Providence they were brought back again to Rome, and laid in precisely the same spot where they were venerated by the Romans the night after his martyrdom. When Antioch fell into the power of the Saracens, under Heraclius, the Christians brought some of their most precious treasures to Rome, and amongst them the relics of St. Ignatius.

Hiero-schemamonk Kuksha

HE modern Russian Elder Fr. Kuksha (1875-1964), after living for some time on Mount Athos, moved to New Athos in the Crimea. When the Bolshevik Revolution struck, the monks of the Crimea and the Caucasus were severely persecuted. Fr. Kuksha was sent to Siberia. The following is an extract from his journal.

* * *

Several men loaded us on a steamship, and we sailed to Russia. The times then were serious—the years 1917-1919. We did not manage to get there, as we were all exiled to Siberia. We labored there for twenty-five years. There was one bishop with me (Averky). Many came there, but at the end few were left. Many could not bear the cold and the hunger, especially when they were building the White Sea Canal. Thus many spiritual persons were buried, hundreds of martyrs.

When they completed the construction, everyone remained right there. Someone called me aside. I came out, and he pushed me from the back—I fell directly into a hole. "Lie down," he said, "until I tell you to stand up." Then they released the water and drowned all those who had just finished digging the canal. They fired at anyone who tried to swim out, and so all remained buried there. God alone knows their names. Then there was a unit of prisoners being conducted away to the taiga. When they passed by, the soldier told me, "Get up!" I got up. He added me to the prisoners, and I departed to the taiga. There we made

rafts to transport cargo. This was by the
shore of the sea—cold, frost, snow, and
we were all hungry, we were freezing,
especially all the monks and priests.
Once I sat down on the edge of a raft
and prayed. I asked the Lord: "Lord,
You see everything. You fed Your
prophets, not forgetting them. And
here Your slave is hungry—do not forget us either, Lord. Give strength in

labor and perseverance in cold." I looked up—a raven was
flying, and in its claws was a loaf of white bread, which we had
not seen for a long time, and some kind of bundle. He carried
it straight to me and dropped it on my knees. I looked in the
package—a sausage, probably more than a kilogram. I called the
bishop, and he blessed and distributed it all. We gave thanks to
the Lord for His great mercy to us sinners. God strengthened
us that entire day. On the third day we were again working in
the snow. I sat down to rest, and I was very hungry. In the
morning before work they gave us each a small crust of bread.
If it hadn't been for God, no one would have been able to endure
the heavy work. I sat and thought: "The Lord does not forget
us sinners." I heard some kind of noise. Not far from us a car
arrived with small pies *(pirogi)* and provisions for the voluntary
workers. They unloaded the pies, evidently for dinner. Ravens
swooped down on them and noise broke out. One raven flew
to me with pies in his claws—two in one claw and three in the
other. He flew to me and set them down on my knees. A convoy
came running for them—a guard with a rifle stood and looked
at me. I said to him, "Take them; I didn't ask him for them."
He stood for a little while musing, and then left. Evidently he
understood God's providence. Later, before the end of work, he
came to me, but this time for conversation: "Father, tell me who

you are." I answered: "A man." "Yes, I know, but you are not an ordinary man." "Yes, I am a sinful monk." Then he took some bread and fish out from his satchel for me, and ordered us to hide so that no one would see, as he was not allowed to talk to us. His daughter was dying at his home. The Lord revealed it to me, but he still did not know about his misfortune. I prayed that the Lord would heal her. I said, "Depart to your home, child. You need to go." He went away to guard his post; in twenty minutes he ran over to me and said: "Father, a telegram came for me. My daughter is dying." With tears he asked: "What shall I do? It is very far; I will not be in time. There are no planes, the taiga is all around us, and it is not summer weather." I blessed him: "Go, you will be in time; your daughter will live, if you make a vow to God to mend your life and become a Christian." "Yes, Father, I will do everything," he said, and bowed to the earth before me.

In a few days the Lord told me that I must return and serve for the people. Towards the evening they sent for me: "Velichko, where do you want a ticket for? Do you want to travel to Kiev?" "Yes, I accept!" I took leave of my brothers and approached the bishop: "Bless me, Vladika, and do not grieve. You will soon serve. We will meet in church. God's will be done in everything."

With God's help I reached Kiev, the Kiev Caves Lavra. My obedience was this: I sat in the vicinity of the caves and sold candles and crosses by the entrance. Sometimes I served molebens there. On the day of the Dormition of the Mother of God, Archbishop Averky came to us for the altar feast. We set off to meet him—I also went. The brethren began to come up for a blessing, and I also approached him. What joy there was—this was my friend from exile! We embraced, we recognized each other. After the service we talked about many things. The Lord did not forget His slaves; such is the mercy of God.

SAINT MACARIUS
OF ALEXANDRIA

Commemorated on January 19

SAINT Macarius is one of the desert fathers. He was born at Alexandria, probably in 296 or 297, possibly of Greek origin. He started as a merchant of sweetmeats and dried fruit. It is not certain when he dedicated himself to religious contemplation and penance. Like thousands of other Christians of that time, he went to live in the desert; first in the Thebaid in Upper Egypt, later in a part of the Libyan desert in Lower Egypt, in the Valley of Natron. This desert was full of Christians who dwelled in cells, some of them dug out in the rock, others built of stones or sun-dried bricks. Some of these men lived far from each other and assembled only on Sundays in the church. Here they were given their provisions for the week. Others lived in small communities. Their lives were severely simple. Only once or twice a week did they eat a cooked meal; the rest of the time they lived on bread and water. All performed some kind of manual work, mostly plaiting baskets of palm leaves. The Natron Valley has its name because here are found six natron lakes. Natron, a valuable salt, has been exploited since ancient times. The Metropolitan Museum of Art made three expeditions to the Natron Valley to investigate the four very old Coptic monasteries which are still inhabited by monks.

Saint Macarius had four cells in different parts of the desert and was priest of "the Cells." His life was written by Saint Palladius, who knew him for three years. The story of the hyena was told to him by Paphnutius, a disciple of Macarius. Saint Macarius, who lived to be nearly one hundred years old, died at "the Cells" in about 393.

It happened one day as he was sitting in his cell, a hyena came to him; her whelp was in her mouth. She set it down beside the door, and knocked on the door with her head. The Elder heard her knock; he came out thinking that a brother had come to him. When he opened the door and saw the hyena, he was astounded, saying, "What does she want here?" She filled her mouth with her whelp and held it out to the old man, weeping. The Elder took the whelp in his hands, steady in simplicity. He turned it this way and that, looking on its body for what ailed it. When he had considered the whelp, behold, it was blind in its two eyes. He took it, he groaned, he spat on its face, he signed it on the eyes with his finger: straightway the whelp saw and went to its mother's dug. It sucked and followed her; they went away to that river…and into the marsh they made their way.

The Lybians bring their sheep once each year into the marsh of Scete to eat the *shoushet,* and the herdsmen that live in the villages over against Pernouj also bring their oxen into the marsh of Scete to eat the green herbage once each year. The hyena left the day before. The next day she came to the Elder, she had a sheepskin in her mouth, thick with wool. Freshly killed, she had it over her; she struck the door with her head. The Elder was sitting in the enclosure. When he heard the knock at the door, he got up and opened it. He found the hyena, the sheepskin over her. He said to the hyena, "Where hast thou been? Where hast thou found this, if thou has not eaten a sheep? As that which thou hast brought me comes of violence, I will not take it."

The hyena struck her head upon the ground, she bent her paws, and on her knees she prayed him, as if she had been a man, to take it. He said to her, "I have but now told thee that I will not take it, unless thou makest me this promise: *I will not vex the poor by eating their sheep."* She made many movements of her head, up and down, as if she were promising him. Again he repeated it to her, saying, "Unless thou dost promise me, saying, *I will not kill a creature alive;* but from today thou wilt eat thy prey when it is dead. If thou art distressed, seeking and finding none, come hither, and I will give thee bread. From this hour, do hurt to no creature." And the hyena bowed her head to the ground, dropped on her knees, bending her paws and moving her head up and down, looking at his face as if she were promising him. And the Elder perceived in his heart that it was the purpose of God Who gives understanding to beasts for a reproach unto ourselves, and he gave glory to God Who gives understanding to the beasts. He sang in the Egyptian tongue "God Who liveth for ever, for the soul hath honor." He said, "I give glory to Thee, O God, Who wast with Daniel in the lion's den, Who didst give understanding unto beasts. Thou also hast given understanding to this hyena, and Thou hast not forgotten

me: but Thou hast made me perceive that it is Thy ordering."
And the Elder took the skin from the hyena, and she went away.
From time to time she would come to seek the Elder. If she had
not been able to find food, she would come to him and he would
throw her a loaf. She did this many a time. And the Elder slept
on the skin until he died. I have seen it with my own eyes.

MALCHUS THE SOLITARY

Commemorated on March 26

ABOUT three miles from Antioch in Syria there is a certain village which is called Maronia, and in this village was an old monk whose name was Malchus, and he was a wonderful and holy man. Now at that time I had travelled far away from the house of my fathers, and I went to Evagrius the priest, where I heard concerning the holy man Malchus, and I desired greatly to see him and to be blessed by him. So I went to him, and he received me gladly, and began to tell me about the habits of life and the works of the monks, and how it is right to fear the Lord. And having rejoiced greatly in the pious words of his doctrine, I besought him to confirm me especially in such things. Then he said unto me, "My son, I will relate unto you concerning the temptations which, in proportion to my presumption and thoughtlessness, have come upon me, in order that they may help you, and also concerning the compassionate grace of the Lord God Who took me out of and redeemed me from them, and Who permitted them to come upon me for the correction of many who should learn of me, and should not become disobedient to the exhortation of their spiritual fathers, because disobedience is the cause of death."

Then having said these things he began to narrate to me his history, and he said: I was born in the village which is called Nisibis, and I was the only child of my parents, who, because I was the only child they ever expected to have, were proud of me. And when I arrived at manhood's estate they were anxious to marry me to a wife, but when I spake against their [wish], saying, "It is right for me to become a monk and to serve the Lord," and they heard of it, they were exceedingly wroth with me. Now my father urged me to marry and threatened me with penalties if I did not, and my mother was always inciting and counselling me to do so. And seeing that their minds were most firmly set upon this, which would become unto me an impediment to my confession of faith before God, I forsook them and treated with contempt all the riches of this world, and took with me only a very small sum of money, which was just sufficient for the expenses of my journey; now I wished to go to the monasteries of the East. And because at that time the Greeks had determined to make war on the Persians, I changed my intention, and made up my mind to go to the West. And whilst I was pondering this matter I learned that between Keneshrin and Aleppo there was a monastery which was situated in a peaceful spot, so I gave up my former intention, and went thither, and I asked them to receive me; and I remained with them, and I wrestled with all their ascetic habits and rules of chastity according to their godly ways of life, and I made good progress therein in the Lord.

And having remained in that monastery for a certain number of years, and having lived blamelessly the life of spiritual excellence, all the brethren rejoiced at the growth of my asceticism. But because the Calumniator, that jealous and envious being, could not endure this, he cast into my mind thoughts [which were apparently] correct ones, saying, "Since thy father is dead, return to thy house, and comfort thy mother so long as she is alive, and after her death sell thy possessions and give some of the price thereof to the poor, and the remainder keep and with it build a monastery, and thou thyself shalt become a father and governor of monks." And to tell the truth to thee, my son, the Calumniator cast within me the passion of avarice, saying, "Keep some of the money for thine old age." And when the war which was caused by these thoughts had been waged against me daily for some time, I felt obliged to reveal this sickness of my soul to the spiritual father, who, when the holy father had heard thereof, said unto me, "My son, hearken not to thy feelings, for this is a snare of Satan who, by means of this cunning device, hath put many monks backward in their course, even as a dog goeth back to his vomit, and hath cast them down and hath made them lose their inheritance, and who, though continually setting before them the hope of that which is good, hath nevertheless brought them down into Sheol. For having raised Adam to a height of error which resembled this, he brought him down to the bottom of Sheol; and our Lord commandeth him that hath laid his hand upon the plough not to turn back."

Now when by means of such testimonies which he brought from the Holy Scriptures he was not able to persuade me to stay, he thereupon fell down before me and wished to swear by the Lord that I would not forsake him. And whilst that merciful and pious father was saying these things for my deliverance, the Enemy was placing in my heart the words, "The father acteth not thus because he would show compassion on thee, but he wisheth that the whole community of the brethren may be glorified by thy staying here"; and by saying words of this kind to me, that evil adviser made me to gain a victory of wickedness, and he made me to come forth out of the monastery....

Then I went from Aleppo to Edessa by the king's highway, and being afraid of the soldiers (i.e., bands of marauding robbers), who had already taken up their abode in the countries round about, I remained in Edessa, hoping to find company for the journey, for so great as this was my watchful fear. And when we had gathered together a company of men and women whose names were seventy in number and had therefore set out on the road, suddenly a band of Arab soldiers swooped down upon us and carried us all away. Then I called to mind the exhortation of the holy father and I said to myself: "O my soul, such are the great riches which I went forth to inherit! O wretched deceiver and destroyer of souls! Inherit thy wealth then, O wretched one, and make thyself happy therewith." And as I was saying these things to myself, one of the Arabs took me and a certain woman and set the two of us on one camel, and having travelled a short distance in the desert, because we were afraid lest we should fall from the camel, we were compelled to hold tightly to each other; and not only did this shame come upon mine unconvincible mind, but I was also obliged to eat with her. And the Arab gave us milk and camel's flesh, and he carried us to his tent, and he commanded me to do homage to his wife and to bow down before her, and he said, "This is thy mistress." Now through these things I, the chaste man and monk, was becoming acquainted with the form of the nakedness of these people, according to the reward which my passion of avarice merited. And the Arab ordered me to gird myself about with woolen garments and to shepherd the sheep, and this occupation became a source of consolation for the tribulations which surrounded me, because after a few days I was released from the evil faces of my masters and companions. But this alone did not bring me consolation, for I remembered that Abel, the Patriarch Jacob and his sons, the holy man Moses, and King David were shepherds of sheep, and I rejoiced in the desert; and I pastured the sheep, and prayed, and sang the Psalms which I learned in the monastery. And I used to eat cheese made of goats' milk, and I drank milk, and I gave praise to God that I had obtained such a [light] penalty for my disobedience. And remembering that the Apostle said, "Servants, be submissive to your masters, not only to the good, but also to the wicked" (Col. 3:22; Eph. 6:5), I took care of my master's sheep with the utmost diligence.

Now in all these things I kept in mind always the envy of the Calumniator, which hateth that which is good.

And when my master saw that I was acting rightly towards him, he wished to reward me well therefore, and he wanted to marry me to that woman who had been taken captive with me. And when I spake against his proposal, saying, "I am a monk, and I cannot do this, besides this woman hath a husband who was taken captive with us, and who hath passed into other ownership," his wrath went up, and he drew his sword, and he set his gaze upon me and would have killed me, had it not been that I ran and took hold of his wife's hand. And having married me to the woman, he brought me into a cave with her. When, therefore, I knew that this was indeed the captor of my soul, I cried aloud and wept and said, "Woe unto me the sinner! What hath happened unto me? For having grown old in the life of virginity, a terrible evil now cometh upon me, and I must, forsooth, become the husband of a wife! Where now is my mother? And where are the possessions and riches of my fathers?"...

Then I took the sword in my hands and saluted that woman, saying, "Mayest thou remain in peace, O wretched woman, and acquire for thyself rather a martyr than a husband, for because I would not marry a wife I fled from and forsook my parents." Now when the woman saw the sword which was shining in the darkness, she fell down before my feet and said unto me, "I will make thee swear by Jesus Christ, the Lord of praise, that thou wilt not kill thyself for my sake; and if thou wishest to do this turn the sword against me. Why shouldst thou wish to kill thyself so that thou mayest not take me to wife? Knowest thou that I am far more anxious than thou art to preserve my chastity unto Christ, and must guard it not only against thee, but also against my lawful husband, for even if he were to come I would keep myself chaste. This is what this captivity wherein I am teacheth me, for this affliction should teach us to take refuge in the Lord. Take me then to thyself as a companion of thy chastity, and let us love each other in spiritual love, so that when our masters see us they may think that our intercourse is carnal. Now God, Who knoweth hearts, recognizeth spiritual brotherhood, and we can easily persuade these people when they see us together in this wise that we love each other." Then whilst marvelling at the understanding of the woman, I received her good advice gladly in Christ, and henceforward I loved her as a spiritual helpmeet, and as a pure and chaste helper. I never saw her body naked, and I never approached her couch, for I was afraid lest, having been victorious in time of war, I might receive a severe wound through the arrows of the Enemy in time of peace. In this wise then our masters left us for a long time, and they were not afraid that we were preparing to run away from them, for it happened on several occasions, sometimes for a whole month together, that I was alone [with the woman] in the desert. And my master used to come, and when he saw that I was taking good care of his sheep, he would go back [to his place] rejoicing.

And it came to pass one day when, according to my custom, I was sitting in the desert, that I began to meditate upon the peaceful life of the brethren who were in the monastery, and I saw also the face of our holy father as if it had been an image; and I thought of his perfect and abundant love for me, and how anxious he was in every way that I should not be separated from him, and how I would not be persuaded [to stay with him] by the divine revelation, and how he bore witness beforehand concerning the things which would happen to me—Whilst, then, I say, I was pondering upon these things in my mind and was greatly afflicted thereby, I saw an ants' nest, and I saw multitudes of these insects working with the greatest diligence and care in their various ways, and I saw how they were all making their way into the nest through a narrow entrance, without impeding each other. Some of them were bringing seeds for their winter food, and others were bringing loads which were larger than their bodies; others were carrying on their backs those which had been wounded, and others were expelling from the nest those which had settled themselves inside, and they were cutting them up into small pieces, lest being drenched in the winter they should have to return to the grass, and should die of hunger and be destroyed; and others were carrying dust, so that when the winter rains fell with violence they might be able to block up the entrance to their nest firmly. Now this sight was in my opinion worthy to wonder at, because everything which these small creatures did was done in perfect order, and I spent the whole of the day in watching them, and so enjoyed some relaxation from my afflictions, and I said, "Well did Solomon counsel us to be like these creatures, for he [wished] to stir up our lazy and sluggish understandings in this wise [to perform] with a ready mind the things which befit our redemption."

Whilst then, I say, I was pondering upon these things in my mind and was greatly afflicted thereby, I began to have sorrow concerning myself, because my lazy and sluggish mind lacked the great sense of order and arrangement which the ants possessed, and also the faculty of not being disturbed by the thoughts of laziness, which the brethren possessed in common with the ants, and also because the Calumniator had hunted me down like a child and had set me in captivity, and had hurled me into such [great] temptations. And I thought of those who were offering their souls with all their hearts to Christ, and who were being guided on their way in all the monasteries by submission and spiritual grace, through the righteous redemption of our Redeemer, and who were anxious to preserve their souls blameless, and who were laboring diligently and without hindrance and with all their strength to do their work and to minister unto one another, and who were not saying about any possession which was theirs, "It is mine";...and who enjoyed sufficiently that which they had for their [daily] needs, with all fear or with all praise, and glorified Him Who richly provided them with everything.

And having made my heart sad and low with such thoughts for many days, I went to that woman, who seeing how greatly my countenance was changed, entreated to be allowed to learn the cause thereof; and having confessed to her that it was because I had remembered the regular life of the brethren and that I wished to escape and return to the monastery out of which the Enemy had made me to come, she advised me and besought me to take her [with me] and to place her also in a nunnery. And having together decided upon this plan, we wept and entreated our Lord to help us carry out what we had determined and to deliver us from that wicked people. Now therefore, having firm hope in God's assistance, we took thought for our return, and I slew two large goats which I had with me and made their skins into water bottles. And having loaded their flesh upon our shoulders, I took the woman and we departed. And we travelled the whole night long, and came to an exceedingly great and wide river, and I blew up the water bottles, and I gave one to the woman and kept the other myself; and we laid hold upon them with our hands, and sitting astride of the skins we paddled with our feet and crossed over the river. Then, seeing that we should have to cross a desert wherein there was no water, we drank abundantly of the water of the river, and rose up from that place and went on our way quickly. And we were turning round continually [to look] back behind us because of our horrible expectation that there would be men pursuing us, and that even if we could escape from them we should fall [into the hands of] wicked men like unto them.

Now because of our fear lest this should happen, and because of the heat of the sun, we were obliged to travel by night; and urged by this great fear, and also by our great anxiety, we were looking behind us ceaselessly. And after [travelling for] five days, we turned round suddenly and saw our master and one of his companions riding upon camels and holding drawn swords in their hands and pursuing after us; and by reason of our fear the sun appeared to us to become dark. And whilst we were in this terrible state of fright and did not know where to escape, through the Providence of Christ, the Hope of the hopeless and the Help of the helpless, we peered about in that place and found a frightful cave in the ground wherein had gathered all the numerous kinds of snakes which are found in the desert, ser-pents, and asps, and vipers, and scorpi-ons, which had gone therein because of the burning heat of the sun. Into this cave we tottered, and we hid ourselves in a corner, on the left-hand side thereof, and we said, "If our Lord help us this  cave shall be unto us a house of deliverance, but if He leave us to the sinners it will be our grave."

Now when our master and his companion following in our footprints had pursued us to the cave, they alighted from their camels and stood by the mouth thereof; and when we saw our master, such great fear laid hold upon us that we were unable to move our tongue to utter a word, for owing to the greatness of our fear we were already [as] dead men before the sword-stroke fell upon us. And when our master stood outside the cave and called to us, we were unable to speak to him because of our fear. And he took hold of the camels and commanded his companion to go in and bring us out, whilst he stood [waiting] for us with his sword drawn, so that he might by means thereof quell his brutal madness. Now when the young man had gone into the cave for a distance of five paces he stood [still], and because he had come in from the outside, his eyes had become dazzled by the light of the sun, and he could not see. Now we being quite near him could see him standing [there], but because he was unable to see us he began to terrify us with [his] voice, saying, "Come out, O ye wicked slaves who deserve death, wherefore do ye delay? Behold, your master is outside expecting you." And as he was saying these words, we saw a lioness rise up on the right-hand side of the cave, and she sprang upon him;

and whilst he was yet speaking, she seized him by the throat and strangled him forthwith, and then dragged him in and laid him on her lair, for she had a male cub. And when we saw our enemy lying [there] before our eyes, we glorified God with great joy. Now his master, not knowing what had happened, and thinking that the young man had been overcome by us, and being unable to contain himself for rage, ran forward, holding his drawn sword in his hand, and, standing at the mouth of the cave, cried out in his wrath to the young man, saying, "Quick, quick, bring forth these [slaves] to me that they may die an evil death." And whilst he was speaking, the lioness sprang upon him suddenly, and ripped him up, and threw him headlong on the ground.

And we marvelled at all these unspeakable and inexplicable wonders of the Lord, and we gave thanks to Him; and we rejoiced in the glory of Him Who in this tribulation had risen up and by Whose command the wild beast had destroyed our enemies. Now when the lioness turned back and passed from one side to the other side of the cave where we were, we thought that she would destroy us, but, because of the wonderful thing which had been wrought, we continued to praise the Lord, and we said, "Since the Lord hath delivered us from those wicked men He can, if He willeth, hand us over to the lions; but nevertheless let us praise Him and give thanks unto Him." Now whilst we were thus thinking in our minds, the lioness took up the cub in her mouth and departed from the cave, and left the place to us; but after she had gone, because of the state of fear in which we were, we remained the whole of that day in the cave.

And in the morning we went forth and found the camels that were still laden with provisions which our master had brought for himself and his slave. And we ate and drank therefrom, and for all these things we gave thanks unto the Lord, who had delivered us from our enemies. And we rode upon the camels, and having crossed that desert in ten days, we arrived at a Greek camp, and we drew nigh to the Tribune who was in command of it and related unto him everything which had happened unto us. Then he sent us on to Sabinus, who was at that time Duke of Mesopotamia, and he likewise learned all our affairs and took our camels and gave us their price, and he dismissed us to depart to our country in peace. Now before our return it happened that my spiritual father fell asleep. And the woman who had been [my] helper, and who had given [me] excellent advice and had counselled good actions, I placed in an abode of virgins; and I returned to my own monastery and to my spiritual brethren, where at the beginning the Lord directed me. And I related unto that blessed brotherhood the story of all the things which had happened to me, and I confessed that it was because I had not hearkened unto the admonition of that holy father that the Lord left me so that all these trials might come upon me; and He did this for the correction of many.

Now therefore, O my son, all these trials, which came upon me because of my disobedience, and which I have narrated before thee, are [intended] for the edification and the protection of thy soul; get thou possession of them, because, by the help of God, patient endurance and implicit obedience will deliver a man from all temptations. Obedience to the commandments of God is everlasting life, and the patient endurance which is perfect produceth everlasting life in us, for "he who endureth unto the end shall live" (Matt. 10:22). These things did the old man Malchus himself relate unto me whilst I was a young man, and on account of the law of brotherly love I have written them down....

THE HOLY GREAT MARTYR MAMAS

Saint Mamas

Commemorated on September 2

CHRIST'S Holy Martyr Mamas was born in
Paphlagonia of Asia Minor in the third century. His
parents Theodotus and Rufina were renowned, of a
patrician family, both wealthy and esteemed by all, and radiant
with Christian piety. Unable to hide for long their faith in Christ
and fervent love for Him, they confessed their piety before all
and turned many to Christ. For this reason, then, Alexander,
the magistrate of the city of Gangra, informed against them, as
he had received command from the emperor to spread and
confirm by all possible means the worship of the pagan gods,
and to torture and put to death all Christians who did not obey
this imperial decree.

Alexander called Theodotus to judgment and began to
impel him to make sacrifice to the idols, but the blessed one did
not wish even to hear what the ruler said. Although Alexander
desired to give over Theodotus to torments immediately, yet he
was constrained by the fact of Theodotus' noble birth, for he
did not have the right to dishonor and torture descendants of
patrician families without special permission from the emperor.
Therefore Alexander sent Theodotus to Caesarea of Cappadocia
to the governor Faustus. Now this Faustus was extremely hardened in his impiety, and as soon as Theodotus came, he shut
him in prison. The wife of Theodotus, the blessed Rufina, also
followed her husband, although she was with child at the time;

she went into the prison together with him and there endured suffering for Christ. Now Theodotus knew the weakness of his flesh and perceived the terrible cruelty of his tormentor, but nonetheless he preferred to die rather than to offend in some way against piety. Yet, fearing that he would not possess the strength to endure the severe tortures awaiting him, he turned to God with fervent prayer, saying, "O Lord God of hosts, Father of Thy beloved Son, I thank and glorify Thee that Thou has deemed me worthy to be cast into this prison for Thy name's sake. But I entreat Thee, O Lord, as Thou knowest my weakness, receive therefore my soul in this prison, that mine enemy might not boast against me."

And God, Who alone hath fashioned our hearts and understandeth all our works, heard His faithful servant and quickly sent unto him a blessed repose: leading his soul out of the prison of the body, He made it to abide in His radiant heavenly mansions. But Theodotus' wife, the blessed Rufina, enduring deprivation and suffering in the prison, and seized with great sorrow over the death of her husband, gave birth to a son before her time. Beholding her newly-born son, and the body of her husband lying lifeless, without breath, she prayed with compunction and tears to God thus: "O God, Who didst create man and from his rib didst fashion woman, command that I also journey the same path which my husband hath gone, and having freed me from this brief life, receive me into Thine eternal habitations. But this infant to which I have given birth, do Thou Thyself rear as Thou knowest, and be to him father, mother, and guardian of his life."

Calling thus upon the Lord in the time of her affliction, this venerable and holy woman was heard and freed from the bonds of the body; having given up her soul into the hands of the Lord, she departed into eternal freedom. The child, however, the great Mamas, remained alive between the bodies of his parents.

Then God Who foreknoweth all things sent in a dream an Angel in the form of a young man to a certain most illustrious and pious woman named Ammia, who was also called Matrona, and ordered her to seek out the relics of the Saints, bury them with due honor, and take the child and rear him as her own son. She hastened to the governor to carry out the Lord's command and requested the bodies from him. God inclined the cruel heart of the ruler to mercy, and he did not hinder the renowned woman's desire. Entering the prison she found the relics of both the Saints lying side by side, and between them a beautiful and joyful infant. She took the relics and buried them in her garden in a resplendent and honorable manner, and the child she took to herself. Ammia was a childless widow who lived in chastity; she loved the infant as though he were her own son and raised him a Christian.

The child grew, but until his fifth year he never spoke a word. The first time he spoke was to Ammia, who was a second mother to him, and he said, "Mama"; whence he was given the name *Mamas*. Ammia sent him to school to receive an education, and soon did he so greatly surpass all those of his own age that all wondered at his brilliance.

At that time the emperor of Rome was the impious Aurelian (270-275). He compelled all to worship the idols, not only adult men and women, but even small children; indeed, he paid special attention to children, imagining that because of their simplicity they could easily be deceived and dissuaded from piety. What is more, this impious one thought that if children became accustomed to eat meat offered to idols from their earliest youth, they would later become the more zealous idolaters in their adult years. Hence by diverse enticements he would lead them to his own impiety. Many children and even young men succumbed to this deception and submitted to the will of the emperor. However, those who were fellow-students of the

blessed Mamas imitated him and followed his instructions and
did not obey the imperial decrees. For he demonstrated to his
school fellows the deception of the pagan gods, which have
neither life nor power, and he instructed them in the knowledge
of the one true God, Whom he himself worshipped and to
Whom he offered spiritual sacrifices, that is, a contrite spirit and
a humble heart. Thus from his earliest years Mamas had the gray
hair and wisdom and maturity of old age, an undefiled life
(Wisdom 4:9).

At that time the emperor sent a new governor named
Democritus to Caesarea to replace Faustus. He was a great zealot
for his impious and godless faith and breathed persecution and
murder upon the Christians. The blessed Mamas was denounced to him as not only not worshipping the gods himself,
but also as corrupting the youth with whom he studied and
teaching them the Christian faith. Mamas was at that time
fifteen years old, and he was also an orphan once again, since
his second mother Ammia had reposed in the Lord, having left
great possessions to her adopted son and only heir. She had
departed unto the heavenly riches which God has prepared for
them that love Him. When Democritus heard of the renowned
Mamas, he sent for him, and as soon as he arrived, he straightway inquired whether he were a Christian and if he not only did
not worship the gods, but also dared to corrupt his schoolmates
and companions by teaching them not to submit to the imperial
decree.

The young Mamas fearlessly replied like a full-grown man,
"I am precisely that one who considers thy wisdom to be
nothing. Thou has turned aside from the right path and dost
stumble about in such darkness that thou canst not even gaze
upon the light of truth. Thou hast departed from the true God
and drawn nigh unto demons, and thou now dost worship

lifeless and deaf idols. I shall never renounce my Christ, and I endeavor to turn unto Him all whomever I can."

Astounded by such a bold reply from the blessed Mamas, Democritus became enraged, and perceiving that he could not dissuade him by meekness, commanded that he immediately be led away to the altar of their god Serapis and there offer sacrifice, even if it were against his will. But Mamas did not in the least fear the threat of the governor, and replied to him calmly, "Thou hast not the authority to punish me or to make these threats, for I am the son of parents of a renowned senatorial family."

Then Democritus inquired of those present concerning Mamas' lineage, and having learned that he was the descendent of ancient Roman nobility and that Ammia, a most illustrious and wealthy woman, had reared him and made him the heir of her vast possessions, he decided not to give him over to tortures, seeing that he did not have the right to do this. Rather, he bound him with iron fetters and sent him to the emperor Aurelian, who at that time was in the city of Ega, and wrote to the emperor concerning his actions.

When the emperor received and read the letter of Democritus, he ordered that the youth be brought before him. He employed much cunning, at times threatening him and at times promising him great honor and precious gifts, saying, "O splendid youth, if thou wilt draw nigh and make sacrifice to the great god Serapis, thou shalt live with us in the palace and be treated in a royal manner. All will revere and praise thee. Truly thou shalt be most fortunate. However, if thou dost not obey me, thou shalt bitterly perish."

But the courageous Mamas replied, "Let it not be that I should worship the lifeless idols which thou dost venerate as gods. How foolish thou art, to worship wood and stone which have no feeling instead of the living God! Cease to tempt me with cunning words, for when thou thinkest that thou doest unto me an act of kindness, in reality thou tormentest me; and when thou tormentest me, thou becomest my benefactor. Be it known to thee, therefore, that all the favors, gifts, and honors which thou dost promise unto me would become torture for me if I should love them instead of Christ; but those harsh torments with which thou threatenest me for the sake of the name of Christ, they shall be for me a great benefaction, since death for my Christ is dearer to me than all honors and possessions."

At this the enraged Aurelian commanded that the youth be beaten with rods. Although the delicate and tender body of the most-wise Mamas was torn by the blows, yet he endured all this without uttering a word, as though someone else were being tortured. The emperor tried to soften and change the mind of the youth even at the time of the beatings by saying to him, "Just say that thou wilt make sacrifice to the gods, and I shall immediately free thee from these torments." But the Martyr answered him, "Neither with my heart nor with my lips will I renounce my God and King Jesus Christ, even though thou shouldst give me ten thousand more wounds. These wounds unite me with my beloved Lord, and I wish that the arms of my tormentors would never grow tired, for the more they beat me, so much the more do they store up riches for me with Christ the setter of the contest."

When Aurelian perceived that the great Mamas was not at all frightened by these tortures, he ordered that he be stripped and his body gradually burned with torches, in order that from the slowness he be made to feel the most harsh and bitter pain. Thus also was this severe torment applied to the indomitable youth, and the lighted torches were brought near unto his martyric body. Yet the fire reverenced the athlete of Christ and did not touch him, but rather turned back into the faces of his tormentors. When the tyrant beheld this and the unshakenness of the Martyr, it was he rather that was kindled and consumed with wrath, for the less attention the blessed Mamas paid to the fire, the more the emperor burned with rage. He then ordered that the Saint be stoned, but this suffering was so pleasant for the Martyr, who was sheltered with the love of Christ, that it seemed as though sweet-smelling flowers had been strewn upon him. Seeing that nothing could persuade the Saint and that he remained invincible through all the tortures, the emperor finally gave command that he be put to death by casting him into the sea. The servants of the emperor fastened lead weights about the Martyr's neck and led him to the sea. But neither at this moment did the Lord—Who hath commanded His Angels to keep us—abandon His servant, for suddenly there appeared upon the way an Angel whose countenance was like unto lightening, and with a human voice he threatened the soldiers, who became terrified and fled. The Angel then took the weight from around the neck of the glorious Martyr of Christ and led him to the top of one high mountain in the wilderness not far from Caesarea and ordered Mamas to remain there.

St. Mamas began his life in the wilderness with a fast; he fasted for forty days and forty nights upon the mountain and was manifested as a second Moses. In a marvelous vision our Saviour bestowed upon him a shepherd's staff and the Holy Gospels. Then he built himself a small chapel in which to pray and read the Holy Gospels. At one divine command the godly Mamas gathered about himself wild beasts from the wilderness in which he abode, as a shepherd his sheep; they listened to him and obeyed him as though endowed with reason. He nourished himself on the milk of his animal companions and also prepared cheese, not only for his own need but for the poor as well.

Soon the report of the blessed one spread throughout all of Caesaria. At that time another governor named Alexander (different from the previous one) ruled in Cappadocia; he, like his predecessors, was exceedingly cruel and impious. When he heard of the divine Mamas, he thought him to be a sorcerer and sent soldiers on horseback into the wilderness to seek him out and bring him before his presence. Now Mamas foreknew by the divine grace dwelling within him of the coming of these men, and therefore he descended a little way from the mountain and met them, and asked them whom they sought. Supposing him to be a shepherd who was tending sheep on the mountain, they replied, "We seek Mamas, who lives somewhere in this wilderness. Knowest thou him and where he might be?" "Why seek ye him?" answered Mamas. "It has been reported to the governor that he is a sorcerer, and therefore he has sent us to seize him and bring him for torture." Then the blessed one said to them, "I shall point him out to you, my friends, but first come to my dwelling to rest from your labor and refresh yourselves with some food."

The soldiers entered his hut, and he offered them cheese. While they began to eat with great appetite, the doe and wild  she-goats gathered that the ascetic might milk them. Mamas offered the fresh milk to the soldiers to drink, while he himself stood apart at prayer. At this many more wild animals began to gather, and the soldiers became terror-stricken, cast aside their food, and hastened to the blessed one. He calmed them and, wishing to free them from their concern for finding him, declared unto them, "I am Mamas whom ye seek." But hearing this they replied, "If thou dost wish to come to the governor, then accompany us; but if thou dost not wish, then permit us to depart without thee, for we do not dare to take thee against thy will. And we entreat thee that the beasts do us no harm." Mamas reassured the soldiers and ordered them to go ahead, saying that he would soon follow them into Caesarea.

Thus the servants of the emperor departed immediately from the presence of the divine servant of God and awaited his arrival at the gates of the city, for they wholly believed the words of such a marvelous man and could not think ill of him. Mamas took a lion with him and followed the soldiers to the city. When he drew nigh into the city gates, he had the lion wait outside the walls, and he himself passed through the gates. The soldiers met and guided him to Alexander, who when he saw the Saint said, "Art thou the notorious Mamas the sorcerer of whom I have heard so much?" Mamas answered saying, "I am the servant of Jesus Christ, Who saveth those who believe on Him and do His holy will, but Who delivereth sorcerers, magicians and those who worship idols unto eternal fire. But tell me, why didst thou send for me?" "Because I cannot understand by what sorcery and magic thou hast so tamed wild and ferocious beasts that thou livest among them, and as I have heard, commandest them as though they were reasonable beings," retorted the governor. The Martyr said to this, "Whoever serves the one, true, and eternal God can never consent to live together with idol-worshippers and workers of evil, for he disdains both magic and idolatry. Therefore I have chosen rather to live with wild beasts in the wilderness than with thee in the habitation of sinners. Animals are tamed and obey me not through sorcery, as thou thinkest—for I do not even know of what sorcery is composed—but though they have not the gift of reason, yet they fear God and reverence His servants. But this is the thing worthy of wonder, that thou who hast before thee such an example still dost not wish to know the truth, showing thyself to possess less reason than they. Thou dost not worship the true God, and thou dishonorest His servants, torturing and murdering them mercilessly." The governor, inasmuch as he could not make answer to this, began to constrain the Martyr even more, saying, "Why hast thou become so impudent and foolish that thou resistest the commands of the emperor and shamelessly revilest us? Yet torments and punishment shall teach thee what is fitting." And he ordered that the blessed one be taken out immediately, hung up, beaten, and raked with iron claws.

Christ's glorious Martyr, although he was grievously wounded, endured these things with such courage that it seemed as though he felt no pain whatever, for neither did he groan nor cry out, but only raised his eyes unto the heavens from whence he awaited succor. Seeing his perseverance, the godless Alexander commanded that he be raked with even greater cruelty. At this a divine voice was suddenly heard from heaven saying, "Mamas, be strengthened and take courage!" Many of the Christians who were standing in that place beholding the contest of the Martyr also heard this voice and were greatly strengthened in their faith. The holy Mamas, being perfectly fortified by this voice, paid no attention at all to the torments, although they continued to rake his body for a long time. Finally Alexander, suffering frenzy and rage and being more tormented in his heart than Mamas in his body, gave command to heat a furnace in which to cast the Martyr, and to take him out meanwhile and hold him in prison until it should be ready.

In the prison were forty other Christians; and as they had become weakened from hunger and thirst, Saint Mamas prayed, and behold, suddenly a dove flew through the window into the dungeon carrying in its beak food which was like unto a pearl in color and sweeter than honey. Having placed the food before the Saint, the dove flew away out of the window. This substance was multiplied, as once also in the wilderness a few loaves of bread were sufficient to feed thousands. When the prisoners had partaken of this food, they were fortified and refreshed. Moreover, through the prayers of the divine Mamas, at midnight the doors of the prison were opened, and all the captives save Mamas departed.

After these things the governor called Mamas to the tribunal and said to him, "Because of our care for other matters we have given thee leisure that thou mightest consider what is to thine advantage; but if thou has not yet come to thy senses, behold the furnace into which thou shalt be thrown." At this the brave Mamas replied, "O governor, I have already made known to thee my resolve; why then dost thou senselessly trouble thyself? Come, therefore, make an end and tarry not to execute those things which thou hast threatened." Hearing this, the governor cast him straightway into the furnace.

The All-good God, however, even as He once bedewed the furnace for the three youths, here also annihilated the power of the fire. The Martyr stood in the flames as though he were in a garden of abundant flowers washed with dew; for the whole period of time that he remained in the furnace he chanted and glorified God. After three days, when the fire was extinguished and the coals had become ashes, the governor ordered the executioners to bring out of the furnace whatever remained of the Martyr's body. As they approached the furnace they heard the divine Mamas glorifying God with a loud voice, and they immediately ran back in terror to make known unto the governor this supernatural wonder. But being darkened in mind, he said, "By the great Serapis and all the gods, this is clearly sorcery"—so foolish was this imperceptive one! But when such as were receptive to the light and the truth saw the athlete of Christ well and unharmed, they gave glory unto God Who works such miracles. While the most senseless governor, seeing the Martyr standing at the tribunal unshaken and having not even a hair of his head singed by the flames, called this sorcery and deceit. The great Mamas would not even make answer to the ruler.

The impious tyrant then commanded that the Saint be thrown to the wild beasts, that they might rend him to pieces, and to this end he was led to the arena. A hungry she-bear was loosed upon him. However, this bear approached the Saint, bowed down before him, and lay at his feet embracing them. Then they released a leopard, but it only embraced the neck of the Martyr, kissed his face, and thus wiped the sweat from off his brow. At that moment a lion sprang into the arena and ran towards the Saint, the same lion that had accompanied him from the wilderness. The lion spoke to the blessed Mamas with a human voice—for manifesting His almighty power, God opened the mouth of the beast as once He opened the mouth of Barlaam's ass—"Thou art my shepherd who tended me on the mountain!" Having uttered this, he leaped upon the crowd, for there was present a numberless multitude of both  pagans and Jews, adults and children. By God's will the gates of the arena locked themselves, and the lion mangled a great number of people, so much so that even the governor barely escaped death, and only a few others were able to flee the wrath of the beast which seized and tore all to pieces.

Afterwards the governor again laid hands on the Saint and confined him once more in prison for some while. Then for a second time he led him out into the arena and unleashed a most ferocious lion upon him, but this lion also became meek and lay at the feet of the blessed one. When the people beheld this, they gnashed their teeth from their great rage at the Saint and cried out to the governor, "Lead away the lion and we shall stone this sorcerer." Then they began to hurl stones at the Martyr. One of the pagan priests at the command of the ruler struck the Saint with a three-pronged spear in such a manner that his belly was opened and his intestines spilled upon the ground. The Martyr gathered them up with his own hands and walked out of the city. His blood, which poured forth like water, was collected by a certain pious woman in a vessel. Having gone about two furlongs from the city, he found a cave in a cliff and lay down there. Shortly thereafter he heard a voice from heaven calling him to the heavenly dwellings of the saints, and with great joy he gave up his holy soul into the hands of the Lord, for Whom he so valiantly had suffered, and to Whom be glory, now and ever, and unto the ages of ages. Amen.

In this manner the great Mamas received the martyr's crown. His holy relics were buried at the place of his repose by the faithful, and many healings and miracles were wrought there, as is evident from a sermon to the Saint by St. Basil the Great. "Have the holy Martyr in remembrance, ye who live in this place and have him as your benefactor, ye who have been helped by him at the calling of his name, who being in error have been guided unto life by him, who have been healed by him, whose children have been returned to life by him though they had died, whose life has been lengthened through his intercessions. Wherefore let us all come together in one body and praise the Martyr."

When Julian the Apostate was still a youth, he wished to leave a memorial of his piety, and he began to erect a magnificent church over the grave of the holy Martyr Mamas, although he did this not out of true piety but rather out of vainglory and hypocrisy. Then a most glorious miracle was seen. Whatever was built during the day was destroyed at night. The pillars that had been erected would fall into a heap. Some of the stones in the wall could not be made to lie correctly; other stones became so hard that they could not be hewn; others turned into dust; the cement and the bricks were found each morning blown from

The Prayer of St. Mamas

To Be Said Over Beasts

Behold, I, Mamas, the sinner and the least, while being in the mountains, and by the might of our Lord Jesus Christ, was milking does and making cheese. I distributed to the poor and lived in the mountains and caves until my martyrdom. As I was living there, John and Philotheos came to me, beseeching and saying, "The malice of the devil hath fallen upon the flocks and herds and they die evilly, and we beseech thee, Saint of God, pray for them, that they be healed of every evil, as an everlasting memorial to the glory of God." But I said unto them, "My spiritual brethren, I am a sinner and God hearkeneth not unto a sinner." But they persisted in beseeching me. Wherefore, giving way to their entreaties I prayed unto the Lord and said:

"We beseech Thee, our Lord Jesus Christ, the true God, Who came down from the bosom of the Father and was incarnate of the Theotokos and Ever-virgin Mary, and Who, by Thine own will endured the Cross and death and arose on the third day, granting life unto the race of mortals: Heaken unto me, Thy sinful and unworthy servant Mamas, and for whomsoever be in grief and much affliction and call upon Thy name, O Lord our God, and remember the name of Thy servant Mamas: let there not come upon his flock nor upon his herd of cattle any diabolical catastrophe or any other malady. Amen."

With special permission from the Holy Transfiguration Monastery, Brookline, Massachusetts.

their places as though scattered by the wind. Indeed this was a revealing of the impiety of Julian and a sign of his future persecution against the Church, for the Saint did not wish that a church should be built in his honor by one who would shortly afterwards raise a persecution against the true faith.

There was a great shrine of St. Mamas housing some of his relics on Cyprus from ancient times. Frescoes of St. Mamas are to be found in the monasteries of Meteora and the churches of Mistra as well as many other places. The Saint is depicted as a youth holding a shepherd's crook and carrying a young fawn in his arms. Sometimes he is depicted riding a lion.

An oral tradition reached the days of St. Basil the Great that when St. Mamas would go out to milk the does, they would race one another in order to be the first to reach the Saint, so familiar were they with him.

There is a prayer of St. Mamas which is read when animals are sick. In America relics of the Saint are to be found, among other places, at the Holy Transfiguration Monastery in Boston and at the Brotherhood of Saint Herman of Alaska near Platina, California.

By the intercessions of Thy great Martyr Mamas, O Lord, deliver us from the teeth of the invisible foes, that we may glorify Thee together with the Father and the Holy Spirit unto the ages. Amen.

Saint Martin of Tours

Commemorated on October 12 & November 11

SAINT MARTIN, a soldier's son, was born in what is now Hungary and brought up in Italy, at Pavia. As a young officer at Amiens he gave half his cloak to a naked beggar, in whom he was led to recognize Christ, and soon afterwards he was baptized. About 339 he asked for discharge from the army, for he said, "I am Christ's soldier; I am not allowed to fight." Accused of cowardice, he retorted by offering to stand unarmed between the opposing lines. However, he was given his discharge, and for some time was in Italy and Dalmatia before living as a recluse on an island off the Ligurian coast. In 360 he became one of St. Hilary's clergy at Poitiers, and founded a semi-eremitical religious community at Ligugé, the first monastery in Gaul. Upon being made bishop of Tours in 370 or 371 he lived at a solitary place near by, which soon developed into another monastery, Marmoutier. His example and encouragement led to the establishment of other communities elsewhere.

St. Martin was an extremely active missionary, his preaching being reinforced by his reputation as a wonderworker; he penetrated into the remotest parts of his diocese and beyond its borders, on foot, on donkey-back, or by water.

As an evangelizer of rural Gaul and the father of monasticism in France, St. Martin of Tours was a figure of great importance; and his fame spread far and wide, not least through the biography and three long letters about him written by his friend Sulpicius Severus. He was one of the first holy men who was not a martyr to be publicly venerated as a saint, and his influence was felt

from Ireland to Africa and the East.

One day on the river he saw some diving birds going after fish. Time and time again, the birds would make a capture and stuff their ravenous crops. "Here," he said "is a picture of the demons. They ambush the unwary and capture them before they know it. They devour their victims, yet cannot satisfy their voraciousness."

Then, with a mighty voice, he ordered the birds to leave the whirling waters where they were swimming and to go to some dry, deserted place. He addressed them with the same commanding tone he commonly used in putting demons to flight. The birds then formed a flock and together left the river, heading for the mountains and forests. Many of his disciples were amazed to see that Martin's power was so great that he could command even the birds.

***

Some time after this, we were traveling with Martin while he visited his parishes. Something or other had compelled us to stay behind, and he had gone on somewhat ahead of us. Meanwhile, a vehicle belonging to the imperial treasury, packed with armed officials, was making its way along the public highway. Martin was advancing on the same side of the road, wearing his shabby tunic, covered with a flowing black pallium. The mules were startled at the sight of him and drew over a little to the other side. Then, the traces became tangled and the whole team was thrown into disorder, for the poor animals had been harnessed together in long lines in a way you have often seen. It was not easy to disengage the mules, and this business delayed the officials, who were in a hurry. They were angered by this, jumped to the ground and began to attack Martin with whips and clubs. He said not a word, but with incredible patience gave his back to their blows. This only aroused the madness of the unfortunate officials, who were furious that he took their lashings lightly, as if he did not feel them. When we came on the scene, we found him lying on the ground where he had fallen in a faint. He was bleeding horribly and every part of his body

had been mangled. We at once set him on his donkey and quickly made our departure, cursing the scene of this bloody deed.

The officials, meanwhile, had satisfied their anger and returned to their vehicle. They gave orders to start up the mules and continued the journey. But the mules remained fixed to the ground, rigid, as if they were bronze statues. The drivers shouted louder and snapped their whips on this side and that, but the mules did not so much as budge. All the passengers then rose to join in the lashing. Gallic whips were used up in the punishment the mules received. A whole grove from nearby was pulled up and the beasts were beaten with tree trunks. This savagery accomplished nothing; the

mules remained in the same spot, immobile statues still. The unfortunate men did not know what to do, yet, even their stupid heads could not prevent them from recognizing that they were being held back by divine power.

They finally came to their senses and began asking who it was they had beaten on that spot just a while before. Putting the question to passers-by they learned that the victim of their cruel blows was Martin. The whole thing then became clear to them all. They could not fail to see that they were being held back because of their misuse of him. So, they all set off after us at a rapid pace. They were conscious of what they had done and what they deserved; they were ashamed and confused. Weeping and with their heads and faces covered with the dust by which they had defiled themselves, they flung themselves at Martin's knees, imploring forgiveness and begging that he let them go. They had already been punished enough, they said, by their pangs of conscience. They knew full well that the earth could have swallowed them up alive, or, rather, that they ought to have had their senses snatched from them and been turned into solid rock, as, indeed, they had seen their mules nailed to the ground where they stood. They begged and besought him to pardon their crime and grant them power to go away.

Even before they came up, the blessed Martin knew that they were held fast and had told us so. Now, he mercifully forgave them, gave them back their mules, and permitted them to go away.

About the same time, when Martin was returning from Treves, he encountered a cow tormented by a demon. She had left her herd and was going about attacking people; she had already

dangerously gored a number with her horns. When she came near us, the people who were following her from a distance began calling out with a loud voice that we should be careful. But the raging beast, staring savagely, came nearer to us. Martin raised his hand and ordered her to stand still. At his word the cow halted, motionless. Meanwhile, Martin spied a demon sitting on her back, and rebuked him. "Depart from the beast," he said, "and stop tormenting a harmless animal." The evil spirit obeyed and withdrew. The heifer did not fail to sense that she had been delivered. Having recovered her composure, she threw herself at the Saint's feet. When Martin then told her to go back to her own herd, she rejoined the company of the other cows, quieter than a lamb.

One time, when Martin was making the round of his parishes, we met a band of hunters. The hounds were pursuing a hare. The long course had overcome the poor little beast. Nowhere in all the broad-spreading field was there any way of escape. Its death was imminent. Consequently at the point of being captured, it put off its fate by quick zigzag movements. The blessed man, in his bounty, had pity on the hare's desparate position, and ordered the hounds to give up the chase and let the fugitive escape. Instantly, at the very first word of his command, they halted: you would have thought them chained, or rather rooted in their very tracks. And so, with its pursuers immobilized, the little hare escaped unharmed.

About this same time, my uncle Evanthius, a profoundly Christian man, though much occupied in worldly business, was gravely ill. Since death seemed imminent, he called for Martin. The blessed man hastened to him without delay, but, before he had come half the way, the sick man felt the miraculous power of his approach. He instantly recovered his health and went out to meet us.

The next day, though Martin wanted to return, he remained when Evanthius begged him to do so. A slave boy belonging to the household had been poisoned by a deadly snake bite and was already nearly dead from the powerful venom. Evanthius put him on his shoulders and laid him before the holy man's feet. He was sure that nothing was impossible to Martin. The poison had already spread through the boy's entire body: you could see all the swollen veins standing out and his vital organs tense like wineskins. Martin stretched out his hand and touched all the members of the boy's body. Then he placed his finger near the tiny wound through which the beast had poured in its poison. The effect was amazing. We saw the poison stream from every part, attracted to Martin's finger, and then, mixed with blood, ooze out of the tiny opening of the wound. (It was like the long stream of milk which flows copiously from the udder of a goat or sheep when the shepherd's hand squeezes it.) The boy rose, completely cured. Dumbfounded at this great miracle, we declared, in all truth, that there was no one under heaven who could imitate Martin.

SAINT MARY OF EGYPT

Commemorated on April 1

 AINT Mary of Egypt was born in Egypt and lived as a prostitute for 17 years until repenting before an icon of the Mother of God and venerating the Cross of Christ. Afterwards the Holy Spirit led her across the Jordan into the desert, where she spent 48 years in repentance and

struggle against her passions. Near the end of her life an elder named Zossima found her in the desert and convinced her to tell him of her life and struggles. She then begged him to return one year later, bringing Holy Communion to her. He did so, and she received the Holy Gifts. Then she asked him to come to the desert again the next year.

* * *

SO when a year had again passed, he went again into the huge solitude of the desert, having done everything according to custom, and he hurried towards that marvelous sight. He walked through the desert without finding any indications that this was the place he was looking for, so he looked right and left, turning his gaze in all directions as if he were a huntsman wanting to capture a much-coveted animal. But seeing no movement anywhere he began to weep bitterly. And looking up to heaven he began to pray, "Show me, O Lord, that angel in the flesh of whom the world is not worthy."

Having prayed in this way, he came to the place which looked like a stream and on the other side he saw the rising sun, and when he looked, he saw the holy one lying dead, her hands folded and her face turned to the east. Running up to her, he watered the feet of the blessed one with tears; otherwise he did not dare to touch her. He wept for some time and said the appropriate psalms, then the prayer for the dead, and then he said to himself, "Is it right to bury the holy body here?" And then he saw by her head these words written in the earth: "Father Zossima, bury in this place the body of Mary the sinner, return me to the earth of which I am made, dust to dust, having prayed to the Lord for me, who died on the first day of the Egyptian month of Pharmuti called the fifth of the Ides of April by the Romans, on the self-same night as the Passion of the Lord after making her communion of the Divine and Mysterious Supper."

When he had read what was written, the Elder wondered who it was that had written these words, since she had told him that she was unlettered, but he rejoiced to know the name of the holy one. He realized that as soon as she had received Communion from the divine mysteries by the Jordan, in that same hour she had come to the place where at once she had

passed from this world. The same journey which had taken
Zossima twenty days with difficulty, Mary had covered in an
hour and then at once passed on to God. So Zossima glorified
God and shed tears on the body, saying, "It is time, Zossima,
to fulfill the command. But how, wretched man, are you going
to dig out a grave with nothing but your hands?" Then he saw
not far away a small piece of wood, thrown down in the desert.
Picking it up he set about digging. But the ground was dry and
very hard, and would not yield to the efforts of the old man. He
grew tired, and poured with sweat. He sighed from the depths
of his soul, and raising his eyes he saw a great lion standing by
the body of the holy one and licking her feet. When he saw the
lion he trembled with fear, especially because he remembered
that Mary had said she had never met any animals. But protect-
ing himself with the sign of the cross, he believed that he would
be kept from harm by the power of the one who lay there. As
for the lion, it walked up to him, expressing friendliness in every
movement. Zossima said to the lion, "Greatest of the beasts, you
have been sent by God, so that the body of the holy one should
be buried, for I am old and have not enough strength to dig her
grave. I have no spade and I cannot go back all that distance to
fetch suitable tools. So do the work with your paws, and we shall
be able to give to the earth the mortal tabernacle of the Saint."

While he was still speaking the lion had already dug out with
its front paws a hole big enough to bury the body in. Again the
Elder watered the feet of the holy one with tears, and then, with
the lion standing by, he called upon her to pray for everyone,
and covered her body with earth; it was naked as it had been
before, except for the torn monastic cloak which Zossima had
thrown across her and with which Mary, turning away, had
partially covered her body. Then they both withdrew. The lion
went off into the depths of the desert as meekly as if it were a
lamb, and Zossima went home, blessing and praising God and

singing hymns of praise to our Lord Christ. When he reached the monastery, he told the monks everything that he had heard and seen, hiding nothing. From the very beginning he told them everything in detail and all marvelled to hear of God's wonders and kept the memory of the Saint in fear and love. As for Abbot John, he did find a few in the monastery in need of correction, as St. Mary had said, so that none of the Saint's words proved useless or inexplicable. Zossima lived in that monastery until he was a hundred, and then he went in peace to God, thanks be to our Lord Jesus Christ, Who with the Father is one in power and honor and glory, with the adorable and life-giving Spirit, now and forever and to the ages of ages, Amen.

Saint Mavra of Ceahlău

THIS spiritual daughter of the Romanian Orthodox Church (17th-18th century) and offspring of the Romanian land, sanctified through the sacrifice and prayers of so many saints and monastics that loved Christ, was from a village in the Bistriţa valley, not far from Ceahlău Mountain. Her parents brought her up from the time she was little in the fear of God, accustoming her to prayer, fasting, and regular attendance at the church services. In summer, especially, the parents took her on pilgrimage to the great monasteries of the Neamţ region, and on feast days they allowed her to worship at the sketes of nuns around Ceahlău....

Arriving at the age of twenty years and her heart being wounded with the love of Christ, she renounced transitory things and, leaving her parents' house, she chose eternal things, that is to say, the humble monastic life of prayer and dispassion, which helps the most for the salvation of the soul. First she lived in asceticism in the community of nuns at Silvestru Skete, where there labored some souls who loved Christ, under the guidance of a meek and humble abbess.

After some years she took the monastic schema, receiving the name of Mavra in place of that of her baptism, Maria. And Mother Mavra was very ascetic, meek, and humble, loving the most: silence, church, and unceasing prayer. She slept a few hours on a chair, made hundreds of prostrations, ate once a day at evening, and was content with some dried bread soaked in water and with a few vegetables.

Desiring more silence, the blessed Mavra made herself nearby a small cell of wood and earth. During the day she took part in church and did her obedience in the skete, and at night she labored in her cell with unknown spiritual labors. And St. Mavra advanced so much in this paradise of prayer and silence that even the birds of the sky and the animals of the forest loved her and were tame before her. The deer honored her the most.

The old folks around Ceahlău say that blessed Mavra always went on the road, on the paths of the mountain and even through the villages with a deer behind her....

From Silvestru Skete, St. Mavra withdrew to even harsher asceticism, in a clearing under the peak of Ceahlău, named Ponoare (i.e., Steep). Here she was alone with the one God. Only her beloved deer, that was like a worthy disciple to her, accompanied her, and the hand of the Lord covered her from all evil. And she labored, blessed as a true bride of Christ, on Ceahlău Mountain, enduring with firmness the cold, strong winds and deep snows, as well as the fire of temptations of all kinds, since here she warred face to face with the devil, with thoughts, and with the weaknesses of nature. Her disciples, searching everywhere for her, found St. Mavra on the mountain and gathered one by one around her. Then, praying and weeping together, with the help of the faithful in the villages, they made in the clearing many desert cells and a small church of wood dedicated to the Feast of Tabor, the Transfiguration. This clearing is called to this day the "Clearing of the Mothers." In this oasis of silence and prayer St. Mavra lived in asceticism up to the end of her life, enduring troubles with joy and thanking God for all things. She also gave wise advice to the disciples and faithful who came up the mountain to ask for words of salvation and to bring them food and necessities.

Feeling the approach of her passing away, she asked for the Most Pure Mysteries, then, calling around her all her disciples, she gave them much spiritual advice and gave them the final kiss, shedding many tears.

After a short time they found her in her cell, asleep in the Lord, and, with all the nuns under Ceahlău weeping over her, they buried her in Ponoare Clearing. Her relics, as also those of other women ascetics, are hidden here in the "Clearing of the Mothers" until the end of the ages, and her soul delights in the band of the saints in heaven.

Holy Mother Mavra, pray to God for us!

SAINT MELANGELL

Commemorated on January 31

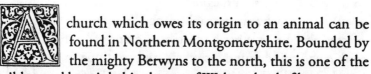 church which owes its origin to an animal can be found in Northern Montgomeryshire. Bounded by the mighty Berwyns to the north, this is one of the wildest and least inhabited parts of Wales; a land of barren crags and desolate moorlands, rivers and waterfalls and little secret valleys into which strangers seldom penetrate. It is therefore not surprising that at the top of one such valley, so narrow that there is only just room for a river and a little land to wind between the mountains, towering up on either side, there is an ancient church with a history as strange and wild as its surroundings, and a story, connected with a hare and stretching back over a thousand years.... The church is called Pennant Melangell, St. Melangell's church at the top of the stream.

According to tradition, in Ireland about the seventh century there lived a king with a most beautiful daughter called Melangell. The princess had vowed herself to celibacy, so rather than be forced into marriage by her father she fled from his kingdom, and after many wanderings found refuge near the source of the river Tanat, in this lonely Montgomeryshire valley, where she lived in perfect peace and seclusion for some fifteen years without ever seeing a man. She scorned all material comforts and slept in a crevice in the rocky mountainside, some way above the present road. One day, Brochwell Yscythog, Prince of Powis, was out hunting, and his hounds started up a hare and pursued it into a dense thicket. Bursting through it, the prince was amazed to find in a clearing a most beautiful girl on her knees, deep in prayer, the hare sitting on the folds of her garment, facing the hounds unafraid. The huntsman urged the hounds on, but they fled  in terror, howling, and when he tried to blow his horn, it stuck to his lips and no sound came.

When Brochwell heard Melangell's story he was so impressed that he gave her a substantial grant of land at Pennant so that she could found a convent and continue to live unmolested. The privilege of sanctuary was also bestowed with the lands and a curse laid on anyone who violated these rights. St. Melangell is said to have lived there as abbess until her death thirty-seven years later and to have performed many miracles "for those who sought refuge in her sanctuary with pure hearts." Because hares were under her special protection, for hundreds of years they were known as "St. Melangell's lambs," and even up to the eighteenth century no one in the parish would kill a hare; and if one was chased by a dog and someone called out "God and St. Melangell be with thee," its escape was assured.

 At the back of the church is the fifteenth-century rood screen which now stands ten feet east of its original position; the elaborate carving on it tells the story of St. Melangell. The man on horseback is clearly the Prince of Powis; the huntsman, his horn frozen to his lips, is kneeling nearby. The Saint herself is sitting in state in a long robe, her hair flowing, in her left hand a staff, and a large hare chased by two hounds is running towards her....

The unique feature of this lonely church is the small room built on at the east end. It is called *cell-y-bedd,* the cell of the grave, and here it seems certain that St. Melangell was buried and later her relics kept; often in bygone centuries, the relics of a saint, or perhaps the whole body, were housed in a shrine in a church instead of being interred, so that they could be more easily venerated. It is a place of beauty and extraordinary peace, and even after the lapse of so many centuries still seems pervaded with the powerful spirit of the indomitable young woman who fled from the comforts of her father's court in Ireland. When I last visited the shrine a vase of fresh flowers on the floor of *cell-y-bedd* showed that she is still remembered by the people of her valley.

Mallwyd church, some twelve miles from Dolgellau [Wales] is also connected with animals through St. Tydecho, its founder, for the Saint was well-known for his power over wild beasts. According to tradition he lived in the fifth or sixth century and was an abbot in Armorica until he came to spread the Gospel in this remote part of Wales, where he lived the life of a hermit, wearing a hair shirt, sleeping on stones and cultivating land sufficient for his spartan needs. But though he lived such a simple life he incurred the wrath of Maelgwyn Gwynedd, a local

chieftain, who, to make things difficult for the Saint, sent him a stud of valuable white horses to look after. Tydecho turned them loose among the mountains where they ran wild and ungroomed. When Maelgwyn wanted them returned they were in such poor condition he was very angry with the Saint and as a reprisal seized

Tydecho's oxen, so that he could not plough and harrow his land.

The Saint must have been in despair, but some stags appeared and allowed themselves to be yoked to the plough, while out of a nearby forest came a wolf, so tame he could be used to draw the harrow. However, things contin- ued to be so unpleasant for St.  Tydecho in North Wales that finally he returned to Brittany, not before he founded two churches, one of them at Mallwyd, the other at Llanymawddwy.

ELDER MELCHIZEDEK
Hermit of the Roslavl Forest

ATHER Melchizedek, a desert-dweller in the central Russian forest in the eighteenth century, was an integral part of the desert-dwelling movement stemming from the disciples of St. Paisius Velichkovsky. Elder Melchizedek was a contemporary of outstanding men of prayer, almost angel-like creatures to whom mystical realities were opened. He was part of the whole phenomenon of the Desert-dwellers of Roslavl, and was actually in no way unique or different from others who pursued monastic love for the wilderness; he followed the standard Orthodox anchoretic experience set up by the 4th-century Egyptian Fathers and repeated by desert-lovers throughout Christendom: Gaul, Ireland, Ethiopia, Mt. Athos, Meteora, Russia, Serbia, Romania, etc. He is to be viewed in the classic context of Eldership. In him was the same freedom of spirit which the Ancient Fathers breathed; he was just as fearless and contemplated the same vision of Adam before the Fall, along with whom he possessed true humanity, the dignified "likeness" of God.

As a young man he journeyed to the small and isolated monastery of Sofroniev Pustin, or the "Desert of Sofrony" in the Ukraine. Here he was accepted as a novice, but did not remain for long.

Owing to the anti-monastic decrees of Peter the Great and the Empress Anne, monastic life as a whole had declined. The best monks were expelled for their criticism of the regime.

While at Sofroniev, he was given the task of looking after the geese and other domestic poultry, and, according to the tradition recorded by Hilarion, these dumb beasts became so attached to him that when he left they drowned themselves in the pond.

New Martyr Nikodim has recorded these episodes from the life of Elder Melchizedek:

"Father Melchizedek had an unusual power over wild animals. One day a forest bear came to him and bent his head before the Elder, and the latter placed on the animal's neck a red collar. It was wonderful to watch this Michailo (or Misha, as that is how the Elder called the bear) of huge stature, quite old and gray-haired and with a red collar, standing at the porch of the Elder's cell and patiently waiting for food for himself. This bear had the habit of visiting Father Melchizedek during the latter's mealtimes, and rarely would he make a mistake in time, for every time his arrival coincided with the usual hour of the Elder's partaking of food. The bear would always wait for his food at the porch until the desert-dweller would bring out to him the remaining food from his table. Having eaten, the bear would go away quite satisfied and consoled.

"Living in this particular desert hermitage, Father Melchizedek (then Maximus) was enduring for a long time various forms of persecution from the brethren, who denied him  even food. But the Most Merciful God, as a consolation, sent him a wild duck. Every springtime she would unfailingly fly back to him and lay eggs near his cell and would sit until they would hatch into fledglings, and for winter she would fly away to warm lands. During the last remaining days of Father Maximus in that desert hermitage, the brethren began to persecute him even more, and, finally, he was told to leave the hermitage altogether. On the last day of his stay in the hermitage there occurred the following incident. The duck, as if feeling the forthcoming separation from her feeder, began to unconsolably make screeching cries while flying from one place to another, and then suddenly together with her fledglings flew way up high over the main church tower, then flew round about there for a long time and, finally, from a remarkable height threw herself against the church dome; her example was followed also by her young ones, and thus they all together hurt themselves to death."

Father Mitrophan, one of Elder Melchizedek's disciples, also records the influence which Melchizedek exercised over wild animals, especially over the giant old bear, *Misha*. On a certain occasion, one of the Staretz's benefactors decided to visit him. Melchizedek, who had the gift of prophecy, said to Mitrophan: "Our benefactor is coming to visit us, and may meet the old bear on the footpath and come to harm." Mitrophan hurried out, and there, sure enough, he saw the old bear attacking the visitor. But as soon as the bear noticed Mitrophan he left the visitor and went away. When the guest reached Melchizedek's cell he said to him: "Father, I now perceive and believe that the Lord is with you. When my life was in danger, I cried out unceasingly, 'O Lord, by the prayers of Fr. Melchizedek save me,' and God preserved me from the beast." To which Melchizedek answered, "You shall receive according to your faith. The Lord is merciful. Because you are merciful to others, He is merciful to you." Then he told the visitor to kiss an icon in thanksgiving. After the death of Melchizedek, the old bear was never seen again.

ABBOT NAZARIUS OF VALAAM

THE Monastery of Valaam, situated on the islands of Lake Ladoga in Russia, with the coming of Abbot Nazarius in 1782 soon became a great monastic citadel, bringing into reality the great Orthodox monastic ideals. Abbot Nazarius led the monks in a renewal of the monastic tradition. Externally, the monastery was rebuilt, and the brotherhood grew from only 18 monks. But more importantly, Abbot Nazarius led the brotherhood in a spiritual revival. He was a Sarov monastery monk initially, in the tradition of the Holy Elder Paisius Velichkovsky, who was responsible for a deep spiritual renewal of the entire Russian and Slavic churches. While on Mt. Athos, Paisius copied, compiled and translated the ancient Patristic texts known as the *Philokalia.* His disciples spread these teachings and the hesychastic practice of "Prayer of the Heart," the Jesus

Prayer. Abbot Nazarius established these traditions and a strict coenobitic life at Valaam. He was also an editor of the first Russian edition of the *Philokalia,* which St. Herman brought to Alaska. It was Abbot Nazarius who sent St. Herman and seven other monks from Valaam with Metropolitan Gabriel's monastic missionaries to Alaska.

In 1801, having earned well a rest from the heavy burden of twenty years of governance of the Valaam Monastery, Fr. Nazarius retired for a life of solitude and divine vision a mile inland from the monastery. But his love for Sarov Monastery, the place where he had laid his ascetic beginnings and had given his monastic vows, kept summoning him to return there. So, after three years of seclusion in Valaam, he decided to retire to Sarov.

Having arrived in Sarov, Fr. Nazarius made a secluded cell in the forest on the river Sarovka, three miles from the monastery, and settled in it. When his strength allowed, he loved in the nighttime to walk in the forest, reciting from memory the ancient Rule of the Twelve Psalms, and he would return to his cell no earlier than sunrise. More than once he encountered bears in the dense forest, but they never touched him, and he would fearlessly walk on, always trusting in the will of God. Many hermits and others living apart from the world came to him to verify their thoughts and their life, to see whether they were of God; and the instruction of the spiritually experienced Elder they accepted as the will of God.

On February 23, 1809, Fr. Nazarius reposed and was buried in Sarov Monastery. O Lord, through the prayers of our most blessed and most honorable Father Nazarius, have mercy on us, preserve us, and save us. Amen.

SAINT PAUL OF OBNORA

Commemorated on January 10

ORN in a pious noble family of Moscow in 1317, St. Paul even from childhood showed leanings toward the contemplative life of a true Orthodox Christian. He avoided noisy children's games and sweet foods; he fasted, gave to the poor everything he had, even the clothes on his back, attended eagerly every church service, and spent whole nights in prayer. When at the age of twenty-two his parents decided to marry him off, he secretly left his home and entered a distant monastery on the banks of the Volga River, where he received the monastic tonsure, surpassing everyone in ascetic fervor. When the good news of the great St. Sergius of Radonezh reached the shores of the Volga, St. Paul felt that his prayer had been answered in obtaining an experienced instructor; and he left his monastery for the Lavra of the Holy Trinity.

St. Sergius received him with love, and seeing that he was full of the fear of God, he made him his disciple. He entrusted him with various obediences: in the kitchen, in the bread-bakery. St. Paul gave up his own will to the God-bearing Abbot and in time acquired the gift of heartfelt feeling and abundance of tears. After several years St. Sergius blessed him to withdraw to a separate recluse's cell, where he spent fifteen years in silence. In this time the study of the Word of God so filled his soul that it began to flow out in a gift of teaching; and the brethren, once having discovered this, began to flock to him for edification—

which only evoked in him a greater desire for silence. He began to beg St. Sergius to bless him for a life of desert-dwelling. Knowing the spiritual maturity of his disciple, St. Sergius blessed him, and bidding farewell with a prayer, he gave him an invincible weapon, a holy Cross. This copper Cross was to accompany the Saint his whole life long, and centuries afterwards it was preserved on the reliquary over the Saint's holy relics.

Having left St. Sergius' monastery, St. Paul went north, deep into the forests beyond the Volga and wandered from place to place, visiting some of the monastic communities scattered throughout the Thebaid of the North. But the heart of the lover of desert-dwelling still thirsted for absolute silence, until finally he settled in a spot in the Komel forests overlooking the little river Griazovitsa, and chose for his abode the hollow of an old linden tree. Here the wondrous Paul spent three years, glorifying God together with the birds, for they alone seconded the hermit's singing in the desolate wilds where no man had yet penetrated. Here he could pray ceaselessly to God. Who can tell of the hardships he endured? Living on grass and roots and enduring all changes of weather, in silence he purified his mind by means of spiritual combat and divine vision.

But it was pleasing to God that St. Paul should serve for the salvation of others, instructing them by word and by his ascetic life. And so, instructed by God, the Saint left his linden tree and went further to the river Nurma, where the Obnora joins it, where he found a spot to his liking, built for himself a little hut no larger than his abandoned linden hollow, and settled therein to spend his days and nights in vigil and prayer. For five days of the week he would remain without food or drink altogether, and only on Saturday and Sunday would he have some bread and water.

Meanwhile, three miles from St. Paul's hermitage, on the same wild banks of the Nurma, another anchorite was laboring: St. Sergius of Nurma, who had received the monastic tonsure on Mount Athos. He had come from the East to the region of Moscow to seek enlightenment from the lamp of

Radonezh. Having matured in spiritual life, the Athonite Sergius, with the blessing of the Russian Sergius, came to settle in this wilderness when the anchorite Paul was still living in his linden hollow....

Having heard of the ascetic labors of Paul, Sergius went to him and saw in the forest a wondrous sight: A flock of birds surrounded the marvelous anchorite; little birds perched on the Elder's head and shoulders, and he fed them by hand. Nearby stood a bear, awaiting his food from the desert-dweller; foxes, rabbits and other beasts ran about, without any enmity among themselves and not fearing

the bear. Behold the life of innocent Adam in Eden, the lordship of man over creation, which together with us groans because of our fall and thirsts to be delivered into *the liberty of the children of God* (Rom. 8:22).

With spiritual joy the two great ascetics became acquainted with each other; they practiced mutual counsel in all their spiritual undertakings and often visited each other, strengthening each other in advanced ascetic labors. Paul chose Sergius as his spiritual father, the latter having been ordained to the rank of presbyter while still living on the Holy Mountain of Athos, and often Paul would receive Communion from his holy hands of the Body and Blood of Christ, confessing to him all his thoughts. But Sergius as well did not hide from Paul what was in his heart; for they were both close servants of the One God, and the Saints helped each other in the tribulations of the wilderness...

Saint Paul the Hermit
and Saint Anthony

Commemorated on January 15

IN the early days of the Church there was a kind of spiritual splendor in the hearts of believers. After the astounding descent of the Holy Spirit, the ensuing miracles, and the inspired preaching and example of the Apostles, the first Christians were, like Stephen, filled with grace and power. In the awful days of the persecutions they lived heroic lives, and thousands died as martyrs. Then came comparative peace and the reaction that often follows. Tempted by the pagan life around them, not a few Christians lost their former zeal and became weak in faith and worldly.

In the Eastern Church many of the faithful, seeing how easy it was to become lax in times of peace, feared for their souls' salvation. They began to withdraw from the world entirely and retired into desert places where they might think of nothing but God and serve Him with all their hearts. At first these men were called solitaries, anchorites, or hermits. Eventually they all became known as monks. The word monk comes from a Greek word meaning alone. By the beginning of the fourth century thousands of monks were to be found in the deserts of Egypt, Syria, Mesopotamia, and Palestine.

It was in Egypt, in the latter part of the third century, that the first of the anchorites appeared. At first they did not go far from home. They lived, each by himself, in caves or rude shelters and tried by penance, mortification, prayer, and labor to order their lives so that they would be pleasing to God. The very first one of whom there is any record is Paul the Hermit.

St. Anthony, mentioned earlier in our book, was another anchorite, younger than Paul the Hermit. He was always a persuasive speaker. At one time while he was living alone in his desert fortress, the emperor Maximian was persecuting the Christians most cruelly. Anthony, who would have been very happy to die a martyr's death, left his tower and hastened to the arena in the city to console those who were condemned to die. Dressed in his white sheepskin tunic, he preached to the martyrs and gave them strength and courage, but he himself, to his disappointment, was not arrested or disturbed. He was banished from the city, however, and had to return sadly to his desert cell.

As he grew older, Anthony longed to go back to the inner desert where he would have more time to pray and meditate. He asked for a pronged hoe, an ax, and some corn. Then far off in a quiet place he tilled a small piece of land near a shallow stream and planted a few vegetables for visitors. He made little ditches or canals to irrigate the dry soil. Then, when the corn was high, some wild horses came and ate it. Anthony took one of them by the ears.

"Why do you eat what you have not sown?" he asked. "Why do you injure one who has not harmed you? Go, in the name of God!"

And the horses went.

When Anthony was ninety years old, he believed that he was the oldest monk in the desert and that God must be well pleased with him, but God, lest Anthony sin by pride, sent him a vision in which he learned of a solitary who was much older and holier than he. This man was Paul the Hermit, and Anthony determined to visit him. It was a two-day journey across the desert, and Anthony didn't know where to look until he saw a wolf go into the entrance to a cave. It turned out to be Paul's cave, but at first Paul would not let Anthony enter. It took Anthony two hours to talk Paul into letting him in, but when at length he did so, he seemed greatly pleased. He asked Anthony for news of the world, who was emperor, and how Christianity was faring. Suddenly, a crow flew down and placed a loaf of bread before them. Paul was delighted.

"Look," said he, "God has sent us our dinner. God the merciful, God the compassionate. For sixty years now I have received a half-loaf of bread every day, but at your coming God has doubled his soldier's rations." Then Paul and Anthony argued politely as to who should break the loaf, Anthony, who was the guest, or Paul, who was the elder. In the end they both took hold of the loaf and together broke it in two.

God must have looked down lovingly at the two dear, holy old men as they accepted the little extra ration so gratefully, hoping to strengthen their bodies and serve Him another day, should that be His will.

As Anthony was leaving, Paul said to him, "My brother Anthony, God promised me that I should see you before I die. He has sent you to me so that you may cover my body with earth. How good God is to me!"

"Oh, take me with you," said Anthony.

"No, wait patiently. Your example is still necessary to the other monks. But bury me like a dutiful son. Go now and bring the cloak that Bishop Athanasius gave you and cover me with it for my burial."

Anthony was astonished that Paul knew about the cloak. He started out immediately to get it, not knowing that Paul had used the cloak as an excuse. He knew that he was about to die, and he wanted to spare Anthony's feelings.

While he was returning with the cloak, Anthony saw a host of angels bearing Paul's soul to heaven. When he reached the cave he found Paul kneeling upright under a palm tree. Anthony wept as he covered the good Elder with the cloak and said the prayers of Christian burial. Afterwards, he began to wonder how he would be able to dig the grave, but two large lions came to him quietly, licked his hands as if they were pet dogs, and proceeded to dig it for him. Then they withdrew as silently as they had come while Anthony blessed them with psalms of praise. He took Paul's penitential garment of woven palm leaves with him in exchange for the cloak of Athanasius and always wore it at Easter and Pentecost. St. Anthony lived to be 105 years old.

SAINT PERPETUA AND
SAINT FELICITI

Commemorated on February 1

THE two Black Carthaginian women being dragged by Roman soldiers did not attract much attention at first. But someone recognized Perpetua, a wealthy, cultured and prominent woman of Carthage. The second woman must have been Feliciti, the maid-servant of Perpetua. A crowd began to follow the Romans and the prisoners. A Roman centurion rode by and saw the possibility of a citizen attack on the Romans. He drove his horse into the crowd, and the Romans carried the women into the courthouse.

Perpetua was married. She had left a nursing baby at home. Feliciti was also married. She was five months pregnant. Even though Perpetua and Feliciti would have walked proudly to the office of the magistrate, the soldiers saw fit to drag them.

Both women stood erect and calm before the magistrate. They knew why they were there. The hot, stuffy, dusty room with the buzzing flies annoyed the Romans more than it did the women. After a long silence, which was to frighten Perpetua and Feliciti, the magistrate ordered them to promise to worship the Roman gods at once. The women did not answer. The magistrate offered them freedom and apologies if they would deny Jesus of Nazareth. He explained that after all Jesus had been dead for more than two hundred years.

Perpetua was said to have stepped forward and said, "As a water pot cannot call itself by any other name, I cannot call myself by any other name than Christian."

Feliciti agreed.

With utmost boredom, the magistrate ordered the women to be thrown into the sports arena with the lions on the following day. He reminded them that they would be torn to shreds by the wild animals.

The next day the stands were crowded with Roman soldiers and hundreds of retired Romans and businessmen from the wide area of Carthage. There were hundreds of Greeks among them. Recreation for them, as in Rome itself, was the fighting events between the gladiators, between the gladiators and wild animals, and sometimes between animals and unarmed captives and Christians.

Today Perpetua and Feliciti were not on the sports agenda. So they were scheduled first into the arena. Two Roman guards led the women past the waiting gladiators under the stands. Perpetua was dragged out onto the field with great speed. At the center of the arena, the guards dropped her to the ground and raced back to the gate. Feliciti, with most of her clothes torn away, was dropped to the ground a few feet from Perpetua.

Suddenly the crowd came alive. There was a loud shout from the stands. The animals were out!

For some strange reason the lions came up to the women and then moved on. The one wild cow in the arena saw them. She lowered her head and charged. The cow sent Perpetua flying

over her back. Perpetua sat calmly on the ground, waiting. The wild cow galloped to another part of the field and stayed there. Feliciti rushed over to Perpetua. The crowd stood and shouted in unison for the women's freedom. It must have been an omen that half-starved lions did not attack human flesh. The crowd continued shouting. There was no ranking Roman official at the stands to make a decision. A Roman tribune standing inside the gate did. He ordered two gladiators to go out and cut off their heads. They did.

Restitua was an African girl who died in the arena with Perpetua and Feliciti. Septimius Severius, a Black man and former Roman general, was the emperor of Rome at the time these women were killed.

Saint Prisca
The Child Martyr

Commemorated on January 18

S AINT PRISCA'S name has always been dearly loved, especially in England. She lived over seventeen hundred years ago and is one of the few child martyrs whose names have come down to us from those early days, although there were many other brave children who suffered and were strong, and who, at last, gave their lives to prove their faith.

St. Prisca was a little Roman girl whose parents were Christians of a noble family. Claudius was the emperor at that time, and though during his reign the Christians were not persecuted in such numbers as they had been before that, still many cruel things were done here and there, and it was a dangerous thing to be a Christian.

It was in the evil times when one did not always dare to say what he really thought, nor publicly to worship as he believed was right. Many of the Christians were not ashamed to conceal their real belief from the heathen Romans, who were everywhere seeking with hatred for the followers of Christ, to torture and slay them.

Prisca's father and mother had managed to keep their secret, and were not suspected of being Christians. They probably went to church in the secret chapels which the Christians had dug deep in the ground under the city. In these dark, gloomy catacombs, as they were called, the Christians held services directly under the feet of the cruel Romans, who were passing overhead without suspecting what was going on so near to them.

But Prisca scorned to use any precaution. Small and defenseless though she was, she did not fear to tell everyone what she believed and Whose Cross she followed. So she soon became known as a firm little Christian maiden. And there were people in the city cruel enough and wicked enough to hate even a little child-Christian and to wish her evil.

These persons reported to the emperor's officers her brave words of faith, and told them how she would not sacrifice to the Roman gods as the other children did. So very soon she was seized by the guards and brought before the emperor.

Claudius looked at the little maid in surprise to find her so young. And he thought: "Ho! I shall easily make this small Christian change her mind and obey me." And he bade his men take her to the temple of Apollo and make her offer incense to the beautiful god of the silver bow. So they carried her to the top of the Palatine, one of the seven hills on which Rome was built.

They first passed under a great marble arch and came into a fair courtyard surrounded by fifty-two marble pillars. In the center of this space stood the temple of Apollo, the most magnificent building in all Rome. With its ivory gates and wonderful groups of statues, its inlaid marble floors and altars wreathed with flowers, its golden tripods breathing incense, its lamps and beautiful silver vases, it was a very different place from the bare, dark caverns in which the Christians worshiped. In front of the temple was a group of four oxen made of bronze, and in the center of this group burned a fire upon a golden tripod. This was the altar to Apollo, the sun-god, whose enormous golden statue, in his four-horse chariot, stood over the door of the temple just above. He was the likeness of a beautiful youth with a wreath of bay about his head, carrying a bow in his hand, with which Apollo was believed to shoot the sunbeams down upon the earth.

They thrust incense into Prisca's hand and bade her throw a few grains into the fire in honor of the beautiful god of the sun. It seemed a very simple thing to do, to save her life—just to scatter a handful of dark powder on the flames. Prisca loved the dear sun as well as any one, but she knew it was foolish to believe that he was a god, and wicked to worship his statue in place of the great God who made the sun and everything else. So Prisca refused to burn the incense.

Then the emperor was very angry, and bade the soldiers whip her until she obeyed his command. But they could not make her yield by cruelty. Even the hard-hearted Romans who had come to look on admired her bravery and pitied her suffering. The women wept to see her so cruelly treated, and the men cried, "Shame! shame! to torture a little child."

And then a beautiful thing happened; for Prisca appeared dressed in a robe of yellow sunshine. A wonderful light shone all about her, and she seemed herself a little star giving out light, so brightly did her brave spirit shine among those cruel men.

It seemed as if no child could bear all this suffering without yielding, and the emperor hoped she would give in, for he did not want to have her killed. But Prisca was firm, and would not make the sacrifice. The emperor was surprised to find a child so brave. He ordered them to drag her away to prison and to keep her there for many days. Here she was most unhappy—lonely and cold and hungry often, wondering what dreadful thing was to happen next. But her heart was always brave, and she was not afraid.

After a long time, one morning the guard came for little Prisca. They led her forth into the dear sunshine, and glad she was to see it and the blue sky once more. But it was only for a short time that they let her enjoy even this little pleasure; for they brought her to the amphitheater, a great open place like the circus, with tiers upon tiers of seats all about, and crowds of faces looking down into the center where she was.

Prisca knew what this meant, for she had often heard how the Christians were put into the arena to be torn in pieces by wild beasts. And kneeling down on the sand she made a little prayer, not that she might be saved from the fierce beasts, but that she might have courage to show her Christian bravery and teach a lesson to these fiercer men and women who were looking on.

Then the keeper opened the grated door of a den at the end of the arena, and out stalked a great yellow lion. With a dreadful roar he rushed into the center of the circle, and stood there lashing his tail and flashing his big yellow eyes all about the place. Then suddenly he spied the little girl standing quietly at one side with her hands clasped in front of her, looking at him without fear. And the great beast strode gently up to her on his padded paws. He bent his head and licked her little bare feet, and then he crouched down by her side, as a Saint Bernard dog might place himself to guard his little mistress. And this is why the old pictures of St. Prisca represent her with a lion by her side.

There fell a great silence on the tented place. The emperor and all the people sat perfectly still, wondering at the strange sight and admiring the courage of the child; for she had reached out her hand and was stroking the yellow head of the lion, playing with his mane. She bent her head and no one heard her whisper into his ear:

"My good friend! You will not hurt me, I know, for the Lord has closed your mouth, just as he did the mouths of the lions into whose den Daniel was thrown by wicked men. These cruel men will put me to death, but you are kinder than they."

And the lion looked up in her face as though he understood, and growled softly. He was quite gentle with her, but when the keeper came towards them he roared and bristled and showed his great teeth, so that for a long time no one dared to come near.

But even the lion could not save her from the death which she had no wish to shun. At last they captured him and took him away. The emperor's heart was softened by Prisca's bravery, and he wished to give her one more chance to save her life. They shut her up for many days in the heathen temple, and tried in every way to make her sacrifice to the gods and give up Christianity. They coaxed her and made her fine promises; they threatened and punished her. But still Prisca stood firm, although she was now very worn and tired and ill because she had suffered so much.

So when she had borne it all patiently and bravely, and they saw it was impossible to make a little Christian turn back again into a little heathen, they led her away down the road which leads south from the Palatine hill, to the place of execution. This was just outside the Ostian gate, an archway in the great wall which surrounded Rome, through which the road led to the town of Ostium and to the sea. Just outside this gate, to show that they were no longer worthy of being Romans and living within its walls, criminals were executed. And here many Christian martyrs lost their lives. Prisca was one of these, for here she was beheaded. And till the very end she neither cried nor screamed nor was in any way afraid. And so she became St. Prisca, a little martyr.

Then another strange thing happened. When she died a great eagle appeared in the sky, hovering over St. Prisca's body far up in the air. And when any of the Romans ventured near her the eagle swooped down upon them with dreadful cries and flapping of his wings. And his round gray eyes looked so fierce and his claws so long and sharp, that no one dared to touch her for fear of the bird. St. Prisca had found another protector in cruel Rome. And this is why many of the old pictures of St. Prisca's martyrdom show a great eagle hovering over her.

The creature guarded her body night and day, driving every one away, until the Christians, who had been waiting for the chance to venture out, came secretly one night and carried her away. They buried her where the Romans could not find her, in their little secret cemetery in the catacombs. This is how St. Prisca lived and died two hundred and seventy years after Christ's birth. But I wish we knew what became of the noble lion and the devoted eagle.

OPTINA ELDER SEBASTIAN
Schema-Archimandrite of Karaganda

ORN In 1884 in the Orel Province of Russia, Elder Sebastian (in the world Stephen) went to Optina Monastery at the age of 19. He served as Elder Joseph's cell-attendant for five years and lived with Elder Nectarius for seventeen years—twelve years of which were in Optina Monastery and five years in the village of Kholmische after the forced closure of the monastery in 1923. Under the guidance of these two Elders, Fr. Sebastian developed the spiritual gifts which he had had since birth and acquired many new lofty gifts: the gifts of meekness, of discernment, of exalted prayer, of clairvoyance, of mercifulness and co-suffering. Later, great love was to lead him to take upon himself the ascetic feat of eldership in an exceptionally difficult time.

In 1933 Elder Sebastian was arrested by the Communists and spent ten years in a Siberian concentration camp. After his imprisonment he lived in a little house in the Michailov suburb of Karaganda. Almost all those in Michailov knew and loved Batiushka. They greatly revered him, and believed in the power of his prayers.

People in other suburbs also heard about him and strove to come to see him. Yea, and not only people, but even the beasts as well. When he, small and insignificant, walked with his quick, light stride along the street of Michailov in his long black overcoat and black cap, from behind all of the fences dogs would crawl out in order to see Batiushka. They rushed, fearing to be late, to have missed him. When the gap in the fence was narrow and they could not crawl through it, then, having sniffed Batiushka, they would dig a hole with their paws under the fence in order to force their heads through and would lie flat like a pancake. Laughing, their owners would tell of this, which I myself saw. "When Batiushka walks by," the people said, "they crawl out like serpents." Where houses had low garden fences, the dogs would fly over them like birds. They all decorously sat in front of their homes, did not run out onto the street, nor did they bark at anyone. They sat quietly, following after Batiushka with their heads as he passed by. What were they trying to express? Oh, the dogs of Michailovka! The dogs of Michailovka! How they impressed me with the keenness and depth of their dog souls and hearts....

SAINT SERAPHIM OF SAROV

Commemorated on January 2

HE best known of the Orthodox saints of modern times, St. Seraphim of Sarov, has much to teach the Orthodox Christians of these last times.

St. Seraphim (his worldly name was Prochor Moshnin) was born in 1759 in Kursk, in the heart of Holy Russia, to a pious merchant family. Raised in the fear of God and strict Orthodox life, he also knew very early the mercies of God at first hand; at the age of ten he was miraculously healed of a serious affliction by the Mother of God through her Kursk Icon.

Once he learned to read, the boy Prochor immersed himself in the spiritual world of basic Christian literature: the Scriptures, Horologion (containing the daily cycle of church ser-vices), the Psalter, the lives of saints. He spent all the time he could in church, where services would go on for many hours every day, and thought only of God and the spiritual world. A deep desire for spiritual things being kindled in him, he began to long to serve God in the monastic calling.

At the age of 19, on a pilgrimage to the holy places of Kiev, he received the counsel of the holy recluse Dositheus (actually a woman) to "go to Sarov"; and after a short time this is what he did—spending the rest of his life in this remarkable monastery.

He lived for many years in coenobitic life with the other brethren of the monastery. Then he received a blessing from the abbot to begin life as a hermit in the forest around Sarov.

St. Seraphim named his new home "Mount Athos," and mentally transformed the dark forest neighboring his barren hut

by giving Biblical names to its various parts: Nazareth, Bethlehem, Jerusalem, Mount Tabor, Golgotha. In this way, as he went about his daily work, gathering moss as fertilizer for his vegetable garden in summer or chopping wood in winter, he could relive these various stages in

the life of Christ, intoning appropriate hymns and occasionally reading relevant prayers or Scriptural passages from the copy of the Gospels, which he always carried with him.

In this northern "Holy Land," the Saint could meet directly with God's creation. He welcomed the mosquitoes that infested the forest swamps where he gathered moss. They were a joy to him, he said, for "the passions are

destroyed through suffering and afflictions." His friendship with the animals of the forest was a source of wonder to his fellow monks. According to Father Joseph—an eyewitness—rabbits, foxes, lynx, lizards, bears, even wolves would gather at midnight around the entrance to the hut, waiting for St. Seraphim to finish his prayers and come out to feed them with bread,

which he always seemed to have left over for them. Several persons told of a bear which would obey his orders and run errands for him, such as fetching honey when there was a visitor. These acts on the bear's part always delighted the Saint.

Martyrs Tharasius, Probus and Andronicus

Commemorated on October 12

ET'S contemplate for a moment a grand and consoling feature of triumph which Almighty God vouchsafed to His servants in the days of persecution. Although hundreds of martyrs have gone to heaven from the arena of the Coliseum, yet few have been killed by the wild beasts. This strange thing is a beam of sunshine amid all the horrors of cruelty and bloodshed. He Who knew how to change the ferocious nature of the animals which prowl through their native mountains and deserts in  search of food, so that they became the protectors and even companions of His hermits and solitaries, made them (instead of being the instruments of the most awful death) the defenders of the chastity of His virgins and the witnesses of the sanctity of His saints. The great Creator of all things intended the dumb animal to be the servant of man, and, with a few exceptions, He refused to allow it to be the executioner of the innocent. One of the most consoling pages in the history of these terrible times, is the oft-repeated miracle of Daniel in the lion's den; not, however, in the silence and darkness of the gloomy cavern into which the youthful prophet was cast, but under the noon-day sun, in the great amphitheater of the capital of the world, and before 100,000 spectators. Miracles have been destined by God to be the handmaids of truth and the medium of conviction. In the visible interposition of His power in preserving His servants from the fury of the beasts in the Coliseum, He presented to the pagans of Rome an incontestable proof of the divinity of Christianity, and a mercy they knew not how to appreciate. If the old walls of the Coliseum could speak, they would tell us some consoling scenes of the triumph of the martyrs and their wonderful preservation. St. Eusebius, who was eyewitness to some of those terrible scenes, describes with eloquence and feeling how the furious wild beasts were unable to harm the Christians, and would turn on the pagans with destructive rage. "Sometimes," he says, "they rushed on the naked and defenseless champions of Christ, but checked as if by some divine power, they returned to their dens. This happened repeatedly, and excited the wonder of the spectators; at their demand the first wild beast having been abashed, a second and third were sent against the same martyr, but to no effect.

"You would have been filled with admiration," he continues, "at the steadfast intrepidity of those holy champions, and at the immovable fortitude displayed by persons of the most tender years. You might have seen a youth who had not yet completed his twentieth year, standing motionless in the midst of the arena with his hands stretched forth in the form of a cross, as he prayed with fervor to God, and not shrinking from the spot in which he stood, even when the bears and leopards, breathing forth rage and death, almost touched his very flesh with their jaws. Again, you might have seen others thrown before an enraged bull, which attacked the pagans who came near him, tossing them with his horns into the air, and leaving them to be taken away half-dead. But when with rage and bellowing he rushed upon the martyrs, he could not approach them, but stamping on the ground with his feet, tossing his horns to and fro, and breathing forth rage and madness, by reason of his being irritated by red-hot goads, the infuriated animal was, in despite of all, held back by an invisible hand. Other wild animals having been tried to no purpose, the Christians were at last put to death by the sword; and their relics, instead of being interred, were consigned to the surges of the deep."

The scenes described by Eusebius were frequent all over the Empire. Wherever the name of Christian was found the persecution raged. It would seem that Almighty God adopted this means to give His infant Church publicity and a sign of the stamp of divinity. Hence in His mercy and goodness He made the persecutions the fruitful harvest of souls. Baronius mentions that in the persecution of Diocletian, when the slain were counted by thousands daily, the holy Pope Marcellus had to appoint twenty-five new parishes in the city, to baptize and instruct the people who multiplied beneath the sword. The hideous and execrable character of the barbarities to which the Christians were subjected, with a view not only to force them to apostatize, but to deter others from embracing the proscribed belief, had the very contrary effect. As to the martyrs, persons of both sexes, and of the tenderest and most infirm age, not only bore their sufferings with superhuman fortitude, but hailed them with joy, as tending to the greater glory of God and the conversion of the pagans. Their very persecutors were forced to applaud the heroism of those whom they so bitterly hated, and to feel disgusted and afflicted at the atrocities they were once so vociferous in demanding.

The reverence which the animals showed the martyrs is touchingly displayed in a scene we will quote from the Acts of three martyrs of Tarsus, given in the Annals of Baronius, under the year 290. They did not suffer in the Coliseum at Rome, yet their martyrdom took place in another amphitheater of the empire, and the records of their death serve as a sample of what generally happened in those days of horror. These martyrs, Tharasius, Probus and Andronicus, had been tortured in a most cruel manner at Tarsus in Cilicia. They were conveyed thence to Mopsueste, and were again submitted to the most horrible barbarities; and a third time they were tormented at Anazobus, so that being covered all over with wounds, and their bones being broken and wrenched from their sockets, when the Governor Maximus wished to have them finally exposed in the amphitheater to the wild beasts, it became necessary for the soldiers to press men from the streets in order to carry thither their almost lifeless bodies.

"When we beheld this," say the three devout Christians who wrote the Acts and interred the relics of the Martyrs, "we turned away our faces and wept. When their mangled frames were cast down from the men's shoulders on the arena, all the spectators were horrified at the sight and began to murmur at the president for this order; and many of them rose up and left the theater, expressing their dislike of this ferocious cruelty, on which Maximus told his guards, who were near him, to take down the names of all who acted thus, that they might be afterwards brought to an account. He then commanded the wild beasts to be let loose on the Martyrs, and, when they would not touch them, he ordered the keepers to be scourged. A bear was then let out which had devoured three men that day; but crouching at the feet of Andronicus, it began gently to lick his wounds, and

continued thus mildly to demean itself, notwithstanding that the Martyr plucked its hair and tried to irritate the animal. Then the president in a fury ordered the lancers to run the bear through the body; and Terentianus (the editor of the games) dreading the president's anger, determined to make sure by letting in on the Martyrs a lioness which had been sent from

Antioch by Herod. But the lioness, to the terror of the spectators, began bounding to the place where they were reclining; and when at length she came to the Martyrs, as it were kneeling down before Tharasius who dragged and annoyed her, she seemed, by cowering down submissively, to attest her veneration, conducting herself less like a lioness than a lamb. Shouts of admiration burst forth from the whole amphitheater, overpowering Maximus with confusion, who screamed to the keepers to infuriate and goad on the lioness. But the beast, with another bound, broke through the palisade back to her den; and the manager, Terentianus, was ordered to proceed without further interlude with the gladiators, directing them first to dispatch the Martyrs with their swords."

Saint Thecla
Equal-to-the-Apostles

Commemorated on September 24

HEN Paul went up to Iconium, after his flight from Antioch, Demas and Hermogenes became his companions, who were then full of hypocrisy. But Paul looking only at the goodness of God, did them no harm, but loved them greatly. Accordingly he endeavored to make known to them all the oracles and doctrines of Christ and the design of the Gospel of God's well-beloved Son, instructing them in the knowledge of Christ, as it was revealed to him.

And a certain man named Onesiphorus, hearing that Paul was come to Iconium, went out speedily to meet him, together with his wife Lectra and his sons Simmia and Zeno, to invite him to their house. For Titus had given them a description of Paul's personage, they as yet not knowing him in person, but only being acquainted with his character. They went in the king's highway to Lystra and stood there waiting for him, comparing all who passed by with that description which Titus had given them. At length they saw a man coming (namely Paul), of a low stature, bald (or shaved) on the head, with crooked thighs, handsome legs, hollow-eyes, and a crooked nose, full of grace; for sometimes he appeared as a man, sometimes he had the countenance of an angel. And Paul saw Onesiphorus and was glad.

And Onesiphorus said: "Hail, thou servant of the blessed God." Paul replied, "The grace of God be with thee and thy family." But Demas and Hermogenes were moved with envy, and, under a show of great religion, Demas said, "And are not we also servants of the blessed God? Why didst thou not salute us?" Onesiphorus replied, "Because I have not perceived in you the fruits of righteousness; nevertheless, if ye are of that sort, ye shall be welcome to my house also."

Then Paul went into the house of Onesiphorus, and there was great joy among the family on that account; and they employed themselves in prayer, breaking of bread, and hearing Paul preach the word of God concerning temperance and the resurrection, in the following manner:

"Blessed are the pure in heart, for they shall see God. Blessed are they who keep their flesh undefiled (or pure), for they shall be the temple of God. Blessed are the temperate (or chaste), for God will reveal Himself to them.

"Blessed are they who abandon their secular enjoyments, for they shall be accepted of God. Blessed are they who have wives, as though they had them not, for they shall be made angels of God. Blessed are they who tremble at the word of God, for they shall be comforted. Blessed are they who keep their baptism pure, for they shall find peace with the Father, Son, and Holy Spirit.

"Blessed are they who pursue the wisdom (or doctrine) of Jesus Christ, for they shall be called the sons of the Most High. Blessed are they who observe the instructions of Jesus Christ, for they shall dwell in eternal light. Blessed are they who for the love of Christ abandon the glories of the world, for they shall judge angels, and be placed at the right hand of Christ, and shall not suffer the bitterness of the last judgment.

"Blessed are the bodies and souls of virgins, for they are acceptable to God, and shall not lose the reward of their virginity; for the word of their (heavenly) Father shall prove effectual to their salvation in the day of his Son, and they shall enjoy rest for evermore."

While Paul was preaching this sermon in the church which was in the house of Onesiphorus, a certain virgin named Thecla (whose mother's name was Theoclia, and who was betrothed to a man named Thamyris) sat at a certain window in her house. From whence, by the advantage of a window in the house where Paul was, she both night and day heard Paul's sermons concerning God, concerning charity, concerning faith in Christ, and concerning prayer; nor would she depart from the window, till with exceeding joy she was subdued to the doctrines of faith. At length, when she saw many women and virgins going in to Paul, she earnestly desired that she might be thought worthy to appear in his presence, and hear the word of Christ; for she had not yet seen Paul's person, but only heard his sermons and that alone.

But when she would not be prevailed upon to depart from the window, her mother sent to Thamyris, who came with the greatest pleasure, as hoping now to marry her. Accordingly he said to Theoclia, "Where is my Thecla?" Theoclia replied, "Thamyris, I have something very strange to tell you; for Thecla, for the space of three days, will not move from the window not so much as to eat or drink, but is so intent in hearing the artful and delusive discourses of a certain foreigner, that I admire, Thamyris, that a young woman of her known modesty will suffer herself to be so prevailed upon. For that man has disturbed the whole city of Iconium, and even your Thecla, among others. All the women and young men flock to him to receive his doctrine; who, besides all the rest, tells them that there is but one God, Who alone is to be worshipped, and that we ought to live in chastity. Notwithstanding this, my daughter Thecla, like a spider's web fastened to the window, is captivated by the discourses of Paul, and attends upon them with prodigious eagerness and vast delight; and thus, by attending on what he says, the young woman is seduced. Now then do you go and speak to her, for she is betrothed to you."

Accordingly Thamyris went, and having saluted her and taking care not to surprise her, he said, "Thecla, my spouse, why sittest thou in this melancholy posture? What strange impressions are made upon thee? Turn to Thamyris, and blush." Her mother also spake to her after the same manner, and said, "Child, why dost thou sit so melancholy and, like one astonished, makest no reply?" Then they wept exceedingly, Thamyris, that he had lost his spouse; Theoclia, that she had lost her daughter; and the maids, that they had lost their mistress; and there was a universal mourning in the family. But all these things made no impression upon Thecla, so as to incline her so much as to turn to them and take notice of them, for she still regarded the discourses of Paul.

Then Thamyris ran forth into the street to observe who they were who went into Paul and came out from him; and he saw two men engaged in a very warm dispute, and said to them, "Sirs, what business have you here? And who is that man within, belonging to you, who deludes the minds of men, both young men and virgins, persuading them that they ought not to marry, but continue as they are? I promise to give you a considerable sum if you will give me a just account of him, for I am the chief person of this city." Demas and Hermogenes replied, "We cannot so exactly tell who he is, but this we know, that he deprives young men of their (intended) wives, and virgins of their (intended) husbands, by teaching: There can be no future resurrection, unless you continue in chastity, and do not defile your flesh."

Then said Thamyris, "Come along with me to my house, and refresh yourselves." So they went to a very splendid entertainment where there was wine in abundance and very rich provision. They were brought to a table richly spread and made to drink plentifully by Thamyris, on account of the love he had for Thecla and his desire to marry her. Then Thamyris said, "I desire ye would inform me what the doctrines of this Paul are, that I may understand them; for I am under no small concern about Thecla, seeing she so delights in that stranger's discourses, that I am in danger of losing my intended wife."

Then Demas and Hermogenes answered both together and said, "Let him be brought before the governor Castellius, as one who endeavors to persuade the people into the new religion of the Christians, and he, according to the order of Caesar, will put him to death, by which means you will obtain your wife; while we at the same time will teach her that the resurrection which he speaks of is already come and consists in our having children, and that we then arose again, when we came to the knowledge of God."

Thamyris having this account from them, was filled with hot resentment; and rising early in the morning he went to the house of Onesiphorus, attended by the magistrates, the jailor, and a great multitude of people with staves, and said to Paul: "Thou hast perverted the city of Iconium, and among the rest, Thecla, who is betrothed to me, so that now she will not marry me. Thou shalt therefore go with us to the governor Castellius." And all the multitude cried out, "Away with this impostor (magician), for he has perverted the minds of our wives, and all the people hearken to him."

Then Thamyris standing before the governor's judgment seat spake with a loud voice in the following manner: "O governor, I know not whence this man cometh; but he is one who teaches that matrimony is unlawful. Command him therefore to declare before you for what reason he publishes such doctrines." While he was saying thus, Demas and Hermogenes (whispered to Thamyris, and) said: "Say that he is a Christian, and he will presently be put to death." But the governor was more deliberate, and calling to Paul, he said, "Who art thou? What dost thou teach? They seem to lay gross crimes to thy charge."

Paul then spake with a loud voice, saying, "As I am now called to give an account, O governor, of my doctrines, I desire your audience. That God, Who is a God of vengeance, and Who stands in need of nothing but the salvation of His creatures, has sent me to reclaim them from their wickedness and corruptions, from all (sinful) pleasures, and from death, and to persuade them to sin no more. On this account God sent his Son Jesus Christ, Whom I preach, and in Whom I instruct men to place their hopes as that Person Who only had such compassion on the deluded world, that it might not, O governor, be condemned, but have faith, the fear of God, the knowledge of religion, and the love of truth. So that if I only teach those things which I have received by revelation from God, where is my crime?"

When the governor heard this, he ordered Paul to be bound, and to be put in prison, till he should be more at leisure to hear him more fully. But in the night, Thecla taking off her earrings, gave them to the turnkey of the prison, who then opened the doors to her, and let her in. And when she made a present of a silver looking-glass to the jailor, was allowed to go into the room where Paul was; then she sat down at his feet, and heard from him the great things of God. And as she perceived Paul not to be afraid of suffering, but that by divine assistance he behaved himself with courage, her faith so far increased that she kissed his chains.

At length Thecla was missed and sought for by the family and by Thamyris in every street, as though she had been lost, but one of the porter's fellow-servants told them that she had gone out in the nighttime. Then they examined the porter, and he told them that she was gone to the prison to the strange man. They went therefore according to his direction and found her; and when they came out, they got a mob together and went and told the governor all that happened. Upon which he ordered Paul to be brought before his judgment seat. Thecla in the meantime lay on the ground in the prison, in that same place where Paul had sat to teach her; upon which the governor also ordered her to be brought before his judgment seat, which summons she received with joy and went.

When Paul was brought thither, the mob with more vehemence cried out, "He is a magician; let him die." Nevertheless the governor attended with pleasure upon Paul's discourses of the holy works of Christ; and, after a council was called, he summoned Thecla and said to her, "Why do you not, according to the law of the Iconians, marry Thamyris?" She stood still, with her eyes fixed upon Paul; and finding she made no reply, Theoclia, her mother, cried out, saying: "Let the unjust creature be burnt; let her be burnt in the midst of the theater, for refusing Thamyris, that all women may learn from her to avoid such practices." Then the governor was exceedingly concerned and ordered Paul to be whipped out of the city and Thecla to be burnt.

So the governor arose and went immediately into the theater, and all the people went forth to see the dismal sight. But Thecla, just as a lamb in the wilderness looks every way to see his shepherd, looked around for Paul; and as she was looking upon the multitude she saw the Lord Jesus in the likeness of Paul and said to herself, "Paul is come to see me in my distressed circumstances." And she fixed her eyes upon him, but He instantly ascended up to heaven while she looked at him.

Then the young men and women brought wood and straw for the burning of Thecla, who, being brought naked to the stake, extorted tears from the governor, with surprise beholding the greatness of her beauty. And when they had placed the wood in order, the people commanded her to go upon it; which she did, first making the sign of the Cross. Then the people set fire to the pile. Though the flame was exceeding large, it did not touch her, for God took compassion on her and caused a great eruption from the earth beneath, and a cloud from above to pour down great quantities of rain and hail, insomuch that by the rupture of the earth very many were in danger and some were killed, the fire was extinguished, and Thecla preserved.

In the meantime Paul, together with Onesiphorus, his wife and children, was keeping a fast in a certain cave, which was in the road from Iconium to Daphne. And when they had fasted for several days the children said to Paul, "Father, we are hungry and have not wherewithal to buy bread"; for Onesiphorus had left all his substance to follow Paul with his family. Then Paul, taking off his coat, said to the boy, "Go, child, and buy bread, and bring it hither." But while the boy was buying the bread, he saw his neighbor Thecla and was surprised and said to her, "Thecla, where are you going?" She replied, "I am in pursuit of Paul, having been delivered from the flames." The boy then said, "I will bring you to him, for he is under great concern on your account, and has been in prayer and fasting these six days."

When Thecla came to the cave, she found Paul upon his knees praying and saying, "O holy Father, O Lord Jesus Christ, grant that the fire may not touch Thecla; but be her helper, for she is Thy servant." Thecla then standing behind him, cried out in the following words: "O sovereign Lord, Creator of heaven and earth, the Father of Thy beloved and holy Son, I praise Thee that Thou hast preserved me from the fire, to see Paul again." Paul then arose, and when he saw her, said, "O God, Who searchest the heart, Father of my Lord Jesus Christ, I praise Thee that Thou hast answered my prayer."

And there prevailed among them in the cave an entire affection to each other: Paul, Onesiphorus, and all that were with them being filled with joy. They had five loaves, some herbs and water, and they solaced each other in reflections upon the holy works of Christ. Then said Thecla to Paul, "If you be pleased with it, I will follow you whithersoever you go." He replied to her, "Persons are now much given to fornication, and you being handsome, I am afraid lest you should meet with greater temptation than the former, and should not withstand, but be overcome by it." Thecla replied, "Grant me only the seal of Christ, and no temptation shall affect me." Paul answered, "Thecla, wait with patience, and you shall receive the gift of Christ."

Then Paul sent back Onesiphorus and his family to their own home, and, taking Thecla along with him, went to Antioch. And as soon as they came into the city, a certain Syrian named Alexander, a magistrate in the city who had done many considerable services for the city during his magistracy, saw Thecla and fell in love with her, and endeavored by many rich presents to engage Paul in his interest. But Paul told him, "I know not the woman of whom you speak, nor does she belong to me." But he being a person of great power in Antioch, Alexander seized her in the street and kissed her, which Thecla would not bear, but looking about for Paul, cried out in a distressed loud tone, "Force me not, who am a stranger; force me not, who am a servant of God. I am one of the principal persons of Iconium, and was obliged to leave that city because I would not be married to Thamyris." Then she laid hold on Alexander, tore his coat, and took his crown off his head, making him appear ridiculous before all the people. But Alexander, partly as he loved her, and partly being ashamed of what had been done, led her to the governor, and upon her confession of what she had done, he condemned her to be thrown among the beasts.

When the people saw this, they said: The judgments passed in this city are unjust. But Thecla desired the favor of the governor, that her chastity might not be attacked, but preserved until she should be cast to the beasts. The governor then inquired who would entertain her, upon which a certain very rich widow named Trifina, whose daughter was lately dead, desired that she might have the keeping of her; and she began to treat her in her house as her own daughter. At length a day came when the beasts were to be brought forth to be seen; and Thecla was brought to the amphitheater and put into a den in which was an exceeding fierce she-lion, in the presence of a multitude of spectators. Trifina, without any surprise, accompanied Thecla, and the she-lion licked the feet of Thecla. The title written which denotes her crime was, sacrilege. Then the woman cried out, "O God, the judgments of this city are unrighteous."

After the beasts had been shown, Trifina took Thecla home with her, and they went to bed; and behold, the daughter of Trifina, who was dead, appeared to her mother and said: "Mother, let the young woman, Thecla, be reputed by you as your daughter in my stead, and desire her that she should pray for me, that I may be translated to a state of happiness." Upon which Trifina, with a mournful air, said, "My daughter

Falconilla has appeared to me and ordered me to receive you in her room, wherefore I desire, Thecla, that you would pray for my daughter, that she may be translated into a state of happiness and to life eternal." When Thecla heard this, she immediately prayed to the Lord, and said: "O Lord God of heaven and earth, Jesus Christ, Thou Son of the Most High, grant that her daughter Falconilla may live forever." Trifina hearing this groaned again, and said: "O unrighteous judgments! O unreasonable wickedness! that such a creature should (again) be cast to the beasts!"

On the morrow, at break of day Alexander came to Trifina's house and said: "The governor and the people are waiting; bring the criminal forth." But Trifina ran in so violently upon him that he was affrighted and ran away. Trifina was one of the royal family, and she thus expressed her sorrow, and said: "Alas! I have trouble in my house on two accounts, and there is no one who will relieve me, either under the loss of my daughter, or my being unable to save Thecla. But now, O Lord God, be Thou the helper of Thecla Thy servant." While she was thus engaged, the governor sent one of his own officers to bring Thecla. Trifina took her by the hand and, going with her, said: "I went with Falconilla to her grave and now must go with Thecla to the beasts." When Thecla heard this, she, weeping, prayed and said: "O Lord God, Whom I have made my confidence and refuge, reward Trifina for her compassion to me, and for preserving my chastity." Upon this there was a great noise in the amphitheater; the beasts roared, and the people cried out, "Bring in the criminal." But the women cried out and said: "Let the whole city suffer for such crimes, and order all of us, O governor, to the same punishment. O unjust judgment! O cruel sight!" Others said: "Let the whole city be destroyed for this vile action. Kill us all, O governor. O cruel sight! O unrighteous judgment."

Then Thecla was taken out of the hand of Trifina, stripped naked, had a girdle put on, and thrown into the place appointed for fighting with the beasts; and the lions and the bears were let loose upon her. But a she-lion, which was of all the most fierce, ran to Thecla and fell down at her feet, upon which the multitude of women shouted.

Then a she-bear ran fiercely towards her; but the she-lion met the bear and tore it to pieces. Again, a he-lion, who had been wont to devour men and which belonged to Alexander, ran towards her; but the she-lion encountered the he-lion, and they killed each other. Then the women were under a greater concern, because the she-lion, which had helped Thecla, was dead.

Afterwards they brought out many other wild beasts, but Thecla stood with her hands stretched towards heaven and prayed; and when she had done praying, she turned about and saw a pit of water and said, "Now it is a proper time for me to be baptized." Accordingly she threw herself into the water, and said: "In Thy name, O my Lord Jesus Christ, I am this last day baptized." The women and the people seeing this cried out and said: "Do not throw yourself into the water." And the governor himself cried out, to think that the fish (sea-calves) were like to devour so much beauty.

Notwithstanding all this, Thecla threw herself into the water, in the name of our Lord Jesus Christ. But the fish (sea-calves) when they saw the lighting and fire, were killed, and floated dead upon the surface of the water; and a cloud of fire surrounded Thecla, so that the beasts could not come near her and the people could not see her nakedness.

Yet they turned other wild beasts upon her, upon which they made a very mournful outcry. And some of them scattered spikenard, others cassia, others amomus (a sort of spikenard, or the herb of Jerusalem or ladies-rose), others ointment, so that the quantity of ointment was large in proportion to the number of people; and upon this all the beasts lay as though they had been fast asleep, and did not touch Thecla. Whereupon Alexander said to the governor, "I have some very terrible bulls; let us bind her to them." To which the governor, with concern, replied: "You may do what you think fit." Then they put a cord round Thecla's waist, which bound also her feet, and with it tied her to the bulls, to whose privy-parts they applied red-hot irons, that so they being the more tormented might more violently drag Thecla about, till they had killed her. The bulls accordingly tore about, making a most hideous noise; but the flame which was about Thecla burnt off the cords which were fastened to the members of the bulls, and she stood in the middle of the stage, as unconcerned as if she had not been bound.

But in the meantime Trifina, who sat upon one of the benches, fainted away and died, upon which the whole city was under a very great concern. And Alexander himself was afraid and desired the governor, saying: "I entreat you, take compassion on me and the city, and release this woman who has fought with the beasts, lest both you and I and the whole city be destroyed. For if Caesar should have any account of what has passed now, he will certainly immediately destroy the city, because Trifina, a person of royal extract and a relation of his, is dead upon her seat."

Upon this the governor called Thecla from among the beasts to him and said to her, "Who art thou? And what are thy circumstances that not one of the beasts will touch thee?" Thecla replied to him: "I am a servant of the living God; and as to my state, I am a believer on Jesus Christ His Son, in Whom God is well pleased, and for that reason none of the beasts could touch me. He alone is the way to eternal salvation, and the foundation of eternal life. He is a refuge to those who are in distress, a support to the afflicted, hope and defence to those who are hopeless; and, in a word, all those who do not believe on him shall not live, but suffer eternal death."

When the governor heard these things, he ordered her clothes to be brought and said to her to put on her clothes. Thecla replied, "May that God Who clothed me when I was naked among beasts, in the day of judgment clothe your soul with the robe of salvation." Then she took her clothes and put them on; and the governor immediately published an order in these words: "I release to you Thecla the servant of God." Upon which the women cried out together with a loud voice, and with one accord gave praise unto God, and said: "There is but one God, Who is the God of Thecla, the one God Who has delivered Thecla." So loud were their voices that the whole city seemed to be shaken; and Trifina herself heard the glad tidings and arose again and ran with the multitude to meet Thecla, and embracing her, said: "Now I believe there shall be a resurrection of the dead; now I am persuaded that my daughter is alive. Come therefore home with me, my daughter Thecla, and I will make over all that I have to you." So Thecla went with Trifina and was entertained there a few days, teaching her the word of the Lord, whereby many young women were converted; and there was great joy in the family of Trifina. But Thecla longed to see Paul, and inquired and sent everywhere to find him. When at length she was informed that he was at Myra, in Lycia, she took with her many young men and women; and putting on a girdle and dressing herself in the habit of a man, she went to him to Myra in Lycia and there found Paul preaching the word of God. And she stood by him among the throng.

But it was no small surprise to Paul when he saw her and the people with her, for he imagined some fresh trial was coming upon them, which when Thecla perceived, she said to him: "I have been baptized, O Paul, for He who assists you in preaching has assisted me to be baptized." Then Paul took her and led her to the house of Hermes; and Thecla related to Paul all that had befallen her in Antioch, insomuch that Paul exceedingly wondered, and all who heard were confirmed in the faith and prayed for Trifina's happiness. Then Thecla arose and said to Paul, "I am going to Iconium." Paul replied to her: "Go, and teach the word of the Lord." But Trifina had sent large sums of money to Paul, and also clothing by the hands of Thecla, for the relief of the poor.

So Thecla went to Iconium. And when she came to the house of Onesiphorus, she fell down upon the floor where Paul had sat and preached, and, mixing tears with her prayers, she praised and glorified God in the following words: "O Lord the God of this house, in which I was first enlightened by Thee; O Jesus, Son of the living God, Who wast my helper before the governor, my helper in the fire, and my helper among the beasts, Thou alone art God forever and ever. Amen."

Thecla now (on her return) found Thamyris dead, but her mother living. So calling her mother, she said to her: "Theoclia, my mother, is it possible for you to be brought to a belief, that there is but one Lord God, Who dwells in the heavens? If you desire great riches, God will give them to you by me; if you want your daughter again, here I am." These and many other things she represented to her mother, (endeavoring) to persuade her (to her own opinion). But her mother Theoclia gave no credit to the things which were said by the Martyr Thecla. So that Thecla, perceiving she discoursed to no purpose, signing her whole body with the sign (of the Cross), left the house and went to Daphine; and when she came there, she went to the cave where she had found Paul with Onesiphorus, and fell down on the ground and wept before God. When she departed thence, she went to Seleucia and enlightened many in the knowledge of Christ.

A bright cloud conducted her in her journey. And after she had arrived at Seleucia she went to a place out of the city about the distance of a furlong, being afraid of the inhabitants because they were worshippers of idols. And she was led (by the cloud) into a mountain called Calamon, or Rodeon. There she abode many years, and underwent a great many grievous temptations of the devil, which she bore in a becoming manner by the assistance which she had from Christ. At length certain gentle-women, hearing of the virgin Thecla, went to her and were instructed by her in the oracles of God; and many of them abandoned this world and led a monastic life with her. Hereby a good report was spread everywhere of Thecla, and she wrought several (miraculous) cures, so that all the city and adjacent countries brought their sick to that mountain; and before they came as far as the door of the cave, they were instantly cured of whatsoever distemper they had. The unclean spirits were cast out, making a noise. All received their sick made whole and glorified God, Who had bestowed such power on the virgin Thecla, insomuch that the physicians of Seleucia were now of no more account and lost all the profit of their trade, because no one regarded them; upon which they were filled with envy and began to contrive what methods to take with this servant of Christ.

The devil then suggested bad advice to their minds; and being on a certain day met together to consult, they reasoned among each other thus: The virgin is a priestess of the great goddess Diana, and whatsoever she requests from her is granted, because she is a virgin and so is beloved by all the gods. Now then let us procure some rakish fellows, and after we have made them sufficiently drunk, and given them a good sum of money, let us order them to go and debauch this virgin, promising them, if they do it, a larger reward. (For they thus concluded among themselves that if they be able to debauch her, the gods will no more regard her, nor Diana cure the sick for her.) They proceeded according to this resolution, and the fellows went to the mountain and as fierce as lions to the cave, knocking at the door. The holy Martyr Thecla, relying upon the God in Whom she believed, opened the door, although she was before apprized of their design, and said to them, "Young men, what is your business?" They replied, "Is there any one within whose name is Thecla?" She answered, "What would you have with her?" They said, "We have a mind to lie with her." The blessed Thecla answered: "Though I am a mean old woman, I am the servant of my Lord Jesus Christ; and though you have a vile design against me, ye shall not be able to accomplish it." They replied: "It is impossible but we must be able to do with you what we have in mind." And while they were saying this, they laid hold on her by great force and would have ravished her. Then she with the greatest mildness said to them: "Young men have patience, and see the glory of the Lord." And while they held her, she looked up to heaven and said: "O God most reverend, to Whom none can be likened, Who makest Thyself glorious over Thine enemies, Who didst deliver me from the fire, and didst not give me up to Thamyris, didst not give me up to Alexander, Who deliveredst me from the wild beasts, Who didst preserve me in the deep waters, Who hast everywhere been my helper, and hast glorified Thy name in me, now also deliver me from the hands of these wicked and unreasonable men, nor suffer them to debauch my chastity which I have hitherto preserved for Thy honor, for I love Thee and long for Thee, and worship Thee, O Father, Son, and Holy Spirit, for evermore. Amen." Then came a voice from heaven, saying, "Fear not,

Thecla, my faithful servant, for I am with thee. Look and see the place which is opened for thee: there thy eternal abode shall be; there thou shalt receive the beatific vision." The blessed Thecla observing, saw the rock opened to as large a degree as that a man might enter in; she did as she was commanded, bravely fled from the vile crew, and went into the rock, which instantly so closed that there was not any crack visible where it had opened. The men stood perfectly astonished at so prodigious a miracle, and had no power to detain the servant of God, but only, catching hold of her veil or hood, tore off a piece of it. And even that was by the permission of God, for the confirmation of their faith who should come to see this venerable place, and to convey blessings to those in succeeding ages, who should believe on our Lord Jesus Christ from a pure heart.

Thus suffered that first Martyr and apostle of God and virgin, Thecla, who came from Iconium at eighteen years of age; afterwards, partly in journeys and travels, and partly in a monastic life in the cave, she lived seventy-two years, so that she was ninety years old when the Lord translated her. Thus ends her life. The day which is kept sacred to her memory is the twenty-fourth of September, to the glory of the Father, and the Son, and the Holy Spirit, now and for evermore. Amen.

SAINT THEODORA OF SIHLA

S AINT THEODORA of Sihla was born in the village of Vanători in Romania, during the first half of the seventeenth century. Her father, Stephen Holdea, was armor-bearer at the castle of Neamț. When she came of age, Theodora was married to a young man from Ismail; having no children, they agreed to retire to monasteries in the Buzău valley. Theodora advanced so rapidly in stillness, prayer and obedience, that in a few years' time she had reached the measure of the elders, had gained the gift of prayer of the heart, and met with many temptations from the enemy. All the sisters loved her, and were constantly edified by her humility, her asceticism and zeal.

When the Turks invaded the Buzău valley, St. Theodora fled to the mountains, together with her spiritual mother, the schemanun Paisia. There they lived for many years in fasting and vigil, valiantly enduring hunger, cold and other unspeakable trials from the devil. The blessed Theodora, arming herself with fervent prayer of the heart, bore all with patience, for she partook of the secret consolation of the Holy Spirit.

After the repose of her spiritual mother, around 1670-1675, the holy Theodora was led by God to the mountains of Neamț. Having venerated the wonderworking icon of the Mother of God in the Lavra, she was directed to seek the advice of the Abbot of Sihăstria Skete, Hieromonk Barsanuphius. Seeing that she longed for the eremetical life, and comprehending her virtues with the grace of the Spirit, he communed her with the Body and Blood of Christ; thereafter he assigned the father confessor Paul as her guide, and said to her: "Go for one year into the wilderness, in the forest of Mount Sihla. If, with the grace of Christ, thou endure the difficulties and cruel trials of the wilderness, remain there until thy death. But if thou canst not, retire to a convent, and labor there in humility for the salvation of thy soul."

Father Paul sought an abandoned hermitage for the blessed Theodora, but without success, until they met an old hermit who lived beneath the cliffs of Sihla. He, possessing the gift of clairvoyance, greeted them, and said to her: "Mother Theodora, remain in my cell, for I am departing to another hermitage." Thus Father Paul left St. Theodora on Mount Sihla and, blessing her, returned to the skete.

In that cell the holy Theodora remained about thirty years, glorifying God unceasingly, and vanquishing with her patience and humility all the attacks of the enemy. With the strength from on high, she never came down from the mountain, nor sought any human aid; only the blessed Paul, her confessor, from time to time climbed up to her cell with the Precious Gifts, and the basic necessities of life. The blessed one so advanced in the angelic life that she would keep vigil all night with her hands raised to the heavens, until the rising sun fell on her face; then she ate some rusks with herbs from the forest, ferns and sorrel. For drink, she collected rainwater in a channel cut in the cliff, called St. Theodora's spring to this day. And, a true miracle, the water in it never dried up. After the repose of the blessed Paul, she remained in the care of God alone.

Once, when the Turks were ravaging the villages and monasteries around Neamţ, the woods filled with villagers and monks. It happened that some nuns found St. Theodora's cell, and the blessed one called to them: "Remain in my cell, for I have another place for refuge." At that time, she moved into a small cave nearby and lived there alone, completely unknown to all. At night she rested a little on the flagstones which are still to be seen there. Once a troop of Turks strayed onto Mount Sihla, and, by the devil's agency, found the cave of St. Theodora. As they fell upon her to slay her, the Saint, raising her hands to heaven, cried, "Save me, O Lord, from the hands of these murderers!" At that moment the wall of the cave opened miraculously, and the bride of God fled into the woods and was saved.

Being completely forgotten by all, and having no one to help her in her old age, she placed all her hope in God alone. She lived as an angel incarnate in her cave and no longer felt the cold or hunger, nor could the devil trouble her further. She prayed without ceasing, until her mind was raised to heaven, while her body at the same time was raised above the ground. Then her face shone, and from her mouth the prayer issued as a flame of fire, as happened with the great saints of old. For St. Theodora reached the greatest heights of prayer, and in ecstasy was ineffably illumined by God.

Her clothes with time became rags which scarcely covered her ascetic body; and when her food ran out, the birds of the sky, at the command of their Maker, daily brought her crumbs and crusts of bread from the trapeza of Sihăstria Skete. The blessed one prayed unceasingly for the world, and rejoiced at her coming repose. Thus, forty days before her death, she besought God to send a priest to bring her the Holy Mysteries; and the Lord did not overlook this longing of her soul.

The abbot of Sihăstria observed flocks of birds coming to the skete, taking little pieces of bread in their beaks, and setting out towards Sihla. Supposing that there must be some holy hermit there, he sent two brothers to see where the birds went. On their way, the monks were overtaken by

night and, losing their way in the woods, they prayed and waited for day. Then, seeing before them a beam of light which ascended to heaven, they advanced and beheld a woman shining with light, raised in the air above the ground, with her hands held high: it was St. Theodora.

"I thank Thee, O Lord, that Thou hast hearkened unto me," said the Saint, then added, "Fear not, brethren, for I am a humble handmaid of Christ. But first throw me something to wear, for I am naked." Then she called them, told them of her life and her approaching end, and said: "Go down to the skete and tell the abbot to send the father confessor Anthony and the hierodeacon Laurence with the Body and Blood of Christ." "How can we reach the skete at night?" replied the brothers. "We do not know the way!" "Follow the light which you will see before you, and you will straightway arrive."

At dawn next day, Father Anthony arrived at Sihla with the deacon and the two brethren, and found St. Theodora at prayer before the fir tree by her cave. She first confessed all the secrets of her life to the priest, then recited the Creed and received the Holy Mysteries. Finally she said: "Glory to Thee, O Lord, for all things!" At that moment the holy one surrendered her blessed soul into the hands of Christ. Her body, filled with fragrance, was buried with great reverence by the fathers in the cave in which she lived.

The news of the repose of St. Theodora went rapidly around all the villages and monasteries of Moldavia, and even abroad. The faithful from afar came to venerate the relics, and many were cured of illnesses. Her body was glorified with incorruption, divine fragrance and miracles. Some kissed her relics, other sick people touched the reliquary, others washed in her spring, and all received healing and comfort.

The relics of St. Theodora remained at Sihla for a hundred years, but between 1828 and 1834 they were removed to Kiev and enshrined in the caves of the Lavra, under the name of "St. Theodora of the Carpathians," and they are to be seen there to this day.

Holy Mother Theodora, pray to God for us!

Saint Theophanes the Confessor

Commemorated on September 9

HEN Theophanes was born to a third-century pagan couple, he was welcomed into the world with a pagan festive celebration. During this many toasts were drunk to the new son and heir of a considerable fortune, the celebrants little realizing that he would grow up to scorn the pagan gods and become a Christian to the degree that has placed him in the sacred company of saints. If there ever was a self-made Christian it was Theophanes. He grew up in the shadows of huge idols found in every corner of a spacious estate, but he was more impressed by the mental image of a humble carpenter from Nazareth.

Theophanes was less than twelve years old when he made a commitment to Jesus Christ after attending Christian meetings with boys whose company he preferred to the unfeeling aristocrats of his father's circle of friends. Too busy with their social pursuits, the parents were unaware that the son they had so gleefully welcomed at birth was a devout Christian. He preferred to kneel before a wooden cross than the imposing statues for which a handsome price had been paid.

On a particularly cold day Theophanes was returning from a meeting with his humble Christian friends when he came upon a boy who was ill clad for such low temperatures. When he learned that the youngster could afford nothing more than he was wearing, Theophanes removed his warm robe and put it around the astounded boy's shoulders. He then ran to his house and was immediately asked by his parents what had happened to the very expensive garment they had just bought for him. He might have said that some ruffian stripped him of it and made off with it, but he told the truth instead. He was then asked upon whom he had lavished such a gift and answered: "I don't know his name. I did it for Jesus Christ."

For this act of charity, construed as weakness by pompous pagans, Theophanes was ordered out of the house by his irate parents. He went to the humble house of Christian friends who praised him for his generosity and who accepted him as one of their own. He had been in the Christian house for several months when he learned of an ascetic who lived on Mt. Diabinos in utter isolation. Theophanes felt a strong urge to seek him out to learn more about Christianity, but on that trackless peak he could spend the rest of his life just looking for the eremite. That night, as he lay sleeping, he was visited in a dream by an angel of the Lord who told him where the hermit was dwelling and exactly how to get there.

Theophanes was off the next day, and before night had fallen he approached the spot where he had been divinely guided. As he was looking about, the eremitic figure appeared as if from nowhere, but actually from a well-hidden cave. After an exchange of greetings, the old man accepted the boy's story of the angelic directions because it would have been impossible to have found him otherwise. The hermit was by then seventy-five years old; but before he died, well into his eighties, he had instilled in the younger man a love for the Saviour. Theophanes would devote his life to Him as the older man had before him.

Alone for the next five years, Theophanes lived in meditation and prayer. He was a mere twenty-one years old when he had acquired the wisdom of a hierarch and the piety through self-denial which gave him the appearance of a man of God in spite of his years. In meditation one day he heard a voice instructing him to descend from the mountain and take up missionary work in the name of the Saviour, inasmuch as he was now thoroughly prepared for holy work. He left behind him a full-grown pet lion whom he had adopted when the animal was a cub and with whom he had become as close as a man with a pet dog.

Theophanes descended to the village to greet old friends and immediately set about preaching the word of the Messiah. Very soon he acquired conversions and a popularity among Christians which was the envy of officials who held ineffective and unpopular sway in the community. Caught in a fresh wave of persecutions, he was thrown into prison and severely beaten. But he was not executed with lesser-known figures; and, finally, under pressure from the general community, the prison officials released him. Unlike most who perish for the Saviour, he was allowed to go back to his beloved mountain where he spent the rest of his life. He died at age seventy-five.

BLESSED THEOPHIL
Fool-for-Christ

Commemorated on October 28

IERO-SCHEMAMONK Theophil (1788-1853), of the Kiev Caves Lavra in Russia, served as a bright lamp of evangelical truth for all Orthodox Christians. As a great teacher of piety, he worked at the improvement of the morals of those nearest him... *warning and admonishing everyone and instructing everyone in all wisdom, that we may present every person mature in Christ, the Anointed One* (Col. 1:28).

By means of spiritual eyes which penetrated the innermost recesses of men's hearts, the Blessed Theophil saw much. He saw how pride, self-delusion, hatred and violence inhabited the darkness of our ignorance. He saw how, plunging into a chaos of passions not penetrated by a single ray of divine light, people forgot God and, being satiated with sins, became filled with material food but starved for spiritual nourishment—Christians in name only, but in deeds and life, far from it.

Starets Theophil saw much and secretly suffered for all souls. In order to support the failing spirit of faith in us, he, out of love, took upon himself the highest podvig of Christian piety—being a fool-for-Christ's sake. He dedicated his whole life to the doctoring of moral ailments.

In general, Theophil used very little food. On Wednesday
and Friday he ate nothing at all except for half a small cup of
honey mixed with cold water and ice. This also composed his
food on Saturday and Sunday of the first week of the Great Lent
and on Saturday of Holy Week. On the other days of Holy
Week, he did not even partake of water. The Starets did not use
tea and instead he used to boil mint and would prepare up to
two cups, but he always drank only half of each cup, pouring
the rest into earthenware pots to treat strangers. The Blessed

One did not eat the rich black bread but used only white or rush, and then he avoided the crust, pinching out bits from the center.

But in addition to all these strange habits, the Blessed One had another original feature: love and sympathy for birds and animals.

There was a small square of land which ran from the fence of the hermitage right up to the edge of the monastery pond. Seeing that the land was not being used, Theophil hired a peasant to plough up the land and seed it with hemp.

"Why do you need hemp, Batiushka?"

"Because the heavenly birds will come here and eat it."

The peasant did as he was told. The hemp grew and whole flocks of birds flew there to feed and nest.

Once a large number of mice invaded the Starets' cell because of the various provisions found in it. Theophil, exas-perated by their nightly raids, de-cided to put an end to them. He called in a young reader and said, "Catch me the superior. Catch him, and I'll give you money for a sweet bun."

"How can he be caught when he always sits in his cell? Go ahead and try it. He'll take a stick to you and you won't forget it as long as you live," the reader answered with a smile. He thought Theophil was talking about the superior, Hiero-schemamonk Iov.

"No! Not that superior, you silly fellow."

"Well, which one, Batiushka?"

 "One that catches mice. Catch an unfortun-ate tramp of a cat. He will be industrious in his work.

A household cat will only put on airs and sleep on the stove-bed."

Soon a tomcat was installed and the mice were suppressed.

But now, alas, cockroaches and beetles began to pester him. Then the Blessed One called his cell-mate and said:

"Here, take this money and buy me a little hen."

The cell-mate went out and, instead of a little hen, he brought a little rooster. The young rooster would walk about the cell, shaking his red comb, picking up insects in every corner. But towards morning, when the tired Starets would doze off after a night of prayerful podvigs, it would suddenly cry, "Cock-a-doodle-doo!"

"This is not monastery life," the Starets decided. "Take it away from here! Take it away!" he said to Ivan, his cell-mate.

"Where shall I take him?" the cell-mate asked, only half awake.

"Take it to the postulant, Nikifor. Give it to him from me."

The cell-mate obeyed without question and took the rooster to Nikifor.

Before entering the monastery, Nikifor had been a serf and served as a lackey for his master. Being inclined towards a religious life, he asked the master to release him. Then he came to Kiev and entered into the brotherhood at the Kitayevskaya Hermitage. He had been living there for three years, but unclean thoughts were confusing him and driving him from the monastery.

Having received the rooster, Nikifor stood and thought, "Why did the Starets send a rooster? I don't eat meat, but people will see this rooster and convict me of it anyway." But because of his humility, he accepted the rooster into his cell.

The rooster being disposed of, Theophil now acquired a little hen. After about a month, the postulant Nikifor came to the Starets for advice. The Blessed One said not a word but gave him the little hen.

"For goodness sake! What is this for, Batiushka? I have more than enough with the rooster."

"Take it; take it, I tell you. This gives you a pair."

Several days later, Nikifor met a beautiful girl by accident and was carried away with passion for her. He secretly slipped away from the monastery and soon married her. Only then did he understand what the rooster signified and why he was given the hen for "a pair."

It was a great distance to the Lavra and the city, and so the Starets had little chance to go there. As a result, the Blessed One acquired a bullock with which to ride to the Lavra and the Bratsky Monastery.

How he happened to acquire the little bull is an incident worth relating.

Ivan Katkov (a butcher from Podol who had brought a horse to Theophil at the Bratsky Monastery) came to the Starets for confession and while telling the Blessed One about his affairs, he mentioned that he had acquired a young bull of a very unstable nature.

"I bought a bullock, Batiushka. I had planned to keep it myself, but I don't know what to do with it. The brute has become stupid and gores at everyone with its horns. I suppose I shall have to butcher it, sorry as I am about it."

"Then give it to me," said the Starets.

"To you? God have mercy, why it's impossible even to approach him! Several people have already been crippled by him."

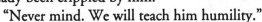

"Never mind. We will teach him humility."

"But how can I..."

"Very simple. Go up to him and say, 'Look here, little bull! From now on you are no longer mine, but Father Theophil's. Prepare to visit him.'"

The butcher did exactly as he was told. Upon returning home, he walked up to the bullock and repeated the words of the Starets; and the bullock, who had been snorting and pawing the ground, became as meek as a lamb. It began to quietly caress and lick the man's hands. Then a worker slipped a rope over his horns, and by dusk the young bull had been settled with Father Theophil at the Kitayevskaya Hermitage.

Now that he had the little bull, the Blessed One built a small cart with a little sailcloth hood set up on hoops in the rear of it. The Starets would travel to the city in this contraption. He never sat in front of the cart, but always in the rear with his back to the bull. He had placed a small analoy under this hood, and he would fall on his knees and read his beloved Psalter as he journeyed. But here is what was so astonishing. The bullock had neither harness nor reins, but only a yoke. The bull went precisely where its master wanted to go without any command, directions, guiding or prodding whatsoever, whether it was to Podol, the Lavra or the Bratsky Monastery. It is said that the bullock even went around stones, ruts, and ditches in order not to jog the Blessed One from his reading.

But we should not be at all astonished that this unreasoning creature obeyed him thus without a whip, that a formerly fierce animal became as tame and meek as a sheep before him. Wild animals have only become fierce because of the cruelty of human nature. Remember the state of our forebears in paradise. All living creatures saw the light of the image of God in their faces and even the most ferocious animals, sensing the wondrous fragrance of this image, peacefully bowed their heads before Adam. When man ceased his obedience to God's commandments, God's image in him darkened. The unreasoning creatures stopped recognizing and obeying him. The fragrance of God's image was exchanged for the stench of passions, and man himself became similar to the unthinking beasts. His disobedience to God was punished by the disobedience to him of the earth's creatures, and man himself now fears beasts which were once submissive to him. But God's holy ones, through obedience to God's commandments, restored the image of God in themselves and, taking unto themselves the gifts of the Lord's grace, radiated the original purity and light. Therefore, the animals, again sensing in man the fragrance of original purity, become obedient to him. What power there is in love and virtue!

In the city everyone knew the Starets. No sooner would he appear on one of the main streets than merchants would begin to run from their shops shouting, "Theophil is coming! Theophil is coming!" And each one hurried to drop something into his cart; one a piece of calico, a second a loaf, a third a handkerchief. It was noticed that anyone who tried to give the Starets something from his own goods, without fail made good profits in his business that day. The Starets kept nothing of this for himself. All that was in his cart he passed out to poor people whom he met on the way. There were many of them, and they would run behind the Blessed One in great crowds.

Many stories are recorded of the odd events which took place on these trips. For example, being aware of Metropolitan Philaret's dislike for him, Theophil tried even more to annoy the venerable Archpastor with his foolishness. Once in summer, when Vladika was spending some time in a cottage in Goloseyevo, Theophil arrived in his cart and drove straight into the Metropolitan's garden. The gardener was amazed.

"God be with you, Father Theophil! Where are you going?"

The Blessed One paid no attention to him and instead turned back towards the way he had come, only this time he travelled down a path lined with grapes on either side and so narrow that one could hardly walk down it. The route lay right below the very window at which Metropolitan Philaret was standing. Vladika was furious. He dashed out onto the porch.

"What is this disgrace? Who dared to let Theophil into the garden? Why did he come here? Send him away immediately. He will ruin my grapes."

The Blessed One, who had gone up the alley almost to its end, met Vladika face to face and, hearing the Archpastor's anger, calmly turned his bullock around.

"If it is not pleasing, then it is not necessary."

And, instead of leaving the garden by a wider path, he turned and travelled back down the same alley, between the grape vines.

"It is a wonder," the terrified gardener later related, "that the Starets was able to travel between the grape bushes, but it is an even greater wonder how he contrived to turn the cart around in such a narrow space where it was hardly possible for a man to even walk through. A miracle! Truly a miracle!"

From that time on Theophil fell into disgrace. The bullock was taken away from him and sent to the pastures of the Lavra.

The Blessed One was forbidden to appear at the Goloseyevskaya Hermitage, or to roam around. But on the day the bullock was placed in the monastery herd, such an unusual loss of cattle took place that the Lavra steward lost all self-control and absolutely did not know what to do. Veterinary doctors were called, and it was thought that some sort of epidemic had broken out in the herd. The doctors examined the cattle and could find nothing wrong with them. Meanwhile, the livestock continued to fall and die. It was decided to report the situation to Metropolitan Philaret. Vladika summoned the Lavra steward and asked to know exactly what day the loss of cattle began. The steward replied that it was the very day when Theophil's bullock was taken from him and put in with the herd.

"Is that so!" Vladika cried out and ordered that the bullock be quickly removed from the herd. When this was done, to the general amazement of everyone, the loss of cattle ended at once. The bullock was led away to Kitayev and returned to his owner. Having received back his pet, the Blessed One gilded his horns and peacefully resumed his daily travels.

In truth, *the ox knows its owner* (Is. 1:3).

The road from Goloseyevo to Katayev used to be unbelievably narrow. At the beginning of the Kitayev woods, the road rose up a steep hill. At this point, a narrow ravine crossed the road, and it was necessary for travellers to descend into the ravine to cross it. It happened once that Metropolitan Philaret and Archimandrite Lavrenty, the Deputy Superior of the Lavra, were hurrying along this road to conduct business at the Kitayevskaya Hermitage. Just as Vladika's carriage reached the middle of the ravine, Father Theophil appeared with his "steed." The Metropolitan's coachman thought that this was an approaching peasant, and he sternly cried out:

"Hey you! Turn back! Turn back, I tell you!"

The Metropolitan, on hearing these stern calls of the coachman, thrust his head out the window and asked, "What is it?"

But, upon seeing Theophil approaching towards him, he at once guessed what it was.

"Ivan, stop!"

The coachman stopped the horses, and Vladika and the deputy superior stepped out of the carriage. Theophil was sitting in the cart, leaning his elbows on its rail, and pretending to be asleep.

"Theophil, get up! Misfortune has occurred!" Metropolitan Philaret said loudly and began to awaken the Blessed One.

"What? Ah! Is it you, holy Vladika?"

"It is. Why are you dozing, you mischievous person? Just take a look at the trouble you have caused us."

And the trouble was great. The meeting occurred at the narrowest place, and it was impossible to turn around either the bullock or the carriage.

"Well, what will we do now?"

"We will do something," Theophil answered peacefully.

There was nothing to do but to unhitch the bullock. Vladika drove him back up the hill with a stick while the Deputy Superior and Theophil pulled the cart after him. The coachman did not participate in this "podvig" since he was holding the horses. After several efforts the road was freed and the Archpastor could finally continue his journey. Vladika was in good spirits, and he laughed upon bidding farewell to Theophil.

"Just see, you mischievous person, how much sweat you have rolled out of us," wiping large drops of perspiration from his forehead.

Soon after this the road was widened, but only slightly, and travellers still ran into difficulty in the ravine. Again the Blessed One and Metropolitan Philaret arrived at that very spot at the same moment. Although this time Theophil could have turned around, he refused to do so. It was as if he premeditatedly blocked the Metropolitan's way. An argument erupted between the coachman and Theophil. Father Theophil argued that it would be more difficult for his one bullock to draw his burden back up the hill than it would for Vladika's four horses to return up with theirs. But the coachman stood his ground.

"Theophil is right," said Vladika, observing the scene. "We should have made way for him. But since it is not possible for a team of four horses to turn around here, be kind enough to turn around with your bullock, Theophil."

But the Blessed One remained stubborn and did not wish to fulfill the request. The Archpastor began to become agitated.

"Well, what about it? Will you stop trying my patience?"

"No, I won't stop, because it is you and not I who must turn back."

"How so?"

"Just so."

At that very moment, a dispatch rider rode up to Vladika with a message from the Lavra. An artisan had fallen from the scaffolding around the belfry of the St. Sophia Cathedral and had been killed.

"He had hung in the air for a long time, holding on to a rail, but did not hold out and fell to the ground," the messenger said, and asked Vladika, in the name of the Lavra Superior, for immediate instructions.

The shaken Archpastor did not say a word in reply, but crossed himself and ordered the coachman to go to the top of the hill to turn around and return to the Lavra. Theophil was no longer there. At the arrival of the dispatch rider he drew back, having finished his mission.

They met again for a third time. On this occasion the Blessed One was returning to Kitayev from the city when the

Metropolitan's carriage overtook him and drew up alongside him on the Dyemiyev Bridge. Vladika called out:

"Theophil! Where are you off to?"

"Wherever God leads and necessity calls. Only there is trouble. The bullock has stopped listening to me. I have ordered a long whip to make him obey."

"And why do you want to ride with him at such a tortoise's pace?"

"The way to the Kingdom of Heaven is slow and steady."

"Here, climb into my carriage, and I'll get you there as fast as a falcon."

"Thank you, I don't wish to. I will get there before you all the same."

Just as Theophil had foretold it, so it happened. Because of the overly fast pace of the carriage, a wheel slipped off Vladika's carriage, and it required a whole hour to repair it. When the Metropolitan arrived at Kitayev, Theophil met him at the gate and, bowing low, he said:

"I wish you health, holy Vladika. I have been waiting for you here for a long time."

"You are right, Theophil," replied the Metropolitan. "The horned bullock overtook my well-fed team. It would seem that in the future I will have to travel in such a manner."

Many people remember this bullock, which usually was not tied, but roamed freely around in the Starets' yard. It is said that the bullock possessed an almost supernatural instinct and could guess, without error, the character of the people who came to the Starets for his blessing. For that reason, he met some visitors in an unfriendly and bellicose manner, while others were treated gently, allowing them to pass unhindered into the Starets' cell.

SAINT TIKHON OF ZADONSK

Commemorated on August 13

AINT TIKHON was born in 1724, in the Russian village of Korotzk, which was in the Valdai district of the Novgorod diocese. He was the sixth and youngest of the family. On May 13, 1761, in the cathedral of St. Peter and St. Paul he was consecrated bishop. His life spanned a turbulent period from 1724-1783. Wars, internal struggles and drastic reforms shook all of Russia.

* * *

He loved to pray in the open, and asked not to be approached when he was walking alone in the garden; if he must be disturbed, he wished to be warned by some little noise or cough. Chebotarev found him once in the garden, kneeling, facing the east, his arms uplifted. The man coughed and, unable to attract Tikhon's attention, he approached him and called him. Tikhon was so violently startled that perspiration appeared on his forehead.

A similar case of Tikhon's ecstatic prayer was witnessed one morning by a monk who was just about to ring the chimes in the belfry. Bishop Tikhon was walking in the little garden near his cell. Suddenly he stopped, looked up, and knelt, pressing his hands to his breast. He looked so radiant that the monk rushed down to tell the brethren, and several of them climbed up to the belfry. Tikhon had already resumed his walk, but the monks thought they discerned in his features the glow of ecstasy.

Once when Tikhon was praying, begging not to be separated from a friend even in after-life, the Virgin Mary appeared to him, "floating in mid-air, with several figures standing nearby." She said, "It shall be done according to your prayer."

St. Tikhon adapted the imagery of the Gospel to the circumstances of everyday life: he spoke of citizens expecting their Tsar; of one being left, another taken; of the gardener cutting down a tree, and so on, and he exhorted people "with zealous hearts to seek eternal bliss, where everything is like the earthly festival, yet everything is celestial: friends, food, singing, praise and love."

"Man is more beautiful than any other creature since he is in the image of God. Through the incarnation he is justified and is no more under wrath. He has become a member of the body of which the heavenly head is Jesus Christ. He mysteriously partakes of the lifegiving Body and divine Blood. He is made worthy to become the habitation of God and the temple of the Holy Spirit. He is in communion with the Father and His Son Jesus Christ. Through faith in Jesus he becomes a son, an heir, a co-heir with Christ. Read the Acts of the Apostles, and you will see that all these titles are ascribed to man by the Holy Spirit.... And what will it be in the future life, according to the unfailing promise of God! What goodness, bliss, honor and glory! The uninterrupted flow of eternal blessedness will be like a river, incomprehensible to the present mind and inexpressible by the tongue, the blessedness which "eye hath not seen" spoken of in I Cor. 2:9. The children of God will shine like the sun in the kingdom of the heavenly Father; they will be as angels, like other gods. Glory be to the Trinity for having so honored and magnified our kind!"

In his social teaching Bishop Tikhon stresses man's dignity, the equality of "the sons of God and brethren of Christ." In his moral teaching he emphasizes the heroic virtues of which man is capable and to which he is called both by his nature—which is in the image and likeness of God—and by adoption as a Christian. One can see in his doctrinal pronouncements how deeply he values this conception of the nature and destiny of man: "All creatures are witnesses to the wisdom and power of God; but man is also honored by being created in the image of God and by his special counsel. Let us learn, brother, our initial nobility and prerogative." He also lays stress on the incarnation as a pledge of God's boundless promises to man: "Jesus assumed to himself a flesh equal to ours."

ELDER ZOSIMA
Hesychast of Siberia

*"I believe that if one departs for the inner desert
overcome and persuaded by a divine love for Christ,
he will truly live as if in Paradise. No longer hindered
by any obstacles, he will be free to delight constantly
in the thought of God and in sweet prayer
of the heart, with God and in his God."*

S O wrote Elder Zosima (1767-1833), one of the many
holy hermits or desert-dwellers who lived in the vast
and wild forests of the Russian North. Written by
his niece and disciple, his biography is a classic of Russian
spirituality, revealing how the grace of God works in one who
is devoted to the labor of unceasing prayer, noetic activity,
unseen warfare, and interior silence (hesychasm). From his
mystical striving in the heart of the wilderness to his work later
in establishing a monastic community for women, Elder Zosima
shines forth with the simple wisdom of Christ-like humility. His
story should be a source of inspiration for all who long for the
heavenly kingdom.

From his youth Elder Zosima longed for the angelic life,
and after living several years at the Konevits Monastery he
became a desert-dweller in the Siberian forests with his Elder
Basilisk.

Although they lived in separate cells, they shared prayers, meals, labors, handiwork, and their meager desert possessions. And when it happened that out of love for deep silence they would not meet for several days, each would inform the other of the times for prayer and food by knocking with a small stick. The other would answer in the same way, thus showing that he was alive and well, and that he heard and would be one with him in prayer or food. They would even wake each other this way during the night, so that in different cells and in different bodies their souls were as one, and they lived one and the same life.

On ordinary days, and especially during fast periods, they maintained strict abstinence, often fasting for three to five days without eating any food, and spending this time in deep silence and seclusion. On the other hand, they honored solemn feasts by permitting themselves to eat the most pleasant of foods. But they took greater consolation in spiritual things, especially following the holy Forty-Day Fast, during which they truly crucified themselves in body and spirit to Him Who was crucified.

They celebrated the bright and joyous Resurrection of Christ most gloriously. Having spent the resplendent night reading and in prayer of the heart, they would sing the Bright Matins service and Hours, and having rested a bit, strengthen themselves to the glory of God with feast food. Then, taking along the Paschal Triodion, Gospel, and some other spiritual book, as well as some of their Paschal food supply, a hatchet, tinder, and a pot, they would stroll deep into the forest and wander about for two or three weeks, leaving their cells unlocked. Passing through forests, mountains, valleys, hills, and woods, they sent the sweet and solemn singing of "Christ is Risen!" filling and resounding through the whole desert, as if announcing to all the creation the Resurrection of its Creator.

With this joyous news they drove out demons from the wild, gloomy, and impassable parts of the wilderness. In these pious journeyings through the forest they would stop when informed by the sun of the dinner hour and build a fire. Having heated their food, they would choose a stump or hillock and eat with great joy. And wherever night would find them, they would lie down on the bare earth for a sweet night's sleep. Not once did either the dawn or a single bird ever precede their morning singing: "Let us arise in the deep dawn" (Irmos of the 5th Song of the Paschal Canon). For it has been said, "To the unfaithful the night is dark, O Christ, and to the faithful it is enlightenment in the sweetness of Thy words" (5th Irmos of the Sunday Canon).

Such was their outward celebration. However, it is impossible to describe the celebration which occurred in the depths of their souls, for no words can accurately describe the inner life of true desert-dwellers, of whom the Church sings, "Blessed is life for dwellers of the desert, who ascend on wings of divine fervor." As a matter of fact, they spent not only each Pascha and Pentecost, but also all summer feast days in this manner. Furthermore, they would often go into the wilderness to work and to gather essentials such as firewood for the winter, berries, and cedar nuts from which they extracted oil. They frequently encountered animals such as deer, wild goats, and sometimes even bears. But the wild beasts lived peacefully with their desert-dwelling friends.

In the following letter, Elder Zosima wrote of how the experience of the goodness of God in His creation helps draw the desert-dweller to his Lord:

"There is nothing in desert-living that would prevent or distract one from the divine services, or would hold one back from studying the Holy Scripture and nourishing oneself by going deeper into the contemplation of God. Instead there is every occasion, and each object forces one here to reach out to God. Around is the deep forest; one's glance may reach without hindrance toward the pure heaven, as one desires to be vouchsafed to be translated to that blessedness. Then again, the voices of singing birds draw the soul together with them to offer a doxology to God the Creator.

"In a word, every occasion, each object seen and heard turns one to contemplation on the omnipotence, the wisdom, the goodness of God—how He, to all of creation, gave its particular abundance, comfort and enjoyment. For if there were no full  satisfaction in all the created things, then there would be no satisfaction and none would rejoice. But instead, we see how trees and all plants grow, and thanks to enjoyment and satisfaction, become verdant, and even, for the abundance of satisfaction, bring forth fruits also. In the same way, one sees also how all beasts and animals and birds, and also all living things mutually admire each other, every kind of them, and enjoy themselves and reproduce. And from much enjoyment, each living kind, according to its nature, in its own voice raises praise of thanksgiving to God Who created it. From all this one can clearly see the good-heartedness of God's Providence, which looks after the whole creation...."

"The path to heaven is clear and pure, and it attracts one's gaze and inspires one's desire to be vouchsafed to be translated to that blessedness. And if one's gaze does turn towards the earth, to behold all the creatures and the whole of nature, one's heart is no less exalted with sweet love towards the Creator of all, with awe at His wisdom with gratitude for His merciful kindness. All creation leads our immortal spirit to unite with its Creator! And what joy and what fear are felt when the soul unites with God! What love, sweetness, consolation, enlightenment, trepidation, warmth, and tears are felt! One forgets himself and all earthly things entirely. This is impossible to describe, for as it has been said, 'Those who dwell in the desert partake of a constant divine aspiration which is free of worldly cares and confusion.' These are the fruits of desert silence!"

To all the Church of God, to all that are sanctified in Jesus Christ, and called to be Saints, with all that in every place call upon the name of Jesus Christ, our Lord.... Grace be unto you, and peace, from God our Father, and from the Lord Jesus Christ. I thank God always on your behalf, for the Grace of God which is given you by Jesus Christ; that in everything you are enriched by Him, in all utterance, and in all knowledge; even as the testimony of Christ was confirmed in you: who shall also confirm you unto the end, that you may be blameless in the day of our Lord Jesus Christ (I Cor. 1:1-8).

333

*"Let my prayer be set forth before Thee as incense;
and the lifting up of my hands as the evening sacrifice"*
(Psalm 141:2).

FOOTNOTES

1. St. Nicodemus of the Holy Mountain, *A Handbook of Spiritual Counsel*, trans. Peter A. Chamberas (New York: Paulist Press, 1989), p. 67.

2. David Winston, *Philo of Alexandria* (New York: Paulist Press, 1981), pp. 15-20.

3. Protopresbyter Michael Pomazansky, *Orthodox Dogmatic Theology* (Platina, California: St. Herman of Alaska Press, 1984), p. 136.

4. *Little Russian Philokalia*, vol. 1 (Platina, California: St. Herman of Alaska Press, 1991), p. 100.

5. *Ibid.*, p. 100.

6. Rev. George Mastrantonis, *A New Style Catechism on the Eastern Orthodox Faith* (St. Louis: The Logos Mission, 1969), p. 75.

7. George Maloney, *Intoxicated with God: A New Translation of the Fifty Spiritual Homilies of St. Macarius* (Denville, New Jersey: Dimension Books, 1978), p. 173.

8. *Little Russian Philokalia*, vol. 1 (Platina, California: St. Herman of Alaska Press, 1991), p. 100.

9. *Ibid.*, p. 99.

10. St. Symeon the New Theologian, *The Sin of Adam* (Platina, California: St. Herman of Alaska Press, 1979), pp. 68-69.

11. *The Lost Books of the Bible—The Forgotten Books of Eden* ("Adam and Eve," World Bible Publishers, Inc., 1927), p. 24.

12. St. John Climacus, *The Ladder of Divine Ascent* (New York: Paulist Press, 1982), p. 179.

13. *Little Russian Philokalia*, vol. 1 (Platina, California: St. Herman of Alaska Press, 1991), p. 99.

14. Constantine Cavarnos, *The Future Life According to Orthodox Teaching*, trans. Hieromonk Auxentios and Archimandrite Chrysostomos (Etna, California: Center for Traditional Orthodox Studies, 1985), p. 57.

15. *The Philokalia*, vol. 4, St. Gregory Palamas (Athens: 1961), p. 156.

16. Bishop Ignatius Brianchaninov, *The Arena*, trans. Archimandrite Lazarus (Jordanville, New York: Holy Trinity Monastery), 1983, p. 95.

17. Fr. Seraphim Rose quoted in "On the Origin of Life and Man" by Ryassaphore-Monk Damascene, *The Orthodox Word*, No. 154 (Platina, California: St. Herman of Alaska Press, 1990), p. 277.

18. *The Philokalia*, vol. 4, St. Gregory Palamas (Athens: 1961), p. 156.

19. St. Isaac of Nineveh, *Mystic Treatises*, trans. A.J. Wensinck (Wiesbaden: 1969), p. 8.

20. St. Gregory Palamas, *op. cit.*, p. 233.

21. St. Augustine, *The Greatness of the Soul*, trans. Joseph M. Colleran (Westminster, Maryland: The Newman Press, 1964), pp. 74-199.

22. St. Basil the Great, *Exegetic Homilies*, trans. Sr. Agnes Clare Way (Washington: Catholic University of America Press), pp. 136-233.

23. *The Philokalia*, vol. 1, St. Anthony the Great, trans. Palmer, Sherrard and Ware (London: Faber and Faber, 1979), p. 354.

24. *The Philokalia*, vol. 2, St. Maximos the Confessor (London: Faber and Faber, 1981), p. 88.

25. St. Augustine, *op. cit.,* pp. 98-105.

26. Sts. Barsanuphius and John, *Guidance Towards Spiritual Life* (Platina, California: St. Herman of Alaska Press, 1990), p. 152.

27. St. Basil the Great, *op. cit.,* p. 142.

28. St. John Climacus, *op. cit.,* p. 238.

29. St. Nicodemus of the Holy Mountain, *op. cit.,* p. 51.

30. St. Isaac of Nineveh, *op cit.,* Homily 71.

31. *The Philokalia,* vol. 1 (London: Faber and Faber, 1979), p. 362.

32. *Ibid.,* pp. 362, 364.

33. *The Philokalia,* vol. 3, St. Peter Damascene, *op. cit.,* p. 106.

34. Bishop Nikolai Velimirovic, *The Prologue from Ochrid,* vol. 3, trans. Mother Maria (Birmingham, England: Lazarica Press, 1986), p. 24.

35. St. John Damascene quoted in *A Handbook of Spiritual Counsel,* St. Nicodemus of the Holy Mountain, *op. cit.,* p. 69.

36. *The Philokalia,* vol. 3, St. Symeon Metaphrastes, *op. cit.,* p. 313.

37. St. Macarius of Egypt, *Pilgrimage of the Heart,* ed. George A. Maloney, S.J. (New York: Harper and Row), 1983, p. 74.

38. *Ibid.,* p. 177.

39. St. Ephraim the Syrian, *Hymns on Paradise,* trans. Sebastian Brock (Crestwood, New York: St. Vladimir's Seminary Press, 1990), p. 72.

40. St. Macarius of Egypt, *Pilgrimage of the Heart, op. cit.,* p. 178.

41. *The Lost Books of the Bible,* "Adam and Eve", *op. cit.,* p. 13.

42. *The Philokalia,* vol. 2, *op. cit.,* p. 139.

43. Aloysius Roche, *Animals Under the Rainbow* (Sheed and Ward, Inc., 1954), p. 136.

44. St. Symeon the New Theologian, *The Sin of Adam, op. cit.*, p. 69.

45. *Little Russian Philokalia*, vol. 1, *op. cit.*, pp. 98-100.

46. St. John of Kronstadt, *My Life in Christ* (Crestwood, New York: St. Vladimir's Seminary Press), p. 122.

47. St. Nicodemus of the Holy Mountain, *Unseen Warfare*, trans. E. Kadloubovsky and G. E. H. Palmer (Crestwood, New York: St. Vladimir's Seminary Press, 1987), p. 101.

48. St. Maximos the Confessor, *Wholeness and Transfiguration, op. cit.*, p. 5.

49. Bishop Nikolai Velimirovic, *The Prologue of Ochrid, op. cit.*, p. 24.

50. Serge N. Bolshakoff, *Elder Melchizedek* (Platina, California: St. Herman of Alaska Press, 1988), p. 37.

51. Hieromonk Seraphim Rose quoted in "On the Origin of Life and Man," Ryassaphore-Monk Damascene, *The Orthodox Word*, No. 154 (Platina, California: St. Herman of Alaska Press, 1990), p. 270.

52. *Ibid.*, p. 277.

53. Abbess Vera Verkhovsky, *Elder Zosima, Hesychast of Siberia* (Platina, California: St. Herman of Alaska Press, 1990), p. 127.

BIBLIOGRAPHY FOR PART I

(References in addition to those in footnotes)

St. Athanasius. *The Life of Anthony.* Translated by Robert C. Gregg. New York: Paulist Press.

Boone, J. Allen. *Kinship With All Life.* New York: Harper and Row, 1954.

Cavarnos, Constantine. *Modern Orthodox Saints: St. Seraphim of Sarov.* Belmont, MA: Institute for Byzantine and Modern Greek Studies, 1980.

Golder, F. A. *Father Herman, Alaska's Saint.* Platina, California: St. Herman of Alaska Press, 1968.

Green, Victor. *Saints for All Seasons.* USA: Avenel Books Crown Public, Inc., 1983.

Gregorios, Paulos Mar. *Cosmic Man.* New York: Paragon House, 1988.

St. Gregory of Tours. *Vita Patrum.* Platina, California: St. Herman of Alaska Press, 1988.

Harris, Mary Corbett. *Crafts, Customs, and Legends of Wales.* London: David and Charles, 1980.

Lynch, Patricia. *Knights of God: Tales and Legends of the Irish Saints.* New York: Holt, Rinehart and Winston.

Septuagint with Apocrypha. Peabody, Massachusetts: Hendrickson, 1986.

Upson, Presbytera Freida. *Women of God.* Brookline, Massachusetts: Holy Cross Orthodox Press, 1978.

BIBLIOGRAPHY FOR PART II

St. Aemilianus
St. Gregory of Tours. *Vita Patrum*. Platina, California: St. Herman of Alaska Press, 1988, pp. 240-242.

Saint Anthony the Great
Poulos, George. *Orthodox Saints,* vol. 4. Brookline, Massachusetts: Holy Cross Orthodox Press, 1982, p. 15.

Thompson, Blanche Jennings. *Saints of the Byzantine World.* New York: Farrer, Straus & Giroux, Inc., 1961, pp. 14, 15, 22-25.

Saint Aredius
St. Gregory of Tours. *Vita Patrum*. Platina, California: St. Herman of Alaska Press, 1988, pp. 309-310.

Elder Athanasius
Archimandrite Cherubim Karamabelas. *Contemporary Ascetics of Mount Athos.* Platina, California: St. Herman of Alaska Press, 1992.

Saint Athenogenes
Poulos, George. *Orthodox Saints,* vol. 4. Brookline, Massachusetts: Holy Cross Orthodox Press, 1982, pp. 91-92.

Hesychast Benjamin
Ierom. Ioanichie Balan. "Ieromonahel Casian Frunza," *Convorbiri Duhovnicesti.* Ruman & Husi, Romania: 1984. In English in *The Orthodox Word,* no. 155, November-December, 1990, p. 377.

Saint David of Garesja
Lang, David Marshall. *Lives and Legends of the Georgian Saints.* Crestwood, New York: St. Vladimir's Seminary Press, 1976, pp. 83-89.

Desert Anchorites
Severus, Sulpicius. *The Fathers of the Church,* vol. 7. New York: Fathers of the Church, Inc., 1949, pp. 178-185.

Bishop Palladius and St. Jerome. *The Paradise of the Holy Fathers,* vol. 1. Seattle: St. Nectarios Press, 1984, pp. 91-93, 187-188, 352-355.

Saint Eleutherius
O'Reilly, Fr. A.J. *The Martyrs of the Coliseum.* Rockford, Illinois: Tan Books and Publications, Inc., 1987, pp. 120-147.

Prophet Elijah
Roche, Aloysius. *Animals Under the Rainbow.* Kansas City, Missouri: Sheed & Ward, Inc., 1954, pp. 130-134.

Saint Eustachius
O'Reilly, Fr. A.J. *The Martyrs of the Coliseum.* Rockford, Illinois: Tan Books and Publications, Inc., 1987, pp. 63-118.

Elder Gabriel
St. Simeon Kholmogorov. *One of the Ancients.* Platina, California: St. Herman of Alaska Press, 1988, p. 106.

Saint Gerasimus
Blessed John Moschus. *Spiritual Meadows.* Sergiev Posad, 1896 (in Russian), pp. 129-132. Translated by R. Monk Gerasim Eliel.

Saint Herman of Alaska
Little Russian Philokalia, vol. 3. New Valaam Monastery, Alaska: St. Herman of Alaska Press, 1989, p. 75.

Saint Hilarion
St. Jerome. *The Life of St. Hilarion*. Willits, California: Eastern Orthodox Books, 1976, pp. 52-55, 64, 70-71.

Saint Ignatius
O'Reilly, Fr. A.J. *The Martyrs of the Coliseum*. Rockford, Illinois: Tan Books and Publications, Inc., 1987, pp. 39-56.

Elder Kuksha
"Modern Patericon: Hiero-schemamonk Kuksha." *The Orthodox Word*, No. 158, May-June, 1991, pp. 130-131.

Saint Macarius
Waddell, Helen. *Beasts and Saints*. London: Constable & Co., Ltd., 1934, pp. 13-16.

Malchus the Solitary
Bishop Palladius and St. Jerome. *The Paradise of the Holy Fathers*, vol. 1. Seattle: St. Nectarios Press, 1984, pp. 226-234.

Saint Mamas
Translated from the Greek by the Holy Transfiguration Monastery, Boston, Massachusetts. "The Life of the Great Martyr Saint Mamas," in *The Orthodox Word*, No. 38, May-June, 1971, pp.100-111.

Saint Martin of Tours
a) Severus, Sulpicius. *The Fathers of the Church*, vol. 7. New York: Fathers of the Church, Inc., 1949, pp. 203-206, 215-216.

b) Attwater, D. *The Avenel Dictionary of Saints*. New York: Penguin Books, Ltd., 1965, pp. 233-234.

Saint Mary of Egypt
Ward, Benedicta, SLG. *Harlots of the Desert*. London, England: Villiers House (A Division of Cassell PLC), 1987, pp. 36-56.

Saint Mavra
Ierom. Ioanichie Bălan. *Romanian Patericon*. Galați, Romania: 1990.

Saint Melangell
Gould, S. Baring. *Lives of the Saints*, vol. 16. Edinburgh, Scotland: John Grant, 1914, pp. 225-226.

Elder Melchizedek
Bolshakoff, Serge N. *Elder Melchizedek*. Platina, California: St. Herman Press, 1988, pp. 11, 27, 55.

Abbot Nazarius of Valaam
Little Russian Philokalia, vol. 2. Platina, California: St. Herman Press, 1983, pp. 11-21.

Saint Paul of Obnora
The Northern Thebaid: Monastic Saints of the Russian North. Platina, California: St. Herman Press, 1975, pp. 36-40.

Saint Paul the Hermit
Thompson, Blanche Jennings. *Saints of the Byzantine World*. New York: Farrer, Straus & Giroux, Inc., 1961, pp. 22-24.

Saints Perpetua and Feliciti
Hyman, Mark. *Blacks Who Died For Jesus*. Nashville, Tennessee: Winston-Derek Publishers, Inc., 1983, pp. 7-10.

Saint Prisca
Farwell, Abbie. *The Book of Saints and Friendly Beasts*. Boston: Houghton Mifflin & Co., 1900, pp. 166-175.

Elder Sebastian
Vladimirovna, Tatiana. "Optina Tradition: Optina Elder Sebastian." *The Orthodox Word*, No. 152, May-June, 1990, p. 140, and No. 153, July-August, 1990, pp. 240-241.

Saint Seraphim
Little Russian Philokalia, vol. 1. Platina, California: St. Herman Press, 1991, pp. 91-99.

Martyrs Tharasius, Probus, and Andronicus
O'Reilly, Fr. A.J. *The Martyrs of the Coliseum.* Rockford, Illinois: Tan Books and Publications, Inc., 1987, pp. 58-63.

Saint Thecla
The Lost Books of the Bible—The Forgotten Books of Eden. World Bible Publishers, Inc., 1927, pp. 99-111.

Saint Theodora
Hieromonk Ambrose Agiokyprianitis, tr. From *Pateric Românesc.* Bucharest: 1980. In *Orthodox Life,* vol. 32, no. 1. Jordanville, New York: Holy Trinity Monastery, 1982, pp. 9-11.

Saint Theophanes
Poulos, George. *Orthodox Saints,* vol. 4. Brookline, Massachusetts: Holy Cross Orthodox Press, 1982, pp. 133-134.

Blessed Theophil
Znosko, Vladimir. *Hiero-schemamonk Feofil.* Jordanville, New York: Holy Trinity Monastery, 1987, pp. 44-51.

Saint Tikhon
Gorodetzsky, Nadejda. *St. Tikhon of Zadonsk.* Crestwood, New York: St. Vladimir's Seminary Press, 1951, pp. 172-173, 200.

Elder Zosima
Abbess Vera Verkhovsky. *Elder Zosima.* Platina, California: St. Herman of Alaska Press, 1990, pp. 132-135, 184.